CONTEXT AND COGNITION IN CONSUMER PSYCHOLOGY

Context and Cognition in Consumer Psychology is concerned with the psychological explanation of consumer choice. It pays particular attention to the roles of perception and emotion in accounting for consumers' actions and their interaction with the desires and beliefs in terms of which consumer choice is frequently analyzed.

In this engaging book, Gordon Foxall extends and elaborates his theory of consumer action, based on the philosophical strategy of Intentional Behaviorism. In doing so, he introduces the concept of contingency-representation to explore the ways in which consumers mentally represent the consequences of past decisions and the likely outcomes of present consumption. The emphasis is on action rather than behavior and the manner in which the intentional consumer-situation, as the immediate precursor of consumer choice, can be reconstructed in order to explain consumer actions in the absence of the environmental stimuli required by behaviorist psychology. The result is a novel reaffirmation of the role of cognition in the determination of consumer choice. Besides the concept of contingency-representation which the author introduces, the analysis draws upon psychoanalytic concepts, theories of cognitive structure and processing, and the philosophy of perception to generate a stimulating synthesis for consumer research.

The book will be of interest to students and researchers in consumer behavior and economic psychology and to all who seek a deeper interdisciplinary understanding of the contextual and cognitive interactions that guide choice in the market place.

Gordon R. Foxall is Distinguished Research Professor at Cardiff University. A Fellow of the Academy of Social Science, the British Psychological Society, and the British Academy of Management, he has published over 30 books and 300 papers on consumer behavior, economic psychology, and marketing theory. His principal research interests are in psychological aspects of consumption and the philosophy of economic behavior.

CONTEXT AND COGNITION IN CONSUMER PSYCHOLOGY

How Perception and Emotion Guide Action

Gordon R. Foxall

Routledge
Taylor & Francis Group

LONDON AND NEW YORK

First published 2018
by Routledge
2 Park Square, Milton Park, Abingdon, Oxon OX14 4RN

and by Routledge
711 Third Avenue, New York, NY 10017

Routledge is an imprint of the Taylor & Francis Group, an informa business

© 2018 Gordon R. Foxall

British Library Cataloguing-in-Publication Data
A catalogue record for this book is available from the British Library

Library of Congress Cataloging-in-Publication Data
Names: Foxall, G. R., author.
Title: Context and cognition in consumer psychology : how perception and emotion guide action / Gordon R. Foxall.
Description: Abingdon, Oxon ; New York, NY : Routledge, 2018. |
Includes bibliographical references and index.
Identifiers: LCCN 2017020326 | ISBN 9781138778191 (hard back : alk. paper) |
ISBN 9781138778207 (pbk. : alk. paper) | ISBN 9781315772103 (ebook)
Subjects: LCSH: Consumer behavior. | Consumers. |
Consumption (Economics)–Psychological aspects.
Classification: LCC HF5415.32 .F683 2018 | DDC 658.8/342–dc23
LC record available at https://lccn.loc.gov/2017020326

ISBN: 978-1-138-77819-1 (hbk)
ISBN: 978-1-138-77820-7 (pbk)
ISBN: 978-1-315-77210-3 (ebk)

Typeset in Bembo
by Out of House Publishing

CONTENTS

LIST OF FIGURES

LIST OF TABLES

PREFACE

My intention is to elaborate aspects of the theory of consumer choice presented most recently in *Addiction as Consumer Choice: Exploring the Cognitive Dimension* (Foxall, 2016a) and *Perspectives on Consumer Choice: From Behavior to Action, From Action to Agency* (Foxall, 2016b).

This book, therefore, forms part of an intellectual endeavor to clarify the explanation of consumer choice through a critical examination of the theoretical position reached in those earlier works. In doing so it draws upon several extraneous research programs which illustrate in varied ways the requirements of a theory of consumer choice that links context and cognition. While none of them is designed to address this problem directly, each is uniquely involved with both philosophy and psychology and each raises issues that an explanation of economic and social action must speak to.

They are, first, Nanay's (2013a) work as a philosopher which interfaces with the psychological, especially in the field of perception and action; second, Brakel's (2009) combination of philosophy and psychoanalysis which is significantly concerned with the nature of psychological explanation; third, work on the Reinforcement Sensitivity Theory (principally Corr, 2008a, but drawing also on Corr & Krupić, 2017; Gray, 1982; Gray & McNaughton, 2000; Smillie, 2008) that links emotion and neurophysiology with contingencies of reinforcement and punishment; and, fourth, theoretical work on the tripartite model of cognitive structure and functioning advanced by Stanovich (2011), but drawing also on Evans (2010) and Stanovich and West (2000). Each of these methodologies and contributions helps refine and develop the synthesis of economic psychology, philosophy of mind, and philosophy of psychology which is germane to understanding contemporaneous consumer choice and hence ourselves.

I take this last point seriously. Although I speak here of the action of consumers as though of occupants of a limited role that might become easily divorced from other aspects of human experience, it seems clear that to discuss consumer action is to adopt a vehicle for the discussion of all human enterprise: for consumption is so central a human concern that it can stand for the whole of human endeavor, and because there is scarcely an aspect of human activity that does not entail consumption of some kind.

Chapter 1 provides an overview of the Intentional Behaviorist research program, including the Behavioral Perspective Model (BPM) which embeds several of the concepts that are central to the research program. Chapter 2 reiterates the main components of the Intentional Behaviorist research strategy, summarizes the theoretical concerns to which this book is addressed, sets out formally the role of temporal context as it influences consumer decision making, which lies at the heart of preference reversal and akrasia (i.e., weakness of will), and thus provides the central *motif* of the book.

The refinement of the intentional consumer-situation that is the book's aim has two further dimensions: first, the introduction of the concept of contingency-representation and, second, the opportunity to develop our understanding of the personal level of exposition. Therefore, in developing the intentional basis of the consumer-situation, Chapters 3 and 4 introduce and refine the original concept of perceptual contingency-representation as a subjective mental depiction of the contingencies of reinforcement and punishment as they have been previously encountered by the consumer and those with which she is currently in contact. As such, contingency-representation has perceptual and emotional components as well as cognitive and conative components in the form of beliefs and desires, respectively. These cognitive, conative, and affective influences on (or at least explicators of) action therefore comprise the conceptual basis of the intentional consumer-situation. The construction of the intentional consumer-situation comprises an account of observed consumer choice that proceeds on the basis that the consumer is a rational system, i.e., one that maximizes a combination of functional satisfactions and social, symbolic, and personal satisfactions from a given pattern of consumption.

Within this theme, I raise also concerns about what role, if any, the traditional *desire x belief* model ought to play in the explanation of consumer choice. This near-ubiquitous depiction of the mental events involved in decision making and action has, as I have noted, recently been called into question, accompanied by the suggestion that it be replaced with a simpler, perception-based understanding of the mental precursors of action (Chapter 6, and especially the "Pragmatic mental imagery" section, returns to this topic but much of the rest of the book bears on it, too). One source of criticism of cognitive approaches is that they posit a process of decision making that is too slow to account for the behavior of both nonhuman animals and human consumers (e.g., Nanay, 2013a). Responses need often to be rapid if opportunities are to be grasped and threats evaded. An account of behavior based on perceptual procedures rather than decision processes might not only serve better the need to explain responding of this kind but also relate human and nonhuman responding insofar as they rely on similar mechanisms. This would require us to propose a mental apparatus and function that applies to animals too, something simpler than the whole cognitive apparatus involved in many depictions of intellectual processing. It is here that the consideration of action in terms of perception and emotion comes into its own. This re-emphasis provides a welcome opportunity to examine the place of cognitive theories in the explanation of consumer choice on the basis of Intentional Behaviorism. The possibility of substituting perceptual experience for cognitive decision making is, therefore, raised in these pages. The outcome is a re-emphasis on perception and emotion and a closer understanding of both the immediate mental antecedents of action and the necessity of retaining both desires and beliefs and the cognitive mechanisms responsible for their generation.

The refinement of the concept of intentional consumer-situation automatically brings with it development of the personal level of exposition, the contribution to consumer theory to our understanding of how consumers process information at the level of the whole person through thinking and feeling and the emergence therefrom of the desires, beliefs, emotions, and perceptions that explain consumer action qua action. I have mentioned that the Intentional Behaviorism research program identifies three points at which the extensional explanation of consumer choice breaks down: in accounting for aspects of the continuity and discontinuity of behavior, in accounting for behavior at the personal level of experience, and in delimiting the behavioral interpretation of consumer choice (Foxall, 2004). The personal level involves both the intentional interpretation that has just been described and the level of cognitive interpretation by which it is in part assessed. It impinges, therefore, on the import of the treatment of the consumer as – in some sense – a utility maximizer, and on the way in which she can be understood as processing the information on which beliefs, be they the kind that are corrigible by reference to how the world is actually constituted or those that build on fantasy and specious internally-generated considerations, depend. The a-rational consumer choice that characterizes the latter is related to akrasia at whatever level it appears in decision making and its action outcomes.

Given the emphasis on the centrality of psychological rationality to the explanation of consumer choice, this investigation develops further the account of the personal dimension as a source of reinforcement and punishment. This provides a further link with the contribution that psychoanalytic thought can make to consumer theory. The aim is the demonstration that the activities of the consumer can be given an intentional interpretation through the ascription of the intentionality that would be appropriate to her given the circumstances in which the observed action occurred. This intentional interpretation then needs to be critically examined in terms of whether cognitive theory and its empirical ramifications supports it or whether what we know of cognitive structure and functioning requires a more sophisticated intentional account to be formulated. Chapters 5 and 6 are devoted to the personal level of exposition. They discuss in detail the content of the intentional consumer-situation in terms of the beliefs and desires of the consumer whose action is characterized by a degree of temporal discounting and preference reversal and the psychological rationality that must be assumed in order to explain such action. The concluding chapter summarizes the argument and provides some thoughts on future directions for the research program.

ACKNOWLEDGMENTS

I am grateful to Cambridge University Press for permission to reproduce Table 4.2 from Corr, P. J. (2008). *The Reinforcement Sensitivity Theory of Personality* (Cambridge: Cambridge University Press); to Oxford University Press USA for permission to reproduce, as Figure 6.1, Stanovich, K. E. (2011). *Rationality and the Reflective Mind* (Oxford: Oxford University Press); and to MIT Press for permission to reproduce Figure 3.1 from Dretske, F. (1988). *Explaining Behavior: Reasons in a World of Causes* (Cambridge, MA: MIT Press). I also thank Professors J. A. Toronchuk and G. F. R. Ellis for permission to reproduce Table 4.1 from their paper, Affective neuronal selection: the nature of the primordial emotion systems, *Frontiers in Psychology*, Vol. 3, Article 589.

I would also like to thank Psychology Press and, especially, Eleanor Reedy for her patience and encouragement.

I am, above all, grateful to my wife, Jean.

1

A PROGRESSIVE RESEARCH PROGRAM

Abstract

The Intentional Behaviorist research program has progressed from the foundation of an empirical base for the explanation of consumer choice to the development of cognitive models of consumer choice that rest on solid conclusions about what it is that makes consumer action action rather than behavior. Recognition that the focus of the research program is henceforth principally on consumer action rather than consumer behavior, appreciation of the role of contingency-representations in the explanation of consumption, and understanding of consumer choice in terms of the temporal considerations that underlie decision processes all indicate the progressive nature of the Intentional Behaviorist research program. The Behavioral Perspective Model (BPM) of purchase and consumption, which provides a *motif* for the Intentional Behaviorist research strategy, proposes that consumer choice is a function of the patterns of reinforcement and punishment which have followed consumer activity. A functional analysis of consumer choice reveals an eightfold classification of the patterns of reinforcement and consumer behavior setting scope that shape and maintain consumer behavior (the contingency categories) and that the consumer-situations that are the immediate precursors of consumer behavior can be defined in these terms. The model accommodates behaviorist, intentional, and cognitive perspectives to portray consumer choice, first, as the outcome of the rewards and sanctions that are the consequences of behavior and, subsequently, as a mode of human action that must be understood in terms of the desires, beliefs, emotions, and perceptions of the consumer and her intellectual functioning. Hence, the BPM provides a vehicle for the exploration of the relationships between the context in which consumer choice occurs (the contingencies of reinforcement and punishment) and the cognitive processes that underlie this choice (decision making) via the construction of an intentional consumer-situation that explains their interaction.

From consumer behavior to consumer action

The Intentional Behaviorism research program has reached an advanced phase: that of constructing and critically evaluating an intentional account of consumer choice, having identified, through the exhaustive testing of a behaviorist model of consumer behavior, the boundaries of extensional explanation (Foxall, 2004, 2016a, 2016b).

The first phase of the Intentional Behaviorist research strategy, exemplified by *consumer behavior analysis*, has accomplished the necessary model building, testing, and evaluation for deciding where intentional explanation, including cognitive explanation, is essential, the form it needs to take, and the functions it needs to perform (Foxall, 2017). This stage, based on a research strategy of *theoretical minimalism*, continues apace for what it reveals of the relation of consumer behavior to its environmental determinants. But, at the same time, we are moving on.

The conduct of empirical research that has tested the central assumptions and explanatory modes of the behaviorist model of consumer choice has also revealed three points at which an extensional explanation of consumer choice breaks down because the stimulus field necessary to sustain it cannot be identified. These are the continuity/discontinuity of behavior across situations, the comprehension of consumer behavior at the personal level of exposition, and the delimitation of behavioral interpretations. All three of these bounds of behaviorism invite an intentional account (Foxall, 2004, 2007b, 2008, 2009, 2016b). The extensional consumer-situation, conceptualized simply as the interaction of the consumer's learning history and the stimulus field provided by the current consumer behavior setting, must give way to an intentional consumer-situation if the explanation of consumer choice is to proceed. An essential methodological aim of the present volume is to clarify the content and role of this *intentional* consumer-situation as part of the explanatory medium that links context and cognition.

The second phase is composed of two stages, the construction of an intentional interpretation and the critical appraisal thereof, which determines whether current cognitive interpretations adequately underpin this intentional explanation. And it introduces three novel concerns.

First, the exploration of this advanced phase, psychological explanation, necessitates a shift in the conceptualization of consumer activity from behavior to action. While behavior is explicable by reference to the antecedent and consequential stimuli through which it can be predicted and influenced, action lacks such a stimulus field and is accounted for in terms of the actor's desires, beliefs, emotions, and perceptions. But this does not imply that consumer action is context-free. Rather, our concern is with how the context within which consumer choice occurs, broadly speaking what behavioral psychology calls the contingencies of reinforcement and punishment, rewards and sanctions, relates to the mental processes that guide or at least provide the explanation for consumers' actions. The stepping-off point is the delineation of consumer choice as activity that entails temporal conflict between alternative courses of action which differ in their objective and psychological evaluation. This understanding of consumer choice is an important element in what makes action action.

Second, the intentional interpretation that forms the second stage of Intentional Behaviorism is the construction of the consumer-situation, the immediate precursor of consumer choice, in intentional terms. It, therefore, embodies the language of intentionality rather than that of extensionally described consumer behavior settings (that consist in stimulus fields) and learning histories (that somehow summate previous exposure to such stimulus fields). The construction of the intentional consumer-situation requires concepts that indicate how the individual represents the contingencies of reinforcement and punishment that have provided the context for previous patterns of consumer choice and those that currently signal the probable outcomes of continued consumer actions. These *contingency-representations* consist in beliefs and desires with respect to the functional outcomes of action and the perceptual experience the consumer has had of previously encountered consumer-situations plus her current perceptual experience with regard to the outcomes that the present consumer behavior setting suggests will eventuate from further consumer action. The quest, therefore, involves the nature of *perceptual* contingency-representation and links it to the emotional experiences consumers report based on their experience of consumer-situations that portray various patterns of contingency. All-in-all, contingency-representation is a second important element in understanding what makes action action.

Third, viewing consumer activity as consumer choice, defined in terms of a temporal conflict between alternative courses of action, introduces the consideration of akrasia into our subject matter and thereby a broader perspective on consumer rationality. In seeking the appropriate desires and beliefs of which the intentional consumer-situation is partially constructed, this book adopts an approach which is amenable not only to the incorporation of rational propositional attitudes of this kind but also of a-rational and even irrational intentionality. Whereas earlier expositions of the Intentional Behaviorist research strategy have concentrated on the role of economic rationality in the explanation of consumer choice, the focus of this volume is on psychological rationality and, given an emphasis on the consumer-as-akrates, it does not rest on the automatic assumption, common among philosophers of mind, that human action is a rational outcome of mentation. Rather, following Brakel (2009), it seeks a more rounded understanding of mental processes and their contents. The nature of the rationality (/irrationality/a-rationality) that is relevant to the intentional explanation of consumer choice is something to be further explored by reference to the structure and functioning of the cognitive procedures that underlay intentional interpretation. Moreover, psychological rationality is the third central component of what makes action action.

The key to the progress of this research program, the generation of its empirical foundation, and its capacity to enhance interdisciplinary understanding of human behavior is the Behavioral Perspective Model.

A model of consumer-situation

The methodology of Intentional Behaviorism exploits the tension between the behaviorist and cognitive perspectives, viewing each as indispensable to the other. At the heart of this Intentional Behaviorist research strategy is the Behavioral Perspective Model (BPM), which can assume behaviorist, intentional, and cognitive perspectives with the aim of rendering consumer activity increasingly intelligible as its empirical base is first explored directly and then through the ascribed phenomenology of the consumer. In its contribution to the initial stage of the research program, the BPM employs a radical behaviorist depiction of consumer activity for two reasons: first, to establish the extent to which a non-cognitive model can uniquely elucidate this aspect of human activity and, second, to identify the points at which such an extensional account breaks down and requires the development of an intentional theory of choice. This delineation of the BPM is based on behavior analysis, a school of psychology that relates the rate at which behavior occurs to the nature of the consequences that similar behavior has generated in the past. Behavior analysis embraces a philosophy of psychology, radical behaviorism, in which the explanation of behavior involves the demonstration that it can be predicted and controlled on the basis of the environmental stimuli that precede and follow it. Nothing else.[1]

This parsimonious version of the model relies on the operant "three-term contingency" of radical behaviorism, which explains behavior by allusion to its predictability and modification by reference to environmental stimuli. A discriminative stimulus is a pre-behavioral event in the presence of which the individual discriminates her behavior, preforming a response that has previously been rewarded rather than one that has not. Better than "rewarded" is "reinforced" in the sense that behavior that is followed by such an event is likely to increase in frequency on future occurrences of the appropriate discriminative stimulus. Discrimination in this sense is simply an observation of an individual's behavior rather than the attribution to her of a mental operation. "Reinforcement" refers, then, to the strengthening of the behavior. Consequences of behavior that eventuate in its being performed less frequently are known as punishers; it is important to bear in mind that it is the behavior that is punished, not the individual. Reinforcers and punishers are post-behavioral stimuli but it is their occurrence in the past, in the consumer's learning history, that accounts for their present potency in shaping and maintaining consumer activity (see Table 1.1).

Positive reinforcement is an increase in the rate of responding due to the receipt of a positive reinforcer; punishment is a reduction in the rate of responding due to the receipt of an aversive consequence. The exposition retains Skinner's (1953, 1974) terminology because it allows more subtle distinctions to be made about

TABLE 1.1 Effects of consequential stimuli on rate of responding

Behavior	Consequential stimulus	
	Positive	Aversive
Approach (generate, produce, or accept the consequential stimulus)	Positive reinforcement	Punishment
Avoidance or escape (prevent or eliminate the consequential stimulus)	Absent	Negative reinforcement

the environmental events that control behavior. Both positive and negative reinforcement involve an increase in the rate of responding: positive reinforcement means working harder, paying more, or performing more responses to obtain the reinforcer; negative reinforcement means increasing the performance of an evasive behavior, one that allows an aversive consequence to be escaped. Punishment and omission involve a decrease in the rate of responding. Punishment is the reception of/approach toward an aversive outcome when this reduces the frequency of the behavior in question. I may still buy fresh fruit when its price increases substantially but I buy less of it. Skinner is meticulous in using the term reinforcement for these instances rather than reward. Behavior is reinforced by an outcome that increases its probability. A person can be rewarded by the adventitious receipt of a gift, say, but her frequency of behaving is not contingent upon this. The same is true of punishment: it is the behavior that is punished when its rate is reduced in the face of its being followed by certain consequences, not the person. In the analysis of consumer behavior which follows, I will use the term reinforcer to refer to a consequence of behavior that increases its rate. I shall speak of emotional reward in referring to the positive emotional outcomes of behaving and receiving reinforcement. This is a subset of the reward as Skinner speaks of it. Correspondingly, emotional punishment will refer to the negative emotional outcomes of behavior.

Another type of pre-behavioral stimulus, the motivating operation, serves to enhance the relationship between a prospective response and the reinforcer which is forecast to follow its performance, making this consequence more attractive, and more valuable insofar as the individual will work harder (or pay more) to obtain the reinforcer. We have seen that the three-term contingency of radical behaviorist explanation comprises a discriminative stimulus (S^D) that increases the probability of a response (R) which has reinforcing/punishing outcomes ($S^{r/p}$) that influence its future rate of occurrence in the presence of the S^D. This may be augmented into a four-term contingency by the addition of an additional pre-behavioral stimulus or state, the motivating operation (MO). While the effect of a discriminative stimulus is on the probability of the response, the effect of the motivating operation is seen in its enhancing the relationship between the response and the reinforcer/punisher.

The response is known as an operant because it operates on the environment to produce consequences (in classical or Pavlovian conditioning, the response is sometimes known among radical behaviorists as a respondent; see Skinner, 1953). An operant response is, therefore, a function of post-behavioral stimuli, but not as these are depicted in the three-term contingency; rather, it is a function of those reinforcing stimuli that have followed similar responses in the past and have thus become elements in the individual's learning history. The learning history is the principal explanatory variable in radical behaviorism because the pattern of prior behavior and the consequences it has generated are the means of predicting future behavior and of seeking to modify it. An operant does not properly refer to a single instance of behavior but to a class of responses all of which generate similar consequences. As an extensional behavioral science, radical behaviorism avoids causal reference to such intentions as desires and beliefs, perceptions and emotions.

The behavior analytic paradigm that has been described commends itself to the pursuit of theoretical minimalism because of the instrumental (or operant) conditioning on which it is based: behavior is a function of the outcomes that are contingent on its performance. This is precisely the stance adopted in the study of economic behavior and is also appropriate to the study of much social behavior. Consumer choice is a function of the economic and social consequences contingent upon it and is, sequentially, controlled by those outcomes. This reliance on the explanatory device of behavior analysis gives rise to the style of theoretical minimalism most appropriate to the first stage of Intentional Behaviorism, namely, consumer behavior analysis. The three- or four-term contingency requires some adjustment, however, if it is to be useful for the comprehension of human consumer choice, and, even in the extensional depiction of consumer choice, there are important conceptual elaborations of traditional behavior analysis (Foxall, 2016b, Chapter 2).

Consumer behavior setting scope

Except in highly restricted experimental settings, people do not respond to a single stimulus but to a selected subset of all the stimuli to which they are exposed. A consumer behavior setting, therefore, is not a single stimulus as in the three- or four-term contingency but a stimulus field, a gestalt, which shapes and maintains a pattern of consumer choice. Moreover, consumer behavior settings differ in the degree to which they encourage or inhibit a particular pattern of behavior; relatively open settings are those that permit a range of consumer behaviors to be undertaken (like being at a party), while relatively closed settings allow only one or at most a few alternative behaviors to be performed (e.g., being in the audience of an opera performance). The continuum of consumer behavior settings is, moreover, a restricted range of the entire spectrum of setting types open to humans (Figure 1.1).

The way in which the consumer behavior setting is perceived, especially in terms of its closed–open scope, reflects individual differences in, inter alia, cognitive

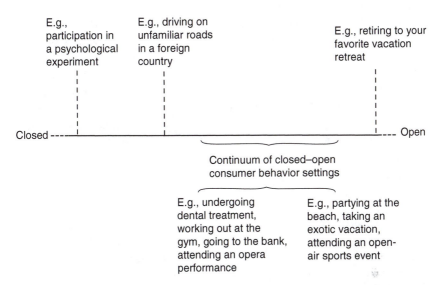

FIGURE 1.1 The continuum of closed–open consumer behavior settings. The diagram is not drawn with any scale in mind but is intended to illustrate the important relationships between the absolute continuum of settings which influence human behavior and the restricted spectrum of settings that are applicable to mainstream consumer behavior. See Foxall (2004, 2010, 2016b).

style, category width, and tolerance of ambiguity. But the consumer's learning history is, within the operant paradigm, the principal device for the prediction and control of their behavior in settings like the operant laboratory, a setting from which all extraneous sources of behavioral control have been eliminated so that only the uncomplicated stimulus–response–stimulus progression of operant conditioning can influence behavior. Such a paradigm scarcely suffices, however, for even the prediction and control of the human activities that comprise purchasing and consuming except in the gross terms of market aggregation. The idea of the consumer-situation in consumer behavior analysis combines the concept of a learning history with that of a consumer behavior setting, the latter comprising the physical (including temporal) and social (including regulatory) stimuli that make up the immediate milieu of consumer choice. It is this context, primed and given meaning by the consumer's learning history, that is the consumer-situation, the immediate precursor and determinant of consumer behavior.

To what does the consumer's learning history refer in addition to the log of behaviors she has previously performed? It incorporates also the outcomes of those behaviors, the log of reinforcers and punishers that have followed the enactment of all those responses. The pattern of reinforcement found in the BPM also differs from the single reinforcer or punisher depicted in this explanatory device. Reinforcers in human experience are of two kinds or sources. Utilitarian reinforcement refers to the functional benefits provided by products and services;

informational reinforcement, to the social feedback on the consumer's perfor-mance, the status or esteem that accrues to the consumer who models behaviors that are socially prescribed and approved. It is the combination of these two kinds of outcome, the pattern of reinforcement that determines the continuity of human complex behaviors such as consumer choice. Although we shall refer to the pattern of reinforcement for simplicity of exposition, it needs to be borne in mind that consumer behavior is always punished (if only through the surrender of so valuable a means of purchasing power as money) as well as reinforced.

Pattern of reinforcement and operant classes of consumer behavior

The enhancement of the three- or four-term contingency that provides the sum-mative BPM of consumer choice is shown in Figure 1.2(a). From the model as depicted here, it is possible to derive hypothetical frameworks for the analysis of consumer choice. The first is a classification of operant consumer behaviors (Figure 1.2(b)) which defines broad operant classes of consumer choice in terms of the pattern of reinforcement that maintains them. The second (Figure 1.2(c))

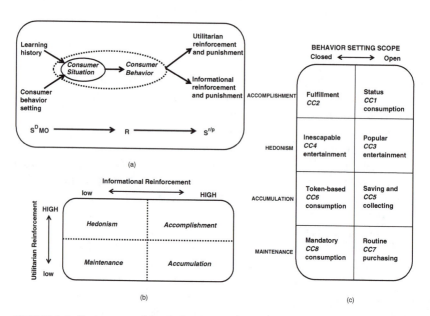

FIGURE 1.2 **Summary of the Behavioral Perspective Model (BPM).** (a) Summative Behavioral Perspective Model. (b) Patterns of reinforcement and operant classes of consumer behavior. (c) The BPM Contingency Matrix. CC = Contingency Category. Note that all of the variables in the model and its derivative analyses are to be relatively comprehended, though for greater elegance of exposition the text refers simply to open and closed consumer behavior settings, high and low utilitarian and informational reinforcement, etc. See Foxall (2016b).

adds the dimension of closed–open consumer behavior settings to this and defines eight categories of contingency to which all consumer behavior can be functionally allocated. Although these are technically hypothetical interpretations of consumer behavior, they have proved remarkably predictive and robust in a wide range of empirical investigations: see Foxall (2017) for a summary.

Accomplishment, maintained by relatively high levels of both utilitarian and informational reinforcement, consists of such consumer behaviors as taking high status vacations, being an early adopter of consumer innovations (in open settings), and attending personal development programs (in closed settings). *Hedonism* includes consumer behaviors maintained by relatively high levels of utilitarian reinforcement and relatively low levels of informational reinforcement. It is typified (in open settings) by watching television, attending movies, going to parties, or a springtime walk in the park, and (in closed settings) by watching an inflight movie or listening to music while waiting on the telephone. *Accumulation* is consumer behavior maintained by relatively low levels of utilitarian reinforcement and relatively high levels of informational reinforcement: like saving up for a treat (open settings) and accumulating points for air travel (closed settings). Finally, *Maintenance* comprises consumer behaviors that are the result of relatively low levels of both utilitarian and informational reinforcement. In open settings this might take the form of doing the weekly supermarket shop; in closed settings, of filling out forms for a passport so that one can travel abroad.

In the extensional understanding of consumer choice, the mode adopted in theoretical minimalism, there is evidence that the ranges of behaviors encompassed by the continuum of consumer behavior analysis settings may not be of identical dimension for each of the four operant classes of consumer choice (Foxall, 1999). Figure 1.3 illustrates stylistically their relationships.

The BPM has inspired a wide range of empirical research (summarized in Foxall, 2017) showing that consumers purchase quantities of utilitarian and informational reinforcement, maximizing specific bundles of these sources of functional and

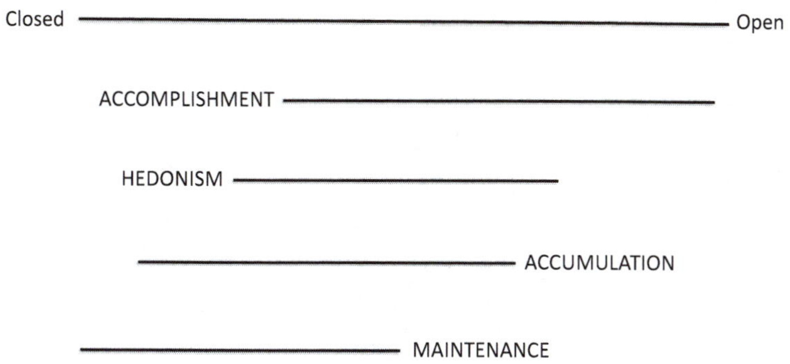

Closed ————————————————————————— Open

ACCOMPLISHMENT ——————————————————

HEDONISM ————————————————

———————————————— ACCUMULATION

———————————————— MAINTENANCE

FIGURE 1.3 Staggered ranges of consumer behavior setting scope. There is no attempt at definitive scale here, just an illustration of an idea. See Foxall (1999).

social benefit through the acquisition and deployment of products and services. Consumer behavior, in the sense of quantity demanded, is sensitive to changes in price but also to the amounts of utilitarian and informational reinforcement consumers acquire and consume. The operant classes of consumer choice defined in terms of pattern of reinforcement (Figure 1.2(b)) and the contingency categories that appear in Figure 1.2(c) are all instrumental in understanding how consumers respond to marketing variables that include not only price, to which economics largely confines itself, but also the elements of branding that are central to modern marketing. Empirical research supports the structure and implications of the BPM and ensures that consumer behavior analysis is a body of knowledge that is highly germane to the development of the intentional and cognitive accounts toward which Intentional Behaviorism strives.[2]

Notes

1 For a treatment of the behaviorist, intentional, and cognitive perspectives that the BPM elucidates, see Foxall (2016b).
2 For an account of this phase of the research program, see Foxall (2017).

2

CONSUMER ACTION

Abstract

The Intentional Behaviorist research strategy has three stages: theoretical minimalism, intentional interpretation, and cognitive interpretation. These involve, first, the construct and testing of a model of consumer choice based on a behaviorist depiction that explains (predicts) consumer behavior in terms of the environmental stimuli responsible for the rate at which it occurs: the aim of this stage is to learn what this methodology can uniquely reveal as the mainsprings of consumer choice and also to identify the point (if any) at which this means of explanation breaks down and must be replaced by an intentional account. The stage of intentional interpretation demonstrates whether consumer activity that is not amenable to an extensional, behaviorist explication can be satisfactorily accounted for in intentional terms. If this proves to be the case, the final stage, cognitive interpretation, critically examines the feasibility of the intentional interpretation as a means of understanding consumer choice. In the course of moving from the first stage of theoretical minimalism to the subsequent stages of psychological explanation, our subject matter ceases to be consumer behavior, a form of activity that is regulated by environmental stimuli, to consumer action which is conceived as resulting from the consumer's mental processes, including the perceptual and conceptual representation of the contingencies of reinforcement and punishment identified in the initial stage. A theme of the analysis undertaken in the present work is that all or virtually all modes of consumer choice involve a degree of akrasia or weakness of will marked by a tendency to reverse preferences over time in accordance with differing rates of discounting future rewards. This is an essential component of the definition of consumer choice.

Intentional behaviorism

A summary of the fundamentals

The initial stage of Intentional Behaviorism, *theoretical minimalism*, is founded on the view that consumer behavior is shaped and maintained by its consequences, the reinforcers and punishers delivered by the products and services consumers acquire and the processes in which they consume them. Theoretical minimalism therefore entails building parsimonious, behaviorist models of behavior and testing them to destruction in order to ascertain the point at which an intentional account becomes necessary and the form it must take. When a satisfactory explanation of observed behavior cannot be made by treating it as a component of a set of contingencies of reinforcement that also includes discriminative and reinforcing/punishing stimuli, the point at which the stimulus field necessary for a behaviorist explanation is not empirically available to the researcher, psychological explanation becomes inevitable. This leads into the second stage, *intentional interpretation*, in which an account of the stimulus-free behavior proceeds by treating it as an idealized system which maximizes utility and ascribing to it the intentionality – desires, beliefs, emotions, and perceptions – necessary to render it intelligible. This idealized interpretation is cashed out in the third stage in terms of a *cognitive interpretation* that demonstrates how far cognitive processing can account for the intentional behavior proposed.[1] This three-stage procedure is the means by which Intentional Behaviorism interrelates the context in which consumer choice occurs – the physical and social surroundings, including temporal and regulatory influences, that comprise the stimulus field, and the pattern of reinforcing and punishing consequences of behavior that regulate its rate of occurrence – to the cognitive concepts required for the explanation of behavior for which any such context eludes observation. In the course of turning to psychological explanation, the principal concern for consumer psychology has become to ascertain how the contingencies of reinforcement and punishment are subjectively processed by consumers prior to their acting, i.e., the explanation of consumer choice by reference to consumers' desires, beliefs, emotions, and perceptions.

Earlier expositions of Intentional Behaviorism have concentrated on desires and beliefs as the central intentional components of explanations of such behavior (Foxall, 2016a, 2016b). In this chapter and the two which follow it, we expand this methodology by concentrating on perception and emotion. This progression is consistent with the fact that, while theoretical minimalism (leading to behaviorological explanation) is concerned with the individual's *behavior*, bodily movement or activity that results from what happens or has happened to her, psychological explanation is concerned with *action*, bodily movement which the individual performs.

A little more detail

Radical behaviorism is a vehicle for theoretical minimalism only so long as we are asking the basic question: what permits us to predict and control behavior, i.e., only as long as we believe that identifying the environmental stimuli that control a behavior is sufficient to explain it. We can then, at least in the closed settings of the operant chamber, discover the environmental stimuli of which behavior is a function. If, however, we ask what mechanisms would be required for an organism to respond in this way, i.e., if we seek to explain environment–behavior relationships, then we must seek a means of ascribing intentionality to the organism.

The psychological explanation that develops as a result of identifying the contributions and limitations of behaviorism has two stages. The first of these, which we have seen involves the development of an *intentional interpretation*, treats the consumer as an idealized utility-maximizing system and derives the desires, beliefs, emotions, and perceptions that are required in order to account for its behavior.[2] The immediate criterion for the appraisal of this depiction is that it renders the behavior of consumers more intelligible and perhaps more predictable. The establishment of this intentional interpretation fulfills the quest for an intentional portrayal of the consumer-situation: no longer simply the extensionally specified interaction of a learning history with a consumer behavior setting, the intentional consumer-situation presents the framework of desires, beliefs, emotions, and perceptions that render observed consumer choice intelligible in the absence of the required stimulus field. This idealized portrayal of consumer activity is subsequently evaluated, in the course of the final stage of Intentional Behaviorism, which we have seen is the *cognitive interpretation*, by reference to its consistency with a broader cognitive interpretation founded upon empirical research on decision making and action. The essence of psychological explanation, which includes both intentional and cognitive interpretations, is that it describes its subject matter using intentional idioms such as desires, believes, and perceives, as well as higher-order cognitive processes such as memory, information processing, and decision making. Each of these intentional attitudes, as they are known by philosophers, is characterized by its being about something other than itself. The consumer desires a product, believes that she can find it at her local supermarket, and when she arrives perceives it on the shelf. Intentional objects do not necessarily exist other than as mental representations – Santa Claus, for instance, or the Golden Mountain: Brentano (1874) pointed out that intentional objects have intentional inexistence. By contrast, the extensional language in terms of which theoretical minimalism proceeds avoids intentional idioms of this kind.[3]

The theories that have provided cognitive interpretation to establish the intentional interpretation of the idealized consumer have taken three forms (Foxall, 2016b, Chapters 8–10). The first draws upon the sub-personal realm that is the subject of neuroscience to establish the content of cognitive theories which have taken the form of dual-process theories of cognitive structure and process. This is the approach I have termed micro-cognitive psychology.[4] The second source of cognitive theorizing appeals to the super-personal realm of the reinforcing and punishing consequences of behavior which determine its frequency of repetition in order to set the content and form of cognitive explanations of behavior. A disciplinary base for this kind of cognitive explanation is found in theories of collective intentionality in which social groups determine for themselves what will act as reinforcers and punishers for their members. This approach I have termed macro-cognitive psychology.[5] The third approach, meso-cognitive psychology, provides necessary links among the sub-personal and super-personal bases of these cognitive psychologies and the personal level at which behavior is conceptualized as well as the desires, beliefs, emotions, and perceptions in terms of which the behavior is explained. Theories that stress the ways in which consumers' competing interests in short- and long-term satisfactions, such as Ainslie's (1992) picoeconomics, have been pressed into service for this level of exposition.[6] In this book, and especially in Chapter 6 which returns to the question of cognitive interpretation, I shall concentrate on micro-cognitive psychology, largely because this is the kind of cognitive theorizing that some authors have argued should be eliminated in favor of an account of action based on perceptual experience.

An action perspective

Bifurcating consumer activity

As a result of the theoretical thrust of the Intentional Behaviorist research program's having moved firmly into its second phase, that of showing what form a psychological explanation of consumer choice should take, it is now principally concerned with action rather than behavior. The adoption of an action perspective means that we are concerned primarily with activities that are performed by the consumer rather than something that happens to the consumer.[7] This focus raises a specific concern with the nature of the cognitive processes that mediate consumer action and their relationship to the ecology of consumption, something of central importance to consumer psychology. We concentrate, therefore, on how the contingencies of reinforcement come to bear on the behavior of the individual through the perceptual aspects of the felt emotion or affect that provide at least a component of her learning history. We are concerned with the contingencies as they exist within the mental processing of the individual rather than in the external environment. This entails forging links between the context of prior behavior and the cognitive framework within which it is perceived, processed, and comprehended, and within which consumer action anticipates the context in which it is performed.

By "consumer activity" is understood whatever consumers do, regardless of how it is explained. It is the activity of consumers as it would be observed by a non-theoretical watcher who took no pains to discover whether the activity resulted from things happening to the consumer or from mental operations occurring within the consumer. Consumer activity subsumes two further categories, consumer action and consumer behavior. Action is activity that is spoken of transitively, my moving my arm, rather than intransitively as my arm's moving or the moving of my arm (Hornsby, 1981). It is activity that I, the agent, bring about (i.e., transitive activity or activity$_T$) rather than something that happens to me (i.e., intransitive activity or activity$_I$), or which at least must be spoken of in these terms in the absence of a stimulus field to which the activity can be attributed. An implication drawn by some philosophers is that there is an agent (an "I") that is responsible for bringing about this movement and that the bringing about is accomplished or at least explained by mental means.[8] All of these implications of an action perspective require multi-faceted philosophical discussion which is beyond the scope of this volume; the only definite implication of employing intentional language that I willingly embrace is that extensional language has failed to provide an explanation of observed behavior and the sole recourse is to intentionality. Making no ontological assumptions on the basis of this shift in explanation, I draw the conclusion that we have two languages, two modes of speaking about our subject matter, and two sources of explanation. But the fact remains that we have only one subject matter, what consumers *do*.

The activities we speak of intransitively, then, are behaviors; those of which we speak transitively, actions. Action and behavior can be topographically identical and it is only as we seek to explain the activity, to trace its causation, that we switch from one appellation to the other. Behavior can be understood in terms of its biology, as is the case for taxa, or behaviorologically, as is the case for Pavlovian and operant conditioning.[9] There are more complex behaviors than these that we account for in broadly similar ways when we resort to the neurophysiology of the organism to find events that are indispensable to the performance of the behavior in question or that correlate with it in ways that make sense from our general biological perspective. We are justified in treating activities as behavior in this way if we can demonstrate that they are caused by, or a function of, environmental stimulation whether this arose, phylogenetically, in the course of evolution by natural selection or during the ontogenetic development of an individual. (See Figure 2.1.)[10]

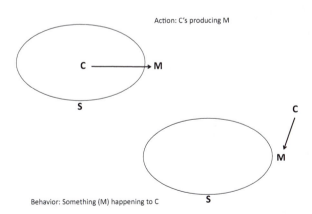

FIGURE 2.1 **Behavior and action.** Action consists in the system's, *S*'s, being the cause (C) of its movement: *S* is the origin of its own movement. This is *activity$_T$*: *S*'s moving all or part of itself. Behavior consists in an external stimulus causing *S*'s movement: *S* is acted upon to move in a particular way. This is *activity$_I$*: *S*'s being moved. See Dretske (1988, p. 3) but note that my depiction and terminology differ from his.

Action, then, is activity for which we are unable to establish antecedent stimuli that would account for it by making it amenable to prediction and control. Action must be accounted for in terms of the intentionality of the individual, her desires, beliefs, emotions, and perceptions, as we reconstruct them from our knowledge of her historical and current circumstances.[11] Having exhausted the explanation of behavior by reference to the extensional sciences of neuroscience and behavioral science, we have no alternative but to explicate any further observed behavior of the organism intentionally. Hence, while "activity" denotes either behavior or action, the topography of the activity in question may be identical whether it is viewed as behavior or action: only its explanation differs. Behavior, by contrast, *can* be traced to a stimulus field. It is only when the discriminative stimuli that would otherwise account for an observed behavior cannot be located that the observed activity is designated *action* and a psychological explanation becomes necessary. Activity for which no such setting variables are apparent requires an intentional explanation. We have no alternative but to go beyond the extensional explanation of behavior because the necessary basis of such an explanation is absent.

Consumer choice

Our focus on action as opposed to behavior has an important consequence. The term "consumer choice" is often used synonymously with "consumer behavior" or "consumer activity," but, in view of the emphasis on action, I should like to define it more closely. Consumer *choice* is marked by a degree of conflict between present and future activities. Should the consumer make purchases at a local convenience store which will charge more but which requires less personal effort than going to the more distant supermarket? Is the consumption of alcohol justified if the expense means eating poorly? Should the student opt for a sports event and so have less money to buy books? Each time the consumer chooses the first option a longer-term and potentially bigger goal has to be displaced. Shopping at the supermarket, even if this requires walking there, will leave more money at the end of the week. Nutritious food is expected to ensure both a healthier life and a longer life: perhaps a single instance in which one selects an alternative product will make no difference to either but a *pattern* of choosing the more immediate payoff may well do so. The student's future depends on studying now and therefore access to books; once again, attending one sports event may not interfere much with this and it may even enhance the process of studying by providing a necessary diversion. But an extended sequence of such choices is likely to impede progress elsewhere. Indeed, it is this temporal conflict that transforms consumer activity, be it behavior or action, into consumer *choice*. Sometimes immediacy seems to be the sole criterion in securing the opportunity to consume. The addict's craving a substance or a behavioral outlet is a case in point even if the satisfaction of the longing fails to bring pleasure. At other times it is relatively easy to pace our consumption. In both cases, however, it is the management of the temporal dimension that enables us to speak of consumer choice.

A degree of akrasia

A recurring feature of the patterns of action which illustrate consumer choice as they extend over time is the reversal of preferences. The choice inheres not just in the objective alternatives available to the consumer in the form of different external rewards: it is to be found also *within* the individual who values the rewards in varying ways over time. (Individual differences in propensity to temporal opportunities and demands stem in part from variations in learning history, personality, and neurophysiology, some of which are discussed in the "Ramsey's claim" section in Chapter 4.) It is easy enough to resolve at the start of the day that you will take a healthy walk to the supermarket and save some money, or study all day without distraction, or forgo more immediate temptations in order to eat well. As lunchtime or the study period or the opportunity to spend a relaxing evening over a drink approaches, however, it is only too easy to switch preferences in favor of the less demanding option that is currently available, even in full knowledge that this will cause a more significant long-term goal to recede further. Sometimes, we modify our preferences yet again, regretting having taken what now looks like the easy option and the consequent loss of a larger reward. Tomorrow, therefore, the cycle may well begin all over again.[12] Some consumers do, of course, choose the delayed but superior option and do so consistently. The point, however, is that most, if not all, consumer choice *can* invite weakness of will or akrasia understood as the selection of a smaller reward that is available earlier over a larger reward that will not appear for some time.[13]

In affluent marketing-oriented economies, where levels of discretionary income run at very high levels, being able to choose immediate consumption rather than delay gratification can exert a strong influence on the pattern of consumer choice. As McGinn (2006, p. 50) comments, "Weakness of will is easy; it is explaining it that is hard."[14] Such behavior is said to be impulsive and is contrasted with that which ignores the immediate but inferior reward by waiting for the superior alternative, thereby exhibiting self-control. Let's not exaggerate: impulsivity does not necessarily lead to serious deleterious effects – indeed, sometimes it is a necessary interlude, adding the spice to life – but if it persists then, in broadly-conceived economic terms, it can be, to say the least, suboptimal. Moreover, an intriguing facet of this kind of choice is that it is not necessarily practiced by people who are generally irrational; as Searle (2001, p. 10) puts it, "akrasia in rational beings is as common as wine in France." But it may entail psychological as well as economic irrationality as well as a-rationality. The exploration of this theme is a central concern of this book because it is closely related to the perceptual means by which consumers evaluate the contingencies of reinforcement and punishment and to the desires and beliefs that shape perceptual experience.

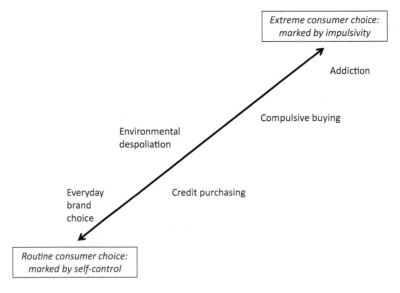

FIGURE 2.2 The continuum of consumer choice.

This emphasis reflects that consumer behaviors form a continuum that ranges from the routine, everyday, and commonplace to the extreme, compulsive, and addictive (Figure 2.2). The selection of a brand of a frequently used foodstuff is, at least in affluent marketing-oriented economies, an example of the former: it involves the choice of a tried, tested, and trusted item and takes place in a context of minimal uncertainty. Even this example of a consumer action may not be entirely conflict-free since it may require that other purchases are delayed and raise considerations that the item purchased may not be strictly necessary given one's budget or that it might be available at a lower price at another store requiring travel. However, for the most part, routine purchasing involves a minimum of conflicting demands. At the other pole of this Continuum of Consumer Choice (Foxall, 2010, 2017) lie the severe compulsive consumer choices involved in addiction. Addiction defies a single-sentence definition but it is likely to involve preference reversal, perhaps to the extent of economic irrationality, and beyond that leading to the loss of friends, spouse, home, or job. The maladaptive behavior involved may also be exacerbated by neurophysiological over-activity (see, for instance, Ross et al., 2008; Foxall, 2016a).

Between these polar extremes, there are consumer actions such as purchasing on some form of credit because it brings consumption forward in time even though it exacts a potentially disruptive price in terms of the eventual repayments that must be made; despoiling the environment through waste disposal or using limited resources such as fossil fuels, which reduce the costs of consuming in the short term but may be responsible for the consumer's incurring more pervasive expense at a later date; and compulsive shopping in which the immediacy of ownership is often divorced even from consumption since the outcome may well be hoarding rather than use. Apart from routine consumer choice, all of these consumer behaviors entail paying more, sooner or later, for the convenience of consuming at once; and even everyday purchasing, as we have seen, is open to these considerations. Moreover, as the analysis will show, routine consumer choice is wide open to the influence of the social, economic, cognitive, and neurophysiological factors that shape its more extreme versions. There is potential for *a degree of* akrasia to be present in most if not all consumer choice.

Is this to say that all or virtually all consumer action is akratic? By no means. *Addiction as Consumer Choice* (Foxall, 2016a) initiated discussion of akrasia in the context of the theory of consumer action, concentrating on the more extreme aspects of consumption that are marked by akrasia. An emphasis there is on the *economic* irrationality of extended akratic choice, and the theoretical developments to which this analysis led were generalized to the broad spectrum of consumer choice, from everyday purchasing to addiction, in *Perspectives on Consumer Choice* (Foxall, 2016b). It is hardly the case that all or even most consumer action involves weakness of will on the scale encountered in compulsion and addiction. But some *degree of* temporal discounting is common and a good deal of consumer choice reflects psychological irrationality and a-rationality even if it is free of economic irrationality. The present work seeks, therefore, to understand better the *psychological* rationality, irrationality, and a-rationality by which consumer choice may be explained. It represents, as we shall see, a further development of the Intentional Behaviorist approach to the cognitive explanation of consumer choice.

Consumer choice that lacks rationality in either an economic or a psychological sense is apparent in the extremes of addiction and compulsion. Addictive consumption, for instance, involves steep temporal discounting: the addict strongly prefers immediate satisfaction to the longer-term benefits of abstinence. In addition, addicts may display economic irrationality, as when they spend large amounts of money on trying to overcome their addiction (on specialist programs and courses, for example) only to relapse at an early opportunity. Severe addiction can be marked by disruptions to the addict's lifestyle: loss of some or all of their livelihood, home, friends, and spouse. Some of these elements of addiction, particularly the compulsion to consume immediately and repeatedly, are likely to be exacerbated by neurophysiological events that generate exaggerated rewards for the continued pursuit of the actions resulting in addiction.

It is tempting to concentrate on the role of economic rationality in consumer choice, partly because it is easier to identify objectively than are deviations from psychological rationality which may be subjective and hidden. (This theme will be examined in detail in the "Psychoanalytical tools for intentional interpretation" section in Chapter 5 and the "A psychoanalytic dimension" section in Chapter 6.) We often hold desires and beliefs that would not be borne out if they were checked against reality and we seek evidence that seems to bolster these mental propositions but which must be spurious. We do not necessarily advertise these thought processes to the world. The so-called "gambler's fallacy," for instance, is the belief that a run of losses must be assuaged by a large success on the basis of the "law of averages." Nicotine addicts smoke what they believe to be their "last cigarette" many times. And we are all prone to the notion that making a New Year's resolution to eat less and get fit will change our behavior. In each case such beliefs begin with a fantasy: of a large win, of a tobacco-free lifestyle, or of a future self who effortlessly pursues a lifestyle marked by eating more moderately and exercising more strenuously. (These aspects of contingency-representation are examined in more detail in the section entitled "Step 4: The ascription of cognition" in Chapter 5.) Spurious evidence can be adduced in favor of all of these fantasies (see Brakel, 2001, 2009): perhaps to the effect that the betting odds have shifted in the gambler's favor, that giving up tobacco, overcoming excessive eating, and working out can be accomplished simply by summoning willpower or obtaining a gym membership. Change is possible, of course, but it is not rationally predictable on the basis of these beliefs, especially if the consumer has a history – as many of us have – of repeatedly trying and failing. Although they look like genuine beliefs that guide action rationally, these fantasies-plus-evidence that never come into contact with reality may be no more than wishful thinking.

There are also consumers who are not addicted but who are open to fantasies with serious consequences not only for themselves but also for others whom they love. For example, some parents avoid immunization for their children in the belief that it will harm them. They do this in the face of demonstrated medical-scientific evidence that inoculation is actually efficacious and that rejecting it puts their own and other parents' children at risk. They may well have reasons for their behavior: information gained online from dubious sources and masqueraded as "evidence" for views which are never tested against reality.[15] Less dramatically, many consumers are influenced by the strong claims of advertising and special offers and consumer deals to over-purchase and/or over-consume, backing up their actions with beliefs, not always conscious, about the social acceptability and functional benefits but especially of the self-enhancement that will follow. These consumer actions do not necessarily reflect psychological *irrationality*, which would require consumers to adopt practices that evince a deliberate negation of common-sense; but they can involve a degree of *a*-rationality where fantasized goals are shorn up by evidence that is not reality-tested.

Now, as long as one avoids seriously compulsive or addictive behaviors, this may not matter. Being somewhat lax in one's devotion to economic theory or psychotherapeutic demands is hardly a crime. But there are two instances in which attention to these deviations is called for. The first is that, for addicts and near-addicts, these are real problems and a theory of consumer choice should seek to understand them better. The second is that an explanation of consumer action that relies on the assumption of a high degree of cognitive rationality ought to be interested in consumer choice that is not so characterized, whether to a large or moderate extent. Many philosophical and social-scientific models of decision making, for instance, assume a rationality that is seldom encountered in reality. The research strategy that has been adopted in devising my own explanation of consumer choice, Intentional Behaviorism, relies at one point, though not ultimately, on the assumption of rationality. It employs the concept of the *intentional consumer-situation* as a theoretical construction that treats the consumer as a rational utility maximizer to whom, given her learning history and current circumstances, appropriate intentionality can be ascribed in order, first, to render her observed actions more intelligible and, second, to demonstrate that an intentional/cognitive explanation of her actions is feasible. Beyond this, it reverts to the possibility that consumer choice may not reach the requirements of optimality, but the temporary assumption of this behavioral objective nevertheless requires further attention.

At this point, it is useful to summarize the nature of akrasia in more formal terms as it is dealt with in the three stages of Intentional Behaviorism.[16]

Consumer decisions in temporal perspective

The following account of how choice is explained, first, by behaviorists and, subsequently, by cognitive psychologists, is presented as an example of how Intentional Behaviorism's strategy of theoretical minimalism identifies the need for an intentional explanation. As Malcolm (1977, p. 89) notes, radical behaviorism is "essentially a philosophical doctrine" that is continuous with physicalism, the view that psychology can be formulated in terms that describe physical entities (Carnap, 1959, p. 165). Psychological laws are therefore a kind of physical law and the meaning of a sentence is its means of verification. In Intentional Behaviorism, this perspective is an essential starting point for the identification of when non-physicalist, intentional explanation is required and the functions it must perform.

This account centers on the activity of the consumer whose behavior exhibits a degree of akrasia and examines how she decides between immediate and delayed behavioral outcomes, be they reinforcing or rewarding, aversive or punishing. Much consumer choice entails decisions of this kind, from the preference for having a product now even though this requires a larger eventual payment for the privilege, through the disposal of waste and consumption of fossil fuels for which subsequent consumers, perhaps generations of consumers, will incur the full costs, to compulsive shopping and the familiar addictions to substances like alcohol and behavior patterns like excessive gambling.[17] The underlying distinctions among these modes of consumer choice derive from the extent to which consumers discount the future consequences of their activities. Only the most commonplace everyday purchasing of familiar brands may escape a degree of akratic preference and even here there is the constant choice of how to obtain the funds to pay for them or whether to forgo them in order to make longer-lasting choices. I do not think it is far-fetched therefore to select this exemplar; insofar as all consumer choice entails the allocation of scarce resources among competing ends, it is all concerned with trade-offs between apparently superior and apparently inferior outcomes.

Theoretical minimalism

Radical behaviorism avoids intentionality as a route to explanation and thus provides an ideal conceptual basis for theoretical minimalism. Hence, choice, in this paradigm, is the relative rate of responding. Current accounts of akrasia, in which an individual chooses between a smaller reward available sooner (SSR) and a larger reward that will not become available until later (LLR), propose comparative evaluation of these alternatives, which appear at t_1 and t_2, respectively. Moreover, they entail that these evaluations occur, first, at t_0, and again at t_1 when the selection of one option excludes the possibility of the other. The resulting explanation, which involves the decision maker in the comparison of representations of the choices, is not a radical behaviorist explanation since it relies on the symbolic manipulation of information, mentally, neurophysiologically, or in private or public verbal behavior. Rather, it is cognitive. We need to consider how the distinct paradigms presented by radical behaviorism and cognitive psychology deal with behavior change that entails the substitution of one pattern of behavior for another. What are the elements of a radical behaviorist explanation of the kind of behavior change that is the goal of the strategies that are commonly advocated as means of overcoming akrasia?

As we have seen, the essence of radical behaviorist explanation is the insistence on extensional language to describe its subject matter, and the corresponding avoidance of intentionality (Foxall, 2004). While this may not be formally enshrined as a principle of radical behaviorism (see, however, Schnaitter, 1999), it seems to me to be its defining mark. Someone who appreciated this was B. F. Skinner (1971), who took pains to point out, for example, that when we say the fisherman spreads nets in order to catch fish we are simply alluding to the order in which these operations occur, rather than to a pre-behavioral resolve to attain a mentally-conceived goal through carrying out a causal act. In line with this, choice in behavior analysis is behavior, or rather the relative rate of responding, not a matter of mental deliberation. As de Villiers and Herrnstein (1976, p. 1131) put it, choice is "behavior in the context of other behavior." There is, accordingly, no room in radical behaviorism for the notion that behavior is a function of representations – in mind, or in verbal behavior, or in neurophysiology – for representation invokes intentionality in the explanation of behavior.

The pre-behavioral mental representation of the environment is actually the central feature of cognitivism, where it includes both relatively simple perceptual and complex symbolic processing (de Gelder, 1996). This presents a quite distinct approach to explanation from that of behaviorism in which the effect of the environment is direct, unmediated by representations. In radical behaviorism, behavior is a function of the external reinforcing and punishing stimuli that have previously followed similar responding. The essence of this psychological paradigm is its insistence that behavior is a function of environmental variables rather than intentionality and that internal states other than physiological events (which can safely be left to the physiologist) play no part.[18] The control of behavior exerted by external stimuli can be fully described in extensional language and resort to description in terms of beliefs and desires, the stock-in-trade of intentional explanation is superfluous (e.g., Skinner, 1950, 1975). The crucial matter, as Compiani (1996, pp. 46–47) notes, is that "[t]his reasoning exclusively in terms of external parameters (stimulus and response) assumes that the processing by the system does not add anything at all to the information content of the input; that is, the performance of the system can be completely characterized externally without recourse to the internal properties of the system."

There is no place here for explanation in terms of intrapersonal desires and beliefs, attitudes, or intentions, information processing or decision making. My theme is how this squares with the explanation of akrasia, weakness of will. I shall examine the implications for explanation of an influential approach to akrasia which proceeds in terms of hyperbolic discounting, which I believe is ultimately cognitive, and compare it with a genuinely behavior analytic approach to explanation. I shall not identify a specific source of this mode of explanation since it is pervasive in behavior analysis.

Hyperbolic discounting

Akrasia is frequently analyzed in terms of hyperbolic discounting. In Figure 2.3, t_1 is the initial choice point, at which Ego may choose either to take a smaller, sooner reward (the SSR) or to wait for a larger, later reward (the LLR) which will be available at t_2. At t_0 the larger reward is said to be valued more highly than the smaller. What can this mean? Neither the SSR nor the LLR is empirically available to Ego at t_0. Where can they exist in order to be evaluated? They can only exist, in a behavior analytic account, in either (a) Ego's learning history and/or (b) the rules with which she has been presented (or has devised for herself).[19] To say they are in the contingencies overlooks the fact that the contingencies are not empirically available to her at this point. Neither formulation actually determines where the SSR and the LLR are. If Ego's learning history is a means of predicting her future behavior, that learning history must be available to the investigator, who is

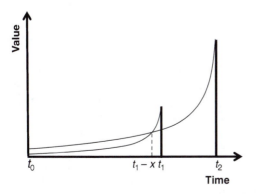

FIGURE 2.3 **Hyperbolic discounting and the point of decision.**

making the prediction, as an inventory of the behaviors Ego has emitted in similar circumstances and their reinforcing (and punishing, though I am not concentrating on these) consequences: the SSRs and LLRs to which they have led. The learning history is not necessarily available to Ego in this form. But there is assumed to be a learning history of which Ego's future behavior is a function. There are behavior analysts who argue that learning history is the only explanatory variable we need to explain behavior.

But knowing these things does not allow us to locate the SSR and the LLR at t_0 in order that we can value them or, rather, know what precisely Ego is valuing. Whether we use Ego's learning history or Ego's rules to predict her behavior, what we actually have is a representation of the SSR and the LLR either in our inventory of her prior choices or in the track, ply, or augmental. This may enable us to predict but it is not useful to explanation. Is the representation of which Ego's next response is a function in her memory of her past behavior and its consequences, in her neurons, or in her internal verbal behavior, perhaps as she privately repeats the rule to herself? Ego can only value the SSR and the LLR if she has a representation of them. Even if she relies on a written record of her learning history or of the rule, her comparison of the SSR and the LLR and their comparative evaluation must take place in verbal behavior, private or overt.

A similar set of circumstances obtains as Ego approaches t_1. We are told that just before the SSR becomes empirically available, its value to Ego rises dramatically, exceeding that of the LLR and that, therefore, the SSR is likely to be chosen at t_1. Again, the SSR is not empirically available at this point, $t_1 - x$, but Ego is said to value it relative to another reward, the LLR, that is equally unavailable. If it is necessary to assume that the imminence of the SSR must be signaled to Ego for the closeness of t_1 to change her valuation, and if this provides some substance to its existence, it still follows that it must be compared with the as yet immaterial LLR. If Ego does not take the SSR but waits for the LLR at t_2, she is said to value the LLR higher than the SSR throughout the period under review, and therefore to discount exponentially (since there is never a point at which the SSR is the more highly valued).

A purely descriptive behaviorist explanation of this behavior is feasible. We can say that the impulsive consumer values the SSR more highly than the delayed LLR at t_1, and that this is an inference from, a re-description of, her actual behavior at t_1. The behavior of selecting the SSR is the valuing; the valuing is the behavior. This avoids the question of how Ego evaluates the SSR in comparison with the LLR except via a representation of the latter because it aims simply to understand the frequency of Ego's choice of the SSR as a proportion of her total number of choices of the SSR and the LLR. Choice is then defined as this rate of relative responding. This is a genuine radical behaviorist explanation since it avoids intentional idioms and is concerned only with behavior. Admittedly, it consists entirely in post hoc description but the relative frequency of responding so obtained could be used to predict further choice. Moreover, its purpose is solely to predict and control Ego's subsequent behavior on the basis of a reconstruction of her learning history.

It may be useful to reiterate how distinct this explanation is from that which the literature of akrasia often puts forward. What is being claimed in the latter is that (a) Ego values the SSR and the LLR first at t_0 where the LLR is the more highly valued, (b) again when the SSR and LLR curves cross just prior to t_1, at $t_1 - x$, that this is the time when Ego comes to value the SSR higher than the LLR. Comparative evaluation of this kind must take place in her private or public verbal behavior. By contrast, the radical behaviorist interpretation precludes Ego's valuing either reward at t_0 and in the interval between t_0 and t_1 because there is no opportunity for her to behave with respect to selecting one or other of the choices. Unless that is, we take any overt verbal behavior of Ego's into consideration. If Ego tells us at t_0 that she values the LLR more highly than the SSR, is this choice behavior? Is this behavior the valuation, her comparative valuation? If so, on what is it based in the face of the SSRs and the LLRs not being empirically available and presenting themselves to Ego only in the form of representations in her learning history or rules? And if her public verbal behavior would count as her comparative evaluation, why shouldn't her private verbal behavior? We are not, after all, predicting her *behavior* now, in which case her private verbal behavior would be of no use to us since it would not be empirically available. We are only trying to understand, explain, why she behaves as she does.

The difficulty with this, from a behavior analytic point of view, is that the valuation is comparative, between the SSR and the LLR. Now the LLR can be no more than a representation at t_0 and t_1 and the SSR is a representation at $t_1 - x$. How does a representation enter into comparative evaluation if it is not a mental (private) representation? To speak in terms of representation means admitting intentionality into one's paradigm and, more than that, to ascribe causal significance to the representation. For Ego's behavior in choosing the SSR earlier or waiting for the LLR must be a function of their comparative evaluation. If we say that the SSR and the LLR are representations in Ego's private verbal behavior at t_0, and between then and t_1, and that thereafter the LLR remains a representation in Ego's verbal behavior, then we make private verbal behavior intentional. If we say that the valuation takes place at $t_1 - x$, then this representative nature of verbal behavior is only confirmed. In any case, the spoken expression "I value...," whether private or public, is itself intentional. To value is a transitive verb. We always value something and therefore our valuations are necessarily about something, intentional. These are not locutions I associate with radical behaviorist explanation.

The distinction between the explanation to which I am drawing attention and that which is a genuinely behavior analytic explanation boils down to the former's molecular analysis of choice, which ignores sequences of responses and reinforcers, and the latter's understanding of choice as a molar pattern of behavior and its consequences. We can describe the relative frequencies of behaviors that lead to the SSR and compare them to the frequencies of behavior the outcome of which is the LLR. That way we can confine our analysis to the behaviors that actually eventuate at t_1 and t_2, and ignore t_0 and the interludes among the temporal points of interest. But the question arises, how are these sequences of behavior inaugurated and how do they change? If learning history is determinative, how can behavior ever deviate from the established patterns it imposes? Yet the behavior of people who have apparently habitually chosen the SSR sometimes is reoriented toward long-term selection of the LLR. How does this come about?

Behavior change

There are three sources of behavioral change: new contingencies; new rules describing contingencies, and new strategies of comparative evaluation. New contingencies need to be discovered in vivo – through exploration, we find out that the arrangement of actions and rewards has changed: for instance, that what was the LLR is now delivered at t_1, while what was the SSR arrives at t_2. This is not, however, the problem of akrasia which is our concern. Such a contingency would in any case induce exclusive choice of the SSR at t_1, and the question of comparative evaluation, however we define it, would be instantly resolved. Taking a behavior analytic perspective, we could simply monitor the behavior of Ego after the contingencies governing her behavior are modified and determine how the sequences of responses and reinforcers are functionally related. This raises interesting questions for research: Would we encounter inflexibility in her behavior after the contingencies had changed, how long would it take for the new contingencies to become operative, how would we explain any insensitivity to the new schedule? New rules leave us in the original quandary of how to explain behavior that is a function of representations.

Strategies are means by which the akrates seeks to change behavior by modifying either the contingencies themselves or how she is thinking about them in order to ameliorate her so-called weakness of will. Most of them take on board the necessity of envisioning behavior in a molar fashion. Bundling, for example, entails bringing all the future outcomes of a stream of choices between the SSR and the LLR to a point prior to t_1 (Figure 2.4). Hence, the akrates is able to contemplate the sum total of the SSRs and LLRs she might reap in the course of an entire sequence of responses. While, for the hyperbolic discounter facing a single instance of choice the SSR > the LLR at t_1, if we bundle future rewards, the sum of the LLRs > that of the SSRs. This makes it easier to commit to the sustained pursuit of the LLR and having made this selection once it becomes more probable that Ego can continue to do so on succeeding occasions of choice. But where does this bundling take place? It can only be in Ego's private or public verbal behavior. Indeed, I would venture to say that the complexity of the task of comparative evaluation which it involves would make private verbal behavior essential whether or not as a prelude to public verbal behavior. However, the required verbal behavior of whatever kind would need to be capable of holding representations of the as yet non-existent rewards as well as calculating their relative values and of engendering consequent overt behavior. The same conclusion must be reached in respect of the other avoidance strategies. Each requires consideration of a future set of circumstances and the behavior they will generate.

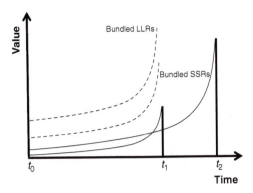

FIGURE 2.4 The principle of bundling.

Source: Foxall (2016a).

Can a behavior analytic explanation be advanced for the development and implementation of strategies such as bundling – one that avoids reference to representation? We are again faced with the proposition that the decision maker must contemplate a set of hypothetical eventualities, compare them critically, and reach a conclusion about the most rational behavior to pursue.

Psychological explanation

This account of behavior and behavioral change stands in contrast to those offered by radical behaviorism. What form would that behaviorist explanation take? Let us put aside the possibility that thought and language are inherently intentional since they are inevitably about something other than themselves, which aboutness is what separates explanations based on them from extensional description. Let us accept that elements of an individual's locutions, private or public, may act as discriminative stimuli for her behavior. This assumption again begs the question whether discriminative stimuli are themselves intentional when they enter our explanations of behavior since they might be said to be about reinforcement or punishment. Let us put this aside too.

Let us suppose that a (more or less) akratic consumer, Ego, who, in order to escape the consequences of the over-frequent selection of the SSR, adopts the bundling strategy. Suppose further that Ego did not come upon this idea as a result of its spontaneous generation within her psyche but was informed of it by either the spoken or written word – that is, as a series of tracks and/or plys, perhaps with the odd augmental thrown in. How do these rules function to alter Ego's behavior? She must somehow compare the outcomes of her own sequence of past behaviors with the promised outcomes of a sequence of alternative future behaviors, calculating their values at the present moment, selecting one and resolving to adhere to the novel program of behavior, or – as Ainslie (1992) puts it – making a side-bet with herself that success will follow. We have noted that, according to this manner of explanation, Ego cannot do any of these things other than through the manipulation of representations.

If we wish to avoid this cognitive explanation, we must identify the potential discriminative stimuli and motivating operations inherent in the rules she has been given and, ultimately, show how they are consistently related to her behavior, how in other words they can be accepted as elements in three- or four-term contingencies. Such an extensional, behavior analytic explanation requires that the elements inherent in rules – the sentences, phrases, words, even phonemes within words – assume the role of discriminative stimuli and motivating operations, understood as components of the environment in the presence of which certain behaviors have been reinforced in the past. These elements cannot however assume these roles in our explanation until Ego has acquired a learning history in which they have figured and in the course of the acquisition of which they have assumed stimulus control over her behavior. We cannot just assume that because these rules are intended to persuade Ego to behave in new ways that they do so by embodying these elements of a behavior analytic account. It does not appear that there is any alternative to taking a cognitive line here.

Intentional interpretation is a depiction of the consumer treated as an idealized system that maximizes a utilitarian and informational reinforcement within the confines of her budget. The assumption is that she will do so by seeking the LLR and that doing this will be her intention at t_0. Taking the decision (at t_0) to accomplish this maximizes utilitarian and informational reinforcement at this time by optimizing the intrinsic benefits of acting consistently with one's highest good. This is consistent with her self-image and maximizes her self-esteem, again at t_0. Suppose that at t_1, however, the consumer opts to consume the SSR. In the idealized interpretation, she still maximizes utilitarian and informational reinforcement, taking the highest level of utilitarian satisfaction available at that time as well as exercising personal power or personal decision, a source of informational reinforcement. If the consumer waits patiently for the LLR at t_2 before consuming, however, she maximizes by selecting the highest level of utilitarian reinforcement at that time and also obtaining the highest level of informational reinforcement by reaping the satisfaction of having exercised self-control.

The rationale of the cognitive interpretation is to ascertain whether the intentional interpretation can be cashed out at the level of cognitive processing. Micro-cognitive psychology suggests that more impulsive decisions result from a neurophysiological system based in the limbic system, while more self-controlled decisions emerge from an executive system based on the prefrontal cortex (PFC). The relative levels of activity found in these systems determine the rate at which the individual discounts future rewards. This is consistent with the intentional interpretation: a hyperactive impulsive system coupled with a hypoactive executive system indicates a tendency toward behavior that manifests in a higher rate of discounting and selection of the SSR; conversely, a hypoactive impulsive system coupled with a hyperactive executive system is likely to eventuate in the exercise of self-control demonstrated by choice of the LLR. The intentional interpretation also squares with the kind of explanation generated by macro-cognitive psychology in terms of the collective intentionality developed within groups that evolve deontic rules that prescribe socially-acceptable actions. Such actions as being patient, showing restraint, and allowing others to make choices first are generally socially rewarded, while impatience, butting in, precluding others from making choices are proscribed and punished. The individual's history of reinforcement and punishment, including the experiences they attract as a result of the degree of conformity with rule-following or rule-breaking their actions evince, account for individual differences in the effectiveness of collective intentionality in terms of their behaviors. Linking these two levels of exposition, the sub-personal which is associated with neuro-physiology and the super-personal which is associated with socially determined contingencies of reinforcement and punishment, is meso-cognitive psychology. Meso-cognitive psychology explains differences in the rate of temporal discounting, behavioral preferences for impulsivity and self-control in terms of conflicting intra-personal interests, one concentrating on short-term reward, the other on long-term reward. All of these cognitive psychologies underpin the intentional interpretation.

The intentional consumer-situation

The difference between the consumer-situation in the extensional model and that in psychological explanation is that the former consists of tangible, physical rewards whether they are utilitarian or informational. They are objectively measurable and can be related systematically to patterns of consumer behavior (Foxall, 2017). Psychological explanation involves the analysis of choice by reference to desires and beliefs, emotions and perceptions, problem solving and decision making rather than contingent environmental stimuli. Hence, the psychological consumer-situation comprises the imagined circumstances in which consumer action occurs and the imagined consequences of acting within them; this consumer-situation is posited to exist in the mind of the consumer (though it may only exist in its formal mode in the mind of the investigator) as it represents the contingencies of reinforcement and punishment intentionally and the action embedded therein (Figure 2.5). These are future contingencies of reinforcement and punishment as putatively perceived by the consumer, perceptual contingency-representations. They may not be tangible but they have empirical substance in that they can be shown to be right or wrong and their truth value inheres in the physical, tangible rewards and sanctions with which the consumer's actions are met. A conclusion is that, in addition to the necessity of evaluating an intentional interpretation according to the requirements of cognitive interpretation, an important criterion of accepting or rejecting the intentional interpretation is its predictive accuracy.[20]

The reason we employ a psychological explanation for consumer activities, treating them as actions rather than behavior, is that we must take the mental representation of the contingencies of reinforcement and punishment into account in the absence of any substantial extensional explanation. To invent a behaviorist explanation that consists of conjectured antecedent and consequent stimuli is the

---

The extensional consumer-situation:

Consumer behavior setting x learning history
(i.e., MOs + S^Ds)   (i.e., log of prior behavior and its
                                reinforcing and punishing outcomes)

The intentional consumer-situation:

Consumer behavior setting x learning history
(i.e., desires, beliefs, emotions, and perceptions representing past
outcomes of consumer actions and the potential outcomes of actions
performed within the present contingencies as they form the content of
the consumer's intentionality)

FIGURE 2.5 **Comparison of the extensional and intentional consumer-situations.**

Note: Like the extensional consumer-situation, the intentional consumer-situation is centered on the interaction of the consumer behavior setting and the consumer's learning history. However, these are now portrayed as entities perceived and interpreted by the consumer's psychological processes. *Key*: MOs = motivating operations; S^Ds = discriminative stimuli.

very approach that behaviorism itself has always explicitly repudiated on the basis that such putative explicatory terms are merely explanatory fictions. The construction of a psychological account of the observed activity which indicates how the individual would perceive the environment and respond to it on the basis of her desires, beliefs, emotions, and perceptions demarcates the explanation so given as of a different order from that of the empirical observation of regularities between acts of consumption and events within a controlling environment.

In doing this we have done much more than account for bodily movements in terms of which basic actions are defined. We have ventured into the realm of what we may understand as "remote contingencies," those that exist only in the intentionality of the consumer as she contemplates future actions – only, that is, in terms of intentional inexistence.

The development of the consumer-situation in intentional terms stems from the inability of the extensional approach to the analysis of consumer behavior that has been the mainstay of the initial phase of theorizing and empirical investigation in Intentional Behaviorism (Foxall, 2017) to explain some aspects of the actions involved in consumer choice of this kind. Reaching this point is a central component of the Intentional Behaviorist methodology, for it is only when extensional explanation has been exhausted that we can know (a) what contribution to understanding consumer choice that methodology can uniquely make, and (b) when, where, and how we are called upon to invoke intentional explanation. These considerations are of the utmost relevance to furthering our understanding and explanation of consumer choice conceived in terms of conflict between imme-diate and delayed outcomes.[21]

If we are to understand in greater detail what is going on when a consumer selects an immediate reward that is smaller than another she could have by wait-ing, we have to posit that she is holding the values of both rewards in the form of perceptions and beliefs that refer to stimuli that are not empirically present at the time. The later, larger reward exists at this time only in the imagination of the consumer: she has no direct empirical access to it. Yet the consumer is able to make a decision concerning it that affects whether she accepts the smaller reward or exercises patience in awaiting the superior outcome. Similarly, if the consumer forestalls an urge to choose the smaller reward, her action is still gov-erned by the imagined later reward on which she now places a higher value than what is currently available. This kind of understanding requires the ascrip-tion of intentionality to the consumer and ultimately a cognitive portrayal of her action. It means bringing together the *context* of behavioral responding (the contingencies of reinforcement and punishment that are the necessary tools of the extensional explanation that radical behaviorism provides) with the *cognition* that must be ascribed in order to make sense of the consumer's actions. It is the *consumer-situation* that brings context and cognition together into a framework of conceptualization and analysis that can handle consumer intentionality. This book is about our conceptual move from the extensional consumer-situation to the intentional consumer-situation.

As the immediate precursor of consumer behavior and consumer action, the consumer-situation links the stimuli that comprise the current consumer behavior setting with the elements of consumer experience of which current behavior is a function. It does so by bringing the consumer's learning history to bear on the significance of these stimuli for continued consumer behavior, the consequences such behavior is likely to yield. In the case of the extensional model of consumer behavior, the consumer-situation is conceptualized as the interaction between, on the one hand, the discriminative stimuli and motivating operations that make up the physical and social setting and, on the other hand, the consumer's learning his-tory, the sum total of previous relevant behaviors and their reinforcing and punish-ing outcomes.

The extensional consumer-situation, then, comprises only the interaction of the consumer behavior setting and learning history, both of which are empirically available. In this case, the extensional consumer-situation can be safely assumed to provide the context of the consumer's behavior. There is no reason to adopt an intentional stance since the behavior is explicable (i.e., predictable) on the basis of the consumer-situation alone. The need to link context and cognition does not arise. This methodology is an elaboration of psychological paradigms in which behavior is predicted on the basis of the observable stimuli that surround it physically and temporally. But when such stimuli are not available to the would-be observer, it is necessary to turn to psychological explanation that employs intentional terms such as *perceives*, *believes*, and *desires* in order to characterize consumer action.

We have seen that, in the extensional model which is a manifestation of theoretical minimalism, it comprises the interaction of the consumer's current behavior setting and her learning history. This is a conceptual definition since the consumer's learning history is often not stipulable other than in generalized terms but it is a potentially empirically-specifiable entity. In psychological explanation, our focus turns from consumer behavior to consumer action, and the consumer-situation comprises the intentionality (desires, beliefs, emotions, and perceptions) and cognitive decision processes that it is necessary to ascribe in order to render intelligible observed consumer activity for which no stimulus filed is empirically available. The consumer-situation now comprises the immediate *mental* antecedents of action.

Psychological explanation proposes two kinds of interpretation of consumer action. The first of these, the *intentional interpretation*, describes consumer-situation predominantly in terms of desires, beliefs, emotions, and perceptions in order to establish an idealized consumer-situation to explicate consumer action, while the cognitive interpretation appraises this in terms of what cognitive theory allows. So, the intentional consumer-situation is an idealized portrayal of the context of consumer choice in which the consumer is treated as an optimizing (utility-maximizing) system; it attributes to the consumer the intentionality she would have in a particular set of circumstances defined by the contingencies of reinforcement and punishment. A key consideration is how the consumer perceives the contingencies that hold the prospects for the reinforcement and punishment of her taking action in the current setting. In other words, what contingency-representations would a consumer in such circumstances have to have in order to maximize utilitarian and informational reinforcement? Insofar as emotions constitute these perceptual contingency-representations, this becomes: what emotional feelings would a consumer in such circumstances have to have in order to maximize utilitarian and informational reinforcement? The aim of the second kind of psychological interpretation, the *cognitive interpretation*, is to ascertain the extent to which the consumer's observed action can be understood in these idealized terms by an evaluation of this pattern of consumer action by reference to the cognitive structure and function available to the consumer.[22]

The intentional consumer-situation links context and cognition by *uniting* them: for the intentional consumer-situation comprises the current consumer behavior setting *as it is represented in the consumer's desires, beliefs, emotions, and perceptions* (especially insofar as these refer to the expected reinforcing and punishing outcomes of consumer action) as primed by her learning history which is itself represented by the consumer's beliefs. The desires, beliefs, emotions, and perceptions (hereafter simply "the intentionality") that compose the intentional consumer-situation are determined by assuming the consumer to be an economically rational system that maximizes utilitarian and informational reinforcement. What existed externally and objectively in the extensional consumer-situation now are transformed into the objects of intentionality.[23] Moreover, since we resort to intentional explanation only when no stimulus field is available, no current consumer behavior setting, the objects of the consumer's intentionality must be memories and mental constructs. We aim to explain consumer action by the ascription of the intentionality the consumer *ought* to have given the behavior setting in which she is located and her learning history. An essential source of integration between context and cognition inheres in emotional responses to consumption environments. These are in turn indicative of consumers' perceptual representations of the contingencies. A central goal of the analysis that follows is to draw perception and emotion more closely into the scope of a theory of consumer choice that draws on behavioral and cognitive psychologies, behavioral economics, marketing science, and philosophy, and seeks their integration as a foundation for an economic psychology of consumption. In this regard, I introduce the concept of contingency-representation as a fundamental component of the intentional consumer-situation.

The applicability of this intentional interpretation more generally to consumer action in natural settings requires its testing via: first, a rigorous delineation, based on empirical observation, of the consumer action to be explained; second, predictions of consumer choice based on the ascribed intentionality, though these are likely to be somewhat simplistic and gross (the full range of desires, beliefs, emotions, and perceptions can be employed in this way); third, the subjection of the perceptual component, namely, contingency-representations in the form of emotional reactions to the rigors of success semantics (clearly, this refers only to one of the components of the intentional consumer-situation); and, finally, the critical evaluation of the content of the intentional consumer-situation in light of theories of cognitive structure and functioning to assess the plausibility of the ascribed intentionality's availability to produce the observed action. This construction of the cognitive interpretation that establishes the viability of the intentional interpretation of consumer choice, the intentional consumer-situation, finally unifies context and cognition in consumer psychology.[24]

Notes

1 This two-stage process of psychological explanation both resembles Dennett's (1987) quest for explanation in terms of intentional systems theory and sub-personal cognitive psychology and differs significantly from it – see Foxall (2016b) for a comprehensive exposition.

2 See Dennett (1978, 1987) for the basic methodology employed here. Foxall (2016b) treats this in detail showing where I adhere to and where I deviate from Dennett's program.

3 See, for instance, Chisholm (1957), Dennett (1969), and Searle (1983). In the context of Intentional Behaviorism, see Foxall (2016a, 2016b).

4 *Micro-cognitive psychology.* Stanovich's tri-process theory elaborates the dual-process models that separate mental processing into a system that relies minimally on working memory and which can respond rapidly to environmental events (often referred to as *system 1* or *S1*) and a system that draws heavily on working memory to produce behavioral alternatives based on consideration of the longer-term outcomes that will ensue (S2). Stanovich (2009) presents a lucid and persuasive account of the tripartite model, and I have described it at some length elsewhere in the context of Intentional Behaviorism (Foxall 2016a, 2016b, 2016c). I will therefore only sketch it here. (Chapter 6 will describe the tripartite model further and discuss its implications for the perceptual understanding of consumer choice.) The minds posited by Stanovich and the relationships among them can be explicated in terms of a business analogy which, in the way of analogies, is not perfect but

provides an initial outline. The reflective mind is the policy-making function which sets out the overarching goals of the enterprise, the styles of managerial behavior that will be employed to achieve them, the kinds of product the firm will bring to market, and the markets it will serve in order to succeed. The algorithmic mind is the strategic planning function which deliberates on how to achieve the objectives of the enterprise, the specific product-markets it will enter, the composition of its marketing mixes, the permitted range of tactical behaviors it will adopt in pursuit of its strategic goals, and the product-markets from which it will withdraw for the same reason. Finally, automatic mind represents the operational level of decision making and action, which recognizes the opportunities and threats currently presented by the marketplace to which it can respond spontaneously by tactical action. In Stanovich's (2009) tripartite model, the automatic mind consists of The Autonomous Set of Systems (TASS) that share a mode of functioning.

The policy-making function of the reflective mind can overrule such tactics if it has the chance, issuing orders to the strategic function of the algorithmic mind, which in turn proposes alternative courses of action and ensures that the operational level of business activities represented by automatic mind will conform to overall corporate objectives. If the operational managers of an actual firm were to respond automatically and on the basis of habit to every apparent opportunity presented by the marketplace, they might score some notable successes but they would also on occasion land the company in deep trouble. Mostly, therefore, the managers responsible for this level are well-briefed and well-trained in following corporate policies and there are mechanisms in place to ensure their conformity. The analogy is not quite accurate in this respect. Automatic mind is assumed *always* to attempt to operate on a more stimulus-response basis, automatically and autonomously reacting to the prospect of immediate gain by behaving on behalf of the entire enterprise. As may be the case in real-world business, the strategic and policy levels of supervision are not always able to countermand such behavior before it has occurred. Similarly, automatic mind's responses to stimuli must be monitored and, where necessary, either terminated before they have disastrous consequences or assuaged by complementary actions.

The dual- and tri-process/tripartite theories of cognitive processing brought to bear on these concerns propose that behavioral responding may be the outcome of either a mental reaction to environmental stimuli that is minimally controlled by working memory, sometimes called the impulsive system (or S1), or by a considered procedure in which alternative courses of action are comparatively evaluated and the one chosen that will be most effective in promoting the individual's long-term welfare (S2). This latter system is deliberative, sometimes known as the executive system, and may act by countermanding the impulsive system.

5 *Macro-cognitive psychology.* This entails looking to social institutions for the sources of decision making. Collective intentionality is an approach to the explanation of shared actions in terms of shared desires, beliefs, emotions, and perceptions. For Searle (1995) it involves deontology, the ascription of status positions and of the roles that are proper to them, and ascription of the rewards and sanctions that will be arranged to follow actions that are considered by the relevant group to be pro- and anti-social. The deontological aspect takes the form of rules that portray, usually verbally, the contingencies that connect specific actions to the situations in which their enactment will attract particular rewards and sanctions. (See Searle's (1995, 2010) exposition of collective intentionality. For other views, see, for instance, Tomasello (2014, 2016). For further discussion in the context of Intentional Behaviorism, see Foxall (2010, 2016b).)

The roles and actions specified in these rules require certain individuals to undertake particular functions for the execution of which they are accorded an appropriate status that is acknowledged by the entire community. Hence, a citizen who has fulfilled particular requirements such as having been successfully elected can be invested with the office of prime minister or president along with the authority and responsibilities that are deemed to go with it. Thereafter, social requirements are met by both the office-holder, who performs tasks assigned by the group and whose performance will be measured and rewarded or punished, and the rest of the community whose actions toward the person assigned to this role, such as due deference, are also laid down and rewarded or punished. Those assuming status functions enjoy *deontic powers* in the form of rights, permissions and entitlements, but they also incur obligations and requirements (Searle, 2010). What this means is that social groups, acting collectively, have some capacity to invent for themselves the contingencies of reinforcement and punishment that will govern their actions, at least as far as the socially-instituted and enforced informational reinforcement is concerned. (A society's capacity to influence the course of the contingencies involved in utilitarian reinforcement is, it goes without saying, more limited.)

Our interest in this capacity of humans to construct contingencies and to specify the collective intentionality that will be expected of members of the social group to which they severally belong lies in there being no reason why the individual group member's mental processing of the deontic outcomes of collective intentionality should take the form only of beliefs-proper. Any individual, any given consumer, may equally fantasize about what is required in particular situations, form beliefs about what the rules are or how they may be fulfilled, and to what extent she will accord the necessary status position to those nominated to hold office. These beliefs may be accurate beliefs-proper insofar as they will lead to actions that are effective and lead to the individual's actions being rewarded and the social group as a whole prospering; if they are erroneous beliefs-proper, they may not have this effect immediately but by their very nature such rational beliefs are likely to be soon corrected. Neurotic beliefs, however, i.e., fantasies that are reinforced by evidence gained only through psychic-reality testing, may be dysfunctional for both the individual holding them and the social group, depending on how centrally they affect the working of the group dynamic. There is a further dimension: the entire social group may entertain neurotic beliefs, religious or political ideas about how the world works that will also prove dysfunctional to the extent of causing the eradication of the society as a whole.

6 *Meso-cognitive psychology.* The consumer's mental experience is not always a matter of the dispassionate weighing of beliefs and desires; often it takes the form of warring internal factions, what Ainslie (1992) envisions as strategically interacting interests whose distinct time-frames lead to their propensity to conflict with one another. The short-range interest (SRI) seeks gratification when it is available even though it is inferior to that which is contingent on the deferment of consumption. This is the conflict between the SSR and LLR that we have already encountered. The long-range interest (LRI) is focused on the attainment of the superior but delayed reward. If we treat these interests in terms of the cognition and other intentionality they are likely to engender in the consumer, we may ask whether they represent beliefs-proper or neurotic beliefs. The intentional interpretations devised in the second stage of the employment of the Intentional Behaviorist research strategy must also cohere with the level of analysis at which this meso-cognitive psychology proceeds. There are several ways in which we can envision these two picoeconomic interests influence one another (Ross, 2012). Our understanding of their mutual effects reflects our assumption of whether they act contemporaneously or sequentially. Ross depicts contemporaneously interacting subagents of this kind as possessing either separate utility functions that are in conflict with each other or contrary time preferences. Each of these gives rise to its own style of economic modeling. For example, the actions of subagents with distinctly different time preferences can be related to their sub-personal neurophysiological functioning that governs their specific hyperbolic time preferences, a matter of the "competition between steeply exponentially discounting 'limbic' regions and more patient (less steeply exponentially discounting) 'cognitive' regions" (Ross, 2012, p. 720). This picoeconomic portrayal depends heavily on the findings of neuroeconomic experiments employing fMRI scans of humans choosing between the SSR and LLR (McClure et al., 2004; for discussion in the present context, see Foxall, 2016a).

7 The question of the nature of action is much more complex than my simple distinction suggests. See, as examples of some recent thinking, Dancy (2000), Hornsby (1981), Sandis (2012), the whole collection of papers in Sandis (2009), and Steward (2012). I have also discussed action and agency at greater length in Foxall (2016b).

8 I discuss action and agency in the context of Intentional Behaviorism and the explanation of consumer choice at greater length in *Perspectives on Consumer Choice: From Behavior to Action, From Action to Agency* (Foxall, 2016b, particularly in Chapters 7 and 11). See also my *Addiction as Consumer Choice: Exploring the Cognitive Dimension* (Foxall, 2016a).

9 For an account of consumer activity that treats it entirely as behavior, see my *Advanced Introduction to Consumer Behavior Analysis* (Foxall, 2017).

10 Some authors argue that actions are the causes of activity rather than the activities themselves: so, for Dretske (1988), actions are the mental states that cause bodily movements. Others, e.g., Steward (2012), argue that there are both mental actions and physical actions. For Dretske, the content or meaning of a belief explains a movement by identifying why this mental state contributes to that movement. So the belief *that s is F* is a neurophysiological event (brain state) that, by virtue of its being selected in the course of operant conditioning, contributes to the causation of a movement because it carries the information *that s is F*. Operant selection of this kind provides the entity, here a brain state, with the function of providing the information and this function confers upon the entity the status of being a representation. Acting "for a reason" in this way allows the explanation of the movement in terms of the content of the belief or other intention.

11 The idea that we construct an intentional account by ascribing the mental operations the system "*ought*" to have given its history and circumstances is a vital component of Dennett's Intentional Systems Theory (IST; 1987). Intentional Behaviorism makes important use of this idea in the construction of the Intentional Interpretation which is its second stage.

12 In the case of compulsive and addictive consumer actions it may seem to stretch the point to speak of choice at all but the same pattern of preference reversal, now accompanied by a striving to overcome the problem – both of which open the pattern of behavior to the charge of economic irrationality – is apparent. The possibility of at least delaying consumption remains and the many instances in which individuals overcome addictions is testimony to the use of the term choice based as I have suggested on the underlying temporal conflict involved.

13 See Radoilska (2013) for an interesting distinction between akrasia and weakness of will.

14 Indeed, for Plato, who argued that the individual who knows what is good is incapable of acting otherwise. See also Davidson (2001).

15 For a recent examination of this kind of social phenomenon, see Nichols (2017).

16 A more comprehensive account is available in Foxall (2016b, Chapter 2).

17 Accounts of the Continuum of Consumer Choice, which summarizes this idea, can be found in Foxall (2010, 2016a, 2016b, 2017).

18 Although it was always Skinner's position that the behaviorist is compiling an agenda for the research program of the physiologist by demonstrating the environmental determination of behavior, other behaviorists have more actively engaged in research that entails the neurophysiological substrates of reinforcement: see, for instance, the special issue of the *Journal of the Experimental Analysis of Behavior* (volume 80, number 3, 2005) devoted to this research.

19 Skinner (1969) makes this important distinction. Contingency-shaped behavior is that which is explained by reference to its concomitant stimulation. An S^D or MO sets the occasion for the performance of a behavior that has previously been reinforced in similar settings. On the basis of knowledge of this stimulus field, the behavior is predictable. Most important from the point of view of Intentional Behaviorism is that no representation is involved in the explanation of contingency-shaped behavior.

Rule-governed behavior is explained by reference to the verbal behavior of an instructor (who can be the behaver herself, giving rise to a distinction between *other*-rules, provided by another person, and *self*-rules, worked out by the individual for herself. The verbal statement is said to specify the elements of the three-term contingency: as in "When you are in the store [consumer behavior setting comprising S^Ds and MOs], please pick up some eggs [response, R], and I will make you your favorite dessert [verbal MO relating the response to a reinforcer]." The only way in which a radical behaviorist can keep such an explanation within the bounds of the operant paradigm is by assuming that the words are S^Ds or MOs that influence behavior by virtue of their having been paired repeatedly with reinforcing or punishing behavioral outcomes. If this is done, there is again no question of representation entering into the explanation.

20 In my *Perspectives on Consumer Choice: From Behavior to Action, From Action to Agency* (Foxall, 2016b), I emphasized the difficulties of employing prediction as a criterion of the validity of an intentional interpretation. However, the development of the concept of contingency-representation and the use of the success semantics of Ramsey ([1927] 1990) permits a more positive appreciation of this source of validation. The need to show how the intentional interpretation is supported, where necessary, by a coherent cognitive interpretation remains.

21 I have written about the distinction between extensional and intentional language and explanations several times (e.g., Foxall, 2016a, 2016b), but the following summary may be useful. Intentionality (with a "t") is simple "aboutness" and refers to the fact that some mentalistic words such as *believes* or *desires*, *perceives* or *fears* refer to something other than themselves. That is, they have an intentional object: no one just *believes*; she believes *that* such and such is the case; similarly we desire *that* the bus will get here quickly, say, perceive *that* the light is brighter here, or fear *that* we have failed the exam. The intentional object in each case (the bus or the light or failing) has, Brentano (1874) points out, intentional inexistence: it exists *in* the proposition. This is the essence of aboutness (see Brentano, 1874, pp. 88–94). It follows that the intentional object need not exist anywhere else. I can believe in Santa Claus without anyone, myself included, having the slightest notion that Santa Claus exists in the real world. If I am to behave successfully as a parent (given particular social norms), it is sufficient that he exists in my imagination and that I can talk to my kids in the knowledge that he exists in theirs too.

Intensionality (with an "s") is a linguistic phenomenon. It has implication for the way in which we employ sentences. For example, intensionality entails that the codesignative propositions cannot be substituted in a sentence that contains an attitude such as believes, desires, or feels without altering the truth value of the statement. Let me illustrate this in the case of a book called *Inside Mr Enderby*, written by Anthony Burgess under the pen-name Joseph Kell. Take the sentence, "*John believes that* Inside Mr Enderby *was written by Joseph Kell.*" It is not valid to state, however, "*John knows that* Inside Mr Enderby *was written by Anthony Burgess,*" for John may not know that Joseph Kell is Anthony Burgess. (Indeed, the editor who asked Burgess to review the book apparently did not! See Burgess (1990, p. 71) for this amusing incident.) The codesignative terms that follow "that" in these sentences are not therefore interchangeable without loss of the intentional sentence's truth value. This is not the case for sentences couched in extensional language. Changing "Anthony Burgess wrote *Inside Mr Enderby*" to "Joseph Kell wrote *Inside Mr Enderby*" does no violence to its truth value.

Another way in which intentional and extensional sentences differ is in the nature of their referring to objects. The object of an intentional sentence has Brentano's intentional inexistence and perhaps may, therefore, not exist outside that sentence, i.e., in the real world. If, speaking extensionally, I say that I am going to drive my car to Cardiff, then, if the sentence is to have any truth value, there has to be a car that is mine and there has to be a place called Cardiff that I can drive to. But if I say that I believe in Santa Claus or am seeking the Golden Mountain or praying for the Elixir of Life, the truth value of the sentence is not affected by the fact that none of these exists in a literal sense.

It is crucial that a person who is to function competently and satisfactorily as a member of society understands the differences in truth value that separate extensional and intentional senses. I might spend some time imagining that the car in which I am going to drive to Cardiff is not the old rust bucket that I actually own but a sparkling new sport car. This is not a problem as long as I know I am fantasizing (or possibly speculating, hypothesizing, supposing) and that I know I must take my own car from the car park rather than the idealized alternative. Problem solving, decision making, and creativity all require the ability to engage in speculation, hypothesizing, and fantasizing from time to time; but all the more do they require, if they are to be successful, in our ability to switch from one of these modes of thinking and feeling to that which is governed by real-world correspondence.

22 This methodology could be said to presume that perception is cognition-laden, a theme to which we shall return.

23 The objects of the ascribed intentionality might be said to exist in the external environment as Dretske (1995) argues, but what influences the actions of the consumer is her perception and conceptualization of the contingencies.

24 I am clearly indebted to Daniel Dennett's (1987) exposition of his research strategy beginning with intentional systems theory (IST), which is followed by sub-personal cognitive psychology (SPCP). Elsewhere (Foxall, 2016b), I explain in some detail what the Intentional Behaviorism research strategy owes to Dennett's formulation and where I diverge from it.

3
PERCEPTUAL CONTINGENCY-REPRESENTATION

Abstract

The mental events by which the consumer represents the contingencies of reinforcement and punishment include desires, beliefs, perceptions, and emotions. While previous expositions of the Intentional Behaviorist research strategy have concentrated on desires and beliefs, the present approach seeks to balance this by exploring the place of perceptual contingency-representations, including emotions, in the consumer's pre-behavioral mental depiction of the contingencies. This is especially pertinent in view of recent arguments that the understanding of human action in cognitive decision-making terms should be wholly or significantly replaced by an account based on simpler perceptual processes. The concept of perceptual contingency-representation is introduced and refined in this chapter and shown to be a necessary component of the conative, cognitive, and affective composite variable contingency-representation, which collectively depicts past and present contingencies of reinforcement and punishment that consumer choice reflects. In seeking the perceptual component of contingency-representation, we consider, first, the nature of perception and representation and, second, the requirements of perceptual contingency-representation. The required concept must represent the consequences of future actions that the consumer can only imagine and do this on the basis of the consumer's learning history with respect to the physical, social, and perceptual outcomes of previously performed actions of a similar kind. In addition, it must incorporate her reflections on this experience and the other-rules and self-rules received/developed in imagination since the actions to which the learning history refers were performed. And it must allow all of these considerations to be combined into a final summative contingency-representation which allows the selection of an appropriate action from among those considered. Contingency-representations that accomplish these tasks include desires and beliefs that represent the contingencies in their specific ways but the analysis focuses on the perceptual component of contingency-representation.

Knowledge by acquaintance and knowledge by description

Before discussing perception in a little detail, I should like to briefly reiterate a crucial distinction which will have implications throughout my argument, that between knowledge by acquaintance and knowledge by description (Russell, 1912; for discussion, see McGinn, 2004; and, in the context of Intentional Behaviorism, Foxall, 2016b, pp. 125–133). Knowledge by acquaintance is founded upon direct experience, e.g., watching the sun rise, whereas knowing by description emerges from the reports of other people, e.g., being told about the rising of the sun over Ben More. Even a recluse who has never left England can recognize the rain falling (and does so directly and non-propositionally) but only through what others say can she know that such precipitation is comparatively rare in certain parts of the world. Knowledge by acquaintance can be translated into propositional knowledge: for instance, having experienced it for myself, I can tell myself and other people that it is raining. Perceptual knowledge is knowledge by acquaintance, while the kinds of knowledge that the classic model of decision making assumes we acquire through internal information processing is knowledge by description. Moreover, knowledge by acquaintance is prerequisite to knowledge by description and propositional knowledge would be impossible without it. Providing implicit understanding of the phenomena of consciousness, knowledge by acquaintance is logically prior to knowledge by description, so much so that without it propositional knowledge would not be feasible (McGinn, 2004). The crucial matter is that *perceptual* experience is a matter of knowledge by acquaintance, while cognition, including believing, information processing, decision making, and other *conceptual* operations, entails knowledge by description.

Perceptual experience

Basic considerations

Perception is conscious awareness of one's environment. It is both intentional and phenomenal. Its definition usually includes the process in which sensory information is received by an organism through one of the senses. It is worth noting at the outset that some authors, such as Prinz (2004), include the emotions within perception. Hence, he writes that "Perceptual states are states in dedicated input systems," where

> A dedicated input system is a mental system that has the function of receiving information from the body or the world via some priority class of transducers and internal representations. Dedicated input systems are perceptual modalities or senses. To count as perceptual, a mental state must inhabit a sense.

Vision, audition, and olfaction are dedicated input systems. They each have their own neural pathways and proprietary representations. If emotions are literally perceptual, they must reside in such a system.

(Prinz, 2004, p. 222; see also Prinz, 2002b)

Behaviorist authors usually restrict perception, if they use the word at all, to sensation; more cognitively-inclined writers expand on this to include the interpretation of the information so received, sometimes to the extent of its being translated into a response. The process of interpretation, linked to the guidance of further activity, presumes the cognitive and conative penetration of perception since these are the vehicles through which interpretation and readiness to act are effected. But perception is inevitably limited and selective: what seems essential is the receipt of information from the environment toward the goal of interacting effectively with that environment. A perceptual system that simply recorded information would be of very limited significance unless the organism's capacity for behavioral response were confined to innate stimulus–response mechanisms, where innate indicates present at birth and unmodifiable by experience. Few organisms could produce adaptive responses to their environment given this state of affairs. There must presumably be some sense in which knowledge and experience can come to exert their influence on perception and behavior.[1]

Direction of fit

Perception is similar to cognition and different from conation in an important respect. Perceptions and cognitions have mind-to-world direction of fit, i.e., they present the way the world *is* and the mind must accept or conform to this. A belief is a propositional statement that one believes that there is a particular state of affairs in the world. The test of the proposition consists in ascertaining whether the appropriate state of the world actually is as the proposition claims it is. Similarly, perception, though non-propositional is an understanding of how the world is constituted. The direction of fit is, again, mind-to-world. This does not signify, of course, that perception is cognitive in itself: perception differs crucially from cognition in being non-propositional, in resting on knowledge by acquaintance rather than knowledge by description. Conation, including desires, wishes, and wants, differs from both perception and cognition in that it has world-to-mind direction of fit: the world is expected to conform to the mind, to become as the individual desires, wishes, or wants it to be. Perceptions do not describe how the world *should* be: they are not therefore conative, though they may, again, be penetrated by conative considerations. Perception is, therefore, often said to be selective: to a degree it reflects the frame of reference laid down for it by cognitive and conative influences. It is probably an exaggeration to say that people generally see what they want to see, hear what they want to hear, but there is influence over whether something is perceived and, if it is, how it is perceived as a result of cognitive biases and strong desires. When people take part in arguments or otherwise consider opposing viewpoints, they may accord overwhelming significance to their own point of view while systematically ignoring or denigrating converse opinions.

Theory-ladenness

This is not to say that perception is wholly independent of cognition, however: perception is theory-laden or cognitively penetrated as its extension into the realm of interpretation suggests. But, at least conceptually, they are distinct. Dretske links perception and cognition in the claim that the conversion of information from analog to digital form is the central rationale of cognitive functioning (see Dretske, 1981, p. 142). Contingency-representation would need to be transformed in this way before it could be useful. Acceptance of this requirement acknowledges that perception and cognition, for all their analytical independence, cannot be precisely demarcated in practice.

In this context, Lupyan (2015) presents a case for the cognitive penetration of perception that can be summarized by the argument that, since the function of perception is to provide information that is useful in guiding behavior, and perceptual inputs are inevitably ambiguous, then, perception depends on knowledge gained through phylogenetic and ontogenetic processes to ensure that inputs become information that can usefully direct behavior. It is not surprising, therefore, that authors differ in the extent to which they implicate perception in their definitions of cognition. Among the many definitions of cognition, one which has been employed in the Intentional Behaviorism research program (Foxall, 2016a) is that of Heyes (2000, p. 4) for whom,

> cognitive states and processes are (1) theoretical entities, which (2) provide a functional characterization of operations of the central nervous system, (3) may or may not be objects of conscious awareness, (4) receive inputs from other cognitive states and processes and from perception, and (5) have outputs to other cognitive states and processes and to behavior.

This definition excludes perception from its understanding of cognition, proposes that cognitions are theoretical constructs, and suggests that cognitive variables provide a functional view of the operation of the CNS. This parsimonious view of cognition may be contrasted with Shettleworth's (2000, p. 43), which positions perception within the bounds of cognition as well as providing additional emphases; hence,

> a full account of the evolution of cognition should embrace all mechanisms that invertebrates and vertebrates have for taking in information through the senses, retaining it, and using it to adjust behavior to local conditions.

Shettleworth makes two observations which are highly relevant to this investigation: (a) that cognition involves the organism's explicitly representing stimuli that are not physically available, and (b) that cognitive explanation employs declarative rather than procedural knowledge. On this understanding, cognition is

> information processing in the broadest sense, from gathering information through the senses to making decisions and performing functionally appropriate actions, regardless of the complexity of any internal representational processes that behavior might imply.
>
> *(Shettleworth, 2000, p. 43)*

This definition makes the possibility of the cognitive penetration of perception more explicit.

Modularity

The meaning of modularity

The delineation of modules is a common biological research strategy in which functions are localized within physical structures; modules emerge from such analysis as the "specialized components" which embody particular kinds of functionality (Bechtel & Abrahamsen, 2002; Bechtel & Richardson, 1993; see also Faucher & Tappolet, 2008; Tappolet, 2016). What is of importance in explaining complex biological phenomena, however, is the way in which a level of macro-organization emerges from the interrelatedness of these components; as Shettleworth (2010, p. 46) points out, modular description treats the organization of a complex whole in terms of its containing "somewhat independently functioning but interconnected subunits." Bechtel and Abrahamsen (2002, pp. 203–204) exemplify this procedure by reference to the subtasks of cell components in facilitating the general task of the cell "to serve as the basic unit of life": the cell membrane functions to control access to and from the cell interior, and mitrochondria make possible energy transfer, while ribosomes enhance protein synthesis. Biological modularity is relatively non-theoretical insofar as it relies on physiological functioning which can be adequately characterized by extensional science. A superficially similar but actually divergent approach is found in cognitive neuroscience, which has embraced modularity as a means of relating brain function and cognitive responding (see, for example, de Gelder & Vroomen, 1994). By linking cognitive and behavioral deficits to damaged brain regions, cognitive neuroscientists ascribe particular functions to neurophysiological modules, especially on the basis of double-dissociations that identify the disparate functions for which separate brain regions are responsible.[2]

The concept of modularity can be also understood insofar as it refers to mental processes. Hence, "When distinct classes of input (domains) are computed on in distinct ways as inferred from behavior, we have a distinct mental module or memory system" (Shettleworth, 2010, p. 47). For Shettleworth, a mental module or memory system entails the inference from behavior of computation on distinct types of input, and she continues: "Computational distinctiveness is the primary criterion for cognitive modularity, although others such as anatomical separability are commonly associated with it."

Kinds of modularity

Several schemes of modularity have been proposed in the attempt to capture the structure of mentality and its functions.[3] A number of these approaches have been constrained by a priori theoretical reasoning or assumption, and their top-down reasoning is valuable insofar as the modular constructs which it generates are relatively precise devices which permit the development of comparatively rigorous and robust theoretical arguments for the nature of cognition and its influence on behavior. However, it is also arguable that top-down modular schemes have placed unnecessary restrictions on cognitive theory by adopting ontological positions which conflate brain and mind. Following the review, therefore, this section suggests a "bottom-up" approach to modularity in which neurophysiology and behavior participate as constraints on intentional explanation.

Samuels (2000, 2006) distinguishes two broad kinds of module, the representational and the computational. The former, which he also describes as "Chomskian," embody domain-specific, representational knowledge (Chomsky, 1980); the latter, which are closer to Fodor's view of modularity, are domain-specific, computational devices, i.e., they manipulate symbolic information, transforming it in the process (Fodor, 1983). He speaks also of Darwinian modules, a subspecies of the latter, which are closest to the modularity proposed by evolutionary psychologists such as Tooby and Cosmides (1992): they are domain-specific, innate, computational, and products of natural selection. Each of these kinds of modularity deserves elaboration before we seek to arrive at a conception of cognitive modules that is suitable for the analysis of animal innovation. Representational modularity forms a template for the simple transference of operations from one representational system to another. The paradigm example is the Chomskian language module, which operates within a single domain to transform words into a structure that conveys meaning by the application of innate rules.

Computational modularity is exemplified by Fodor (1983), who reserves the term modularity for input systems: i.e., perceptual subsystems, and language. Among their other properties,[4] these computational devices display *informational encapsulation* (they contain self-contained information already available to the individual by which perception is guided: see Sterelny 2003, pp. 185–189); *domain specificity* (they are concerned with the solution of a particular kind of problem, e.g., vision, speech); *innateness* (the information they supply is not a consequence of learning or experience but a prerequisite of them: Sterelny, 2003, p. 187); *epistemic boundedness* (each module contains built-in assumptions about how the world works); and *functional autonomy* (modules operate automatically, not as a result of decisions made somewhere else.) A Fodorian module may, therefore, be described in summary as an "informationally encapsulated perceptual system: it acts exclusively on a restricted kind of input" (Shettleworth, 2010, p. 46).

In order to place Fodor's now classic portrayal of modularity in the context of subsequent viewpoints, it is worth considering briefly the nature of *Darwinian modularity*, which, Samuels (2000) argues, is exemplified by evolutionary psychology. Evolutionary psychologists such as Tooby and Cosmides (1992) downplay Fodor's nonmodular central processes in favor of "massive modularity": they stress domain specificity and the evolved nature of modules. According to the massive modularity hypothesis, the human mind is composed of "ensembles of innately specified, domain-specific, operationally autonomous, computational devices," and these *modules* reflect "specific cognitive adaptations" rather than "general-purpose learning capacities" (Sterelny, 2003, p. 191). Tooby and Cosmides differ from Fodor in arguing that domain specificity is more important than informational encapsulation. Samuels (2000) summarizes the *massive modularity hypothesis* as the view that the mind is almost or entirely composed of modules, that is, comprises hundreds or thousands of such modules, and that they are responsible not only for the input–output functions of which Fodor speaks but also his central processing functions. An important point made by Samuels is that cognitive modules of this kind are not necessarily subvenient on neural modules: it is possible that modules map exactly on to "discrete, spatially localized pieces of neural tissue," but it is also feasible that Darwinian modules are "subserved by complex, widely distributed brain structures" (p. 23; see also Samuels, 2005). Hence, Darwinian modules do not entail neural modules: failure to locate a neural basis for a cognitive module does not imply that such a module does not exist.

Fodor's view is further contextualized by returning to the considerations provided by Shettleworth which were quoted above. Crucially, she is clear that a module does not rely on anatomical location in a specific brain area. Moreover, in arguing that "computational distinctiveness is the primary criterion for cognitive modularity," she seems to be saying that we infer modularity on the basis of functions that are themselves inferred from observation of behavior. The implication is that experience can influence modular functioning (via neuronal plasticity), something to which Shettleworth is clearly open: "Experience could modify prefunctionally ('innately') organized cognitive modules in characteristic ways, presumably by rules intrinsic to each module" (2000, p. 48). Shettleworth further argues that "to think sensibly about the evolution of cognition we need to start with the ways in which animals process and use information in nature to adjust individual behavior to local conditions, local on a spatial and temporal scale, from the animal's lifetime to variations from moment to moment" (p. 44). And, "If we take as 'cognitive' all mechanisms that take in information through the senses and lead to behavioral adjustments to conditions that are local in time and/or space, it follows that cognition must be modular" (ibid). The precision with which information has to be appropriated and exploited in order to fulfill such local functions places cognition beyond the scope of a unitary, all-purpose computer. Rather, the mind comprises an amalgam of devices each of which performs a specialized task, transforming inputs in order to meet specific needs with appropriately adaptive behavior. These modules are individually fine-tuned and combined in order to solve problems that crop up in the here and now. The localness of the behavior that entails cognitive modularity is central to her specific criteria. This conception clearly refers to a much more specific and direct operation than does the more general idea of mental structure and functioning to which the label mental mechanism is attached (see Bechtel, 2008).

Representation

Representing the contingencies

The radical behaviorist explanation of behavior adverts to the consequences a response has engendered in the past. Despite the commonplace means of depicting the three- or four-term contingency, the *future* consequences cannot affect the behavior that has not yet produced them; rather, it is the organism's learning *history* that is the key to its present and future behavior. We have noted that such explanatory devices are satisfactory as long as our sole aim is to predict and control the behavior, which are sufficient goals for the extensional study of behavior that is germane to theoretical minimalism. However, as we move from prediction and control to an explanation of consumer activity in terms of action rather than behavior, it becomes evident that there is a missing link in the causal chain from past behavior and its outcomes to current responding. This does not mean that the contingencies of reinforcement and punishment are no longer relevant to the generation of activity when it is conceived as action but it brings into play their internal depiction and its bearing on output. Learning history, the outcomes, reinforcing and/or punishing, of prior activity, must be represented by the organism if they are going to influence the rate of subsequent responding, and this relies on memory. Similarly, the contingencies presented by the current consumer behavior setting must be represented by the individual prior to their influencing choice. Extensional reasoning is unequal to this task since representation invokes intentional explanation or interpretation.

We have seen that understanding the nature of the action-related consumer-situation requires us to be able to ascribe intentionality to the consumer who is viewed as an idealized system, one that maximizes utility (utilitarian and informational reinforcement). What intentionality would such an organism need to have in order to function optimally in its given circumstances? Answering this question requires that we understand what enables the consumer to consume as it does, to continue consuming for a period, and to cease to do so at a particular time. These considerations entail that we explain why environment–action relationships operate as they do. Specifically, if we are to seek to explain the way in which the organism is sensitive to certain stimuli such that they influence the rate at which it repeats the action on which they are contingent, we must understand how organisms represent their environments. The contingent relations between behavior and its consequences remain vital when we consider the explanation of action. Dretske (1981, 1988, 1995) is especially important in this regard because of the link his analysis provides between context (as presented in the radical behaviorist explanation of behavior) and cognition (as it is being developed in the Intentional Behaviorist explanation of action) through the consideration given to what representation is and how it works.[5] Dretske (1988, p. 100) argues that, for all its shortcomings, the law of effect that is at the heart of operant psychology is central to explanation:

> What is important is that *something* (call it what you will), *when* it occurs in the right relationship (whatever, exactly, that may be) to behavior performed in certain stimulus conditions, tends (for *some* behavior and *some* stimulus conditions) to increase the chances that that behavior will be repeated in those conditions. There are *some* consequences of *some* behaviors of *some* organisms that are causally relevant to the likelihood that such behaviors will be repeated in similar circumstances.

Moreover, the explanation of action in terms of its contingent outcomes entails that we posit a sensitivity on the part of the organism to particular external conditions, F. We have seen that in the case of action Dretske (1988) designates M as a movement caused by an internal cause, C (see the "Birfurcating consumer activity" section and Figure 2.1, both in Chapter 2). In the explanation of action he offers, shown in Figure 3.1, he argues, moreover, that this causal relationship is explained by the *meaning* of C, i.e., C's indication of how the world operates. C does this by indicating the external stimulus condition, F. C must not merely indicate that "F causes M." Rather, C's indicating F is "an explanatorily relevant fact about C – the fact about C that explains ... *why* it causes M" (p. 84). F designates, therefore, environmental stimuli. Reinforcers have a tendency to increase the probability that M will be reproduced in conditions, F. If the organism is to learn, it must be able to identify conditions F, possessing, as Dretske (1988, p. 101) puts it, "something *in* the animal to 'tell' it when conditions F exist." This requires that we identify a representation within the organism of F, and this is C.

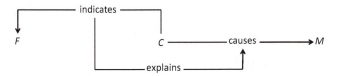

FIGURE 3.1 The relationships involved in indication and causation. The relationship that underlies C's semantic nature explains the causal relationship between C and M which defines the behavior (action) in question. F is an external stimulus condition that is indicated by C.

Source: Dretske, F. (1988). *Explaining Behavior: Reasons in a World of Causes*. Cambridge, MA: MIT Press, p. 84. Reproduced by kind permission of MIT Press.

Types of representational system

In what Dretske calls "Type I representational systems [RSI]," representation is achieved by any system that operates to indicate "how thing stand with respect to some other object, condition, or magnitude" (1988, p. 52). An example of these *conventional systems* is using pebbles to indicate the positions and actions of the players in a football game I witnessed. The ability of the stones to represent accurately what happened depends on *me*, especially my memory. The capacity of the pebbles to represent what actually happened is a function of how well I recall and am able to maneuver the medium used to represent the events. Hence, the pebbles (the expressive medium) have no *intrinsic* ability to represent. Other examples of these "conventional systems" are maps, diagrams, road signs, and some natural languages. The representative elements of these systems are *symbols*: they are assigned "indicator functions" that they have no ability to perform intrinsically. "We give them a job to do and then we do it for them" (ibid, p. 54).

Dretske speaks also of a second kind of representational system that inheres in *natural signs* and information.[6] Animal tracks in the snow, for instance, indicate what they do independently of us. They are natural signs. They do not derive their indicative powers from us but from their objective relationship to what they represent. Their use depends on their unconventional constitution being used in a conventional way by us. They are a blend, therefore, of the conventional and the unconventional or natural. In Type II representation, which is still conventional, natural signs replace symbols as the elements of representation. We must bear in mind that what a system represents is not what its expressive elements *mean* but what these elements have the *function* of indicating/meaning. A natural sign can indicate many things but is usually taken to mean only one: that which we have applied special significance to. The dependence on us is only partial (in comparison with RSI, where it is complete). The *signs* are independent of other systems but the *functions* they perform are specified by another system, namely, human beings.

Dretske's final kind of representation, exemplified by Type III representational systems, involves *intrinsic natural indicators*. A natural system of representation has elements (like the elements of Type II systems) whose power to indicate is independent of the interests, purposes, and capacities of other systems, but the *functions* of whose signs are also independent of the interests, purposes, and capacities of other systems (in contrast to those of Type II). These are the environmental elements that indicate to organisms how to locate biologically essential resources such as food and mates. As such, they "have *their own* intrinsic indicator functions that derive from the way the indicators are developed and used *by the system of which they are part*" (Dretske, 1988, p. 62, emphasis in original). These *internal indicators* are essential to sense perception:

> Without such internal indicators, an organism has no way to avoid predators, find food, locate mates, and do the things it has to do to survive and propagate. This indeed is what sense perception is all about. An animal's senses

(at least the so-called exteroceptors) are merely the diverse ways nature has devised for making what happens inside an animal depend, in some indicator-relevant way, on what happens outside.

(ibid)

These indicators result from the phylogenetic history of the species to which an individual animal belongs and from its own ontogenetic development, principally one supposes through operant conditioning. By dint of having come about in these wholly natural ways the representations have the capacity to influence behavior. They are, moreover, functions that are intrinsic to the organisms in which they operate: hence, we observers may *discover* them but we do *not* invent or assign them. These representational systems also account for the cognitive capacities of humans since "it is in so far as these sorts of representations are at the heart of the cognitive powers of humans that humans can generate non-intrinsic indicators (that is, invent conventional symbols or employ natural signs). For it needs cognitive skills to invent or employ something as the sign of something else" (Lyons, 1995, p. 109).

Central to Dretske's understanding of intentionality is the importance he attaches to misrepresentation. Intentionality can misrepresent. A propositional attitude can say that *p* when *p* does not obtain. Dretske argues that Type I and II systems derive their intentionality from humans who display the full panoply of intentionality, "*their* display of intentional characteristics is not surprising"; their intentionality is simply a *reflection* "of the minds, *our* minds, that assign them the properties, in particular the functions from which they derive their status as representations" (1988, pp. 64–65). He argues, however, that Type III systems must possess *original* or *intrinsic* intentionality. Their intentionality is not derived from us and, importantly, such systems possess the capacity to *mis*represent. The reason is that only if the system can misrepresent can it also get things *right*, i.e., have *meaning* (something we cannot say of Type I and II systems: they just represent in the manner they are mechanically designed to do). The first requirement of such a system must be that it have the function of indicating what it indicates. Many indicators that arise in Type II systems (e.g., tree rings) do indicate as far as we are concerned but it is not their *function* to indicate. This is why demonstrating a system's capacity to misrepresent is so important in establishing whether its function is to represent.

In the case of Type I representational systems (RSI), any misrepresentations are really *our* misrepresentations. The same is true, though a bit more complicated, for Type II representational systems (RSII). But Dretske maintains that only in the case of Type III representational systems (RSIII), where he says the function to indicate is intrinsic, do we have a *source* rather than a *reflection* of intentionality. "Only here do we have systems sufficiently self-contained in their representational efforts to serve, in this one respect at least, as models of thought, belief, and judgment" (p. 67). Dretske uses the example of the northern hemisphere bacterium that contains a magnetosome, which, by representing magnetic north, steers the organism toward anaerobic environments ensuring its survival. If the bacterium is relocated to the southern hemisphere, it dies because it is diverted towards oxygen-bearing climes.

The function of magnetosomes is to indicate where anaerobic conditions lie. In the inappropriate hemisphere, they misrepresent. When a representational system has the function of indicating that s is F, Dretske refers to the proposition expressed in this sentence as the *content* of the representation. Representational content has two parts: its reference, i.e., the object, person, or condition that is represented, and the *sense* of the representation, i.e., what it is supposed to indicate. Content and sense capture the essence of intentionality: its *aboutness*.

Symbols (RSI) and natural signs (RSII) rely on knowledge by description. Intrinsic indicators rest on knowledge by acquaintance. Our reconstruction of an agent's likely intrinsic indicators in the course of developing the intentional interpretation is, however, a matter of knowledge by description. Similarly the agent may employ knowledge by description in the reconstruction of any of her natural indictors of which she is aware.

Requirements of perceptual contingency-representation

The concept itself

Perceptual contingency-representation is conceptualized as linking the context of contingencies of reinforcement with consumer action, the immediate precursor of activity or, more accurately, a component thereof, having cognitive, conative, affective, and perceptual components, embodying the individual's learning history, capable of representing probable outcomes of current/future activity, a common currency for representing the probable outcomes of future behavior and for comparing alternatives, and able to link the context of consumer action, namely, the contingencies of reinforcement, with the higher levels of consumer cognitive processing.

Contingency-representations must be informed by the consumer's learning history or experience – indeed, Nanay (2013a) says of pragmatic representations, which he defines as the immediate mental antecedents of action, that they are learned. Contingency-representations must, therefore, form a part of the intentional consumer-situation. Their formation looks back to the learning history that produced them, but also looks forward to the pattern of reinforcement that can be obtained via action with respect to the perceptual object. The question arises, if pragmatic representations are influenced by our actions, that is, if they are learned, revisable, can they be considered modular in Fodor's sense which prescribes that modules are informationally-encapsulated? The same consideration arises with respect to contingency-representations. I think they are modular but that we have to allow for them to be informationally influenced by central processing of experience.

What perceptual contingency-representation represents

Contingency-representations must denote the potential reinforcing and punishing outcomes of behavior in light of both previous experience and the current consumer behavior setting. It is the contingency-representation, therefore, that influences the probability of action on this occasion. In these contingency-representations inheres the capacity to transform bodily movement into action for they embody the goals that agents pursue by performing the actions, the consumer's relevant learning history, and the evaluation of current opportunities for consumer activity in light of internally-perused consequences. In short, what makes bodily movement an action is the representation of a goal in mind as a contingency-representation. It is contingency-representation that makes actions actions.

A major task of consumer psychology is to show how sensory input is related to motor output via cognitive intermediaries that take into consideration the contextual texture of consumer choice. When a consumer becomes perceptually aware of an environment that affords reinforcement and punishment contingent on the performance of particular behaviors, how is this translated into the behavioral output that secures the "correct" response is selected from her repertoire? By making the "correct" choice, I mean the selection of a behavioral route that leads to consequences that enhance the consumer's current wellbeing by optimizing her returns, whilst also contributing to her long-term survival and biological fitness. One answer to this question is to be found in the neurophysiological events that mediate sensation and behavior, and these will find a place in the account that follows. But the principal aim is to explore the psychological mediators, including perception, emotion, and decision making. It is not difficult to ascribe cognitive and affective experiences to behavior on the basis of a sort of folk psychology that assumes consumers do whatever increases pleasure and removes pain, acting therefore in accordance with a set of beliefs and desires that are consistent with these overall aims. We use this approach daily to make sense of our own and others' behavior and can readily apply it also in the more abstract sense of working out what motivates consumers. People behave in ways that serve their economic and social needs and refrain from behaviors that would harm them – don't they? This folk psychological perspective may suggest a starting point for more formal investigation but it is an unconvincing way to explain consumer choice in the context of social and behavioral science. We need a surer foundation for our understanding of what consumers maximize, what behaviors they seek to perform and those they avoid or escape from. And we require a means of explaining why they behave as they do that goes beyond the superficially evident.

This represents a shift, at least in emphasis, from the notion that action is the outcome of a deliberative process that painstakingly compares all of the prospective activities open to the individual in terms of an objective function. A normative model of rational decision making pervades, in one form or another, the social and behavioral sciences as well as marketing and consumer research and, perversely, does not accurately predict the individual actions in terms of which its measures of pre-actional mental processing and action are couched but approximates the aggregate actions of a large number.[7]

Although contingency-representation has three components – cognitive, conative, and perceptual – all of which can be thought of as among the immediate mental precursors of action, it is the perceptual component that is the most immediate.

Contingency-representation must in some way provide a common currency for representing the probable outcomes of future behavior and for comparing alternatives, and the perceptual component is the most obvious candidate for this, albeit guided and constrained by the cognitive and conative elements.

A contingency-representation specifically represents the individual's learning history which enables her to compute the probable outcomes of behaving in the current circumstances in a manner similar to that previously enacted. I use the term "compute" with reservation here: I am not speaking of a major operation of a computational mind but of a far less complicated perceptual comparison of alternative courses of action and their probable consequences. Nevertheless, there must be a means of selecting among these, choosing the one course of action that will be implemented. I defer further consideration of this mechanism until the nature of contingency-representation has been further clarified. A learning history is a record of the behaviors performed by an individual and the reinforcing and punishing outcomes that have ensued. The form it takes might vary: an experimenter in the animal laboratory, using subjects that have since birth given themselves altruistically to the advancement of behavioral science, can know their entire reinforcement history and record simply as a log. Learning histories of this kind are more elusive in the case of the post-pubescent consumer making her way through the complexities of a department store. When learning history is used as an explanatory variable of actions so complex as purchasing and consuming, it is almost impossible to specify except in broad terms. But the explanation of action requires, nonetheless, some conception of how the contingencies of reinforcement and punishment are encoded and how they come to impinge on current performance. Contingency-representation is to be understood, then, as that perceptual event which so encodes both the past and the envisioned future that is contingent on acting in a particular way.

Contingency-representation would be of limited benefit to an organism if it referred exclusively to the past. Its conative function, guiding current behavior, must rest upon a conception of the ways in which current circumstances, always subtly divergent from past encounters with the contingencies, might be instrumental in generating reinforcing and punishing experience.

What kind of representation is perceptual contingency-representation?

Let us recall Dretske's typology of representational systems before discussing the representational status of contingency-representations. Type I representational systems indicate how A stands in relation to B; for example, the circles I draw to indicate the planets of the solar system. Their capacity to represent is entirely dependent on the intentionality we ascribe to them. I set up the system, determine what the *symbols* will be and how they relate to the planets, draw the picture, and tell others what it is actually about as opposed to the possibility that it is a layout of a building, a small housing estate, or whatever. The intentionality that these symbols possess is entirely derived from myself as their author and the collective intentionality involved in their being shared by others with whom I communicate. Type II representational systems do their representing independently of us, however: animal tracks in the snow which are objectively related to what they represent. Natural representations are *signs* rather than symbols. The signs themselves are independent of humans but the functions they serve (allowing us to track the animal in question) are not. Their assuming the status of signs is entirely dependent on the intentionality we ascribe to them, that they derive from another system. Type III representational systems are also natural signs; they represent independently of the interests and functions of other systems (e.g., humans) and their functions are also independent of the purposes, etc. of those other systems. These are biologically-based *internal indicators* of, for example, how to locate food. They possess, indeed they exist solely by virtue of, intrinsic intentionality. Contingency-representations are undoubtedly representational systems of Dretske's third type.

First, they are intrinsic to our acting as animals and guide behavior and actions independently of our willing them to do this or that. Second, they represent the contingencies of reinforcement and punishment independently of the cognitive processes of any other system. I have argued that perception of the contingencies relies on the desires and beliefs we entertain, and that these are themselves representations of the contingencies that may influence perception. But these cognitive and conative processes do not belong to any other living entity that must assign for us the intentionality that provides the content of our perceptual contingency-representations. Rather, the presence of our own cognitive and conative contingency-representations and their penetration of our perceptual contingency-representations argues for a unified conception of contingency-representation based on the interaction of all three. Hence, we have reason to treat the perceptual, cognitive, and conative elements of contingency-representation as a singly-acting whole, a combined influence on action. Third, they can misrepresent as well as represent: this goes for the cognitive and conative elements of contingency-representation as well as the perceptual. Fourth, they are not simply sub-personal biological entities but personal level experiences; hence, their intentionality is partially derived from our selves; they are not simply sensations but cognitively and conatively interpreted actions in their own right, mental actions that have meaning in a way that the mechanistically-operating Type I and Type II representations cannot. Indeed, there seems to be a tendency for Dretske to present his theory at the sub-personal level at which biological mechanisms operate and not to touch on the personal level as that at which people desire, believe, emote, and perceive. He seems also to arbitrarily assign biological mechanisms the designation "beliefs" simply because they, as Type III representational systems, have content. This is a far cry from the personal level of intentionality and action of humans.

Dretske's (1988) approach to the explanation of behavior is particularly relevant to the present inquiry because of the central place it accords operant conditioning. Moreover, its portrayal of operant psychology is, as far as it goes, accurate. It captures correctly the difference between negative reinforcement and punishment, for instance, which is an acid test. It fails, however, to accommodate some important changes in radical behaviorist thought since Skinner's (1953) *Science and Human Behavior* which it reflects. Dretske does not, for instance, take on board Skinner's (1969) distinction between contingency-shaped and rule-governed behavior which has implications for the nature of the learning process involving contingent behavior and neural plasticity that Dretske apparently assumes. Even if Dretske is correct in assuming that, in the case of contingency-shaped behavior, some intra-personal element, *C*, both detects and represents external conditions, *F*, and that *C* is neurophysiologically characterized, the fact is that the representations required for rule-governed behavior are entirely cognitive.[8] Or is he seriously saying that the spoken sounds or written symbols in which socially-conveyed rules consist are translated into neurophysiological means of monitoring behavior and detecting circumstances, and thereby creating representations that determine behavior? Rules may be regarded simply as discriminative stimuli or motivating operations; if this is the case, we might be able to see these stimuli as engendering internalized causes of behavior. This extensional view is only of value if all we want to do is predict and possibly control behavior. However, Dretske is seeking an intentional explanation of behavior, one which is naturalized. In this case, we must accept that rules state propositions: their elements refer, employing sentences that are intensional.[9]

The problem reflects the continuing debate in the philosophy of mind concerning the status of beliefs and the level of exposition to which they belong. What is sometimes called the Standard View maintains that beliefs are physical or at least physiological. In any event, we should understand them as sub-personal; alternatively, approaches such as Baker's (1995) Practical Realism argue that beliefs belong at the level of the whole person and, therefore, to the personal level of exposition. However, the either/or nature of the debate overlooks the necessity of relying on both physicalist and intentional explanations in order to attain the most comprehensive account of human behavior of which we are capable. This is the perspective that Intentional Behaviorism takes in discerning the roles of context and cognition in consumer psychology. A key theme within this debate is the attempt to naturalize intentionality, i.e., to give a physicalist account of intentional phenomena. Dretske (e.g., 1988) and Baker (e.g., 1995) take antipodal approaches to defining the nature of intentionality in the explanation of behavior and the level of exposition at which mentation is ascribed. Baker (1995) argues *against* the Standard View that reason causation is in some way instantiated by neural events and *for* Practical Reality, which argues that intentionality is a property of the whole person. She argues, moreover, that Dretske's account of how beliefs explain is circular (Baker, 1991; cf. Dretske, 1991).

The problem is that Dretske is looking for the mind at the wrong level of exposition. He places it firmly at the sub-personal level when it can only be conceptualized at the personal level.[10] To be sure, any first-person experience of mind must have substrates (it cannot occur in the case of damaged neurophysiology) and superstrates (operant experience), but the third-person ascriptions of intentionality we make to explain behavior attribute it to the person as a whole, just as we ascribe overt behavior at this level. Intentional interpretation is therefore a *third-person*

ascription, even if it is our own account of our own action that is based on knowledge by description. As Lyons (1995, p. 112) points out, "Dretskean beliefs are neural structures." Hence, we are not aware of our beliefs. Indeed, beliefs are inaccessible
to us since brain events cannot be individuated so as to capture any particular belief.
Lyons goes on to argue that the brain is not an epistemic engine. Although it processes syntactically and semantically, it never *knows* or *interprets* the information that
it bears. Only the person does these things (Bennett & Hacker, 2003). The brain as a
causal processor cannot stand alongside its operations in order to monitor or inter-
pret them (Lyons, 1995, p. 117). The brain does not need intentional information to
appreciate what is happening when one steps on a nail because the brain does not
need to know that the cause of the resulting pain is a nail.

Dretske's analysis raises an important consideration with respect to the scope of
psychological explanation: does operant behavior inherently require an intentional
element since it is assumed to rest upon internal representation? This would mean
that even the theoretically minimalist extensional account of behavior generated by
radical behaviorism would be open to interpretation in intentional terms. I should
like to argue that this is true but that its implications for the pursuit of Intentional
Behaviorism are negligible. The point about extensional behavioral science is that
it seeks to *predict* behavior solely on the basis of the empirically-available stimulus
field that the BPM characterizes as the consumer behavior setting. As long as this is
possible and fulfills the requirements of the investigator, there is no need to resort
to intentional explanation. However, the pursuit of the operant account provides
an appropriate test for the necessity of an intentional account when it reaches its
boundaries and can no longer advert to such stimulus conditions. If the investigator
wishes, over and above the prediction of the behavior observed within the operant
paradigm, to *explain* it, she may at any time resort to intentional and cognitive reasoning (to provide understanding at the personal level of exposition), as she might
employ neuropsychology (to provide explanation at the sub-personal level).[11]

Distinguishing perceptual contingency-representation

In order to complete the conceptualization of contingency-representation, which
to date is largely confined to conative and cognitive components thereof, we now
examine the role of a *perceptual* component of contingency-representation which
would include the affective dimension. There are two routes to this refinement of
the concept of contingency-representation. First, Nanay's concept of *pragmatic representation* is critically examined as a source of perceptual experience that guides
action with respect to the physical manipulation of the environment. However,
while this idea embodies a significant advance, it does not capture the consumer's
perceptions of the reinforcement and punishment that are contingent on her acting
in the current consumer behavior setting, given her learning history. In particular,
pragmatic representation does not sufficiently represent the consumer's learning
history and the broader contingencies of reinforcement and punishment that ought
to guide future action; it actually obviates the need for psychological explanation

since the actions to which it is addressed may be readily explicated in terms of a behaviorist model.

Second, I propose that emotional feelings constitute, wholly or in part, the perceptual component of contingency-representation. They are so to the extent that the emotion may be regarded as perceptual, intentional, phenomenal, and modular in most of the respects suggested by Fodor, though perhaps differing importantly as Prinz points out. The argument for the thesis that emotional experience constitutes the principal source of perceptual contingency-representation requires that the link between emotional response and the contingencies of reinforcement and punishment be empirically demonstrated. There is support for this thesis in the form of evidence that consumers' emotional reactions are systematically related to the patterns of reinforcement identified by the BPM and the theoretical and empirical consonance of reinforcement sensitivity theory.

A comparison with pragmatic representation[12]

The essence of an action inheres in its having been instigated and shaped by a mental event or necessitating explanation in intentional terms.[13] Those mental actions that are the immediate precursors of bodily movements must inter alia represent in various ways the nature of the action to be performed, the dimensions of the task this entails, and the capacities its successful execution will require. Hence, before an individual can carry out a simple motor task such as grasping a cup she must be able to represent certain properties of this object to herself. When they are perceptually represented, Nanay (2013a) refers to the attribute properties of objects – their weight, shape, or distance, for instance – as action properties. These are whatever aspects of an object must be represented in order that an agent can carry out actions vis-à-vis that object. The representations themselves are *pragmatic representations* and they are responsible for making actions actions rather than mere bodily movements or behaviors. In a nutshell, "pragmatic representations attribute properties, the representation of which is necessary for the performance of an action"; they are perceptual – "genuine perceptual states". Hence, "we perceptually represent those properties the representation of which is necessary for the performance of an action" (p. 29). Moreover, these pragmatic representations are the perceptual constituents of the mental operations that immediately precede action. They do not fully constitute the immediate precursors of action but they are an indispensable component thereof.

Nanay argues, then, that pragmatic representations are perceptual, the representational component of the immediate mental precursors of action. He is, moreover, concerned with *basic actions*, those that do not require any other action in order to be performed. So booking an online rail ticket to Inverness is not a basic action but clicking the computer key that completes the booking is. Much less is travelling to Scotland by train a basic action but sitting down in one's train seat is. Avoiding an accident is accomplished by depressing the brake pedal but it is pressing the pedal that is the basic action.

Consistent with this, Nanay further defines pragmatic representations (a) in terms of their guiding bodily movements, (b) being contentful without being propositional, and (c) being capable of being correct or incorrect. The first of these is what transforms bodily movements into actions: they are mentally directed activities rather than behaviors automatically determined by genetic causation or stimulus control. The second demarcate pragmatic representations as perceptual and therefore intentional in the sense of having content about the world but, unlike desires and beliefs, not propositional. Not only do they not conform to the syntactical structure of proposition; they also defy description as sentences inscribed in a mental language. We may infer from this that they are the outcome of knowledge by acquaintance rather than knowledge by description (Russell, 1912).[14]

Finally, pragmatic representations can be adjudged correct if they guide bodily movements advantageously and appropriately and incorrect if they accomplish the reverse. This last suggests a connection with the success semantics methodology of determining the correctness of both propositional and non-propositional perceptions (Ramsey, [1927] 1990). By contrast with the desires and beliefs that are to the fore in decision-processing explanations of action, mediating sensory inputs and motor outputs, Nanay argues that pragmatic representations perform this function in the case of the vast majority of actions people perform and almost all of the behaviors of non-human animals. That the desire/belief model – what Searle (2001) calls the Classical Model of Rationality – applies assuredly to those human actions that are highly intellectualized is, he says, taken as license by cognitive theorists to apply the model generally. Nanay argues that, for most of our actions, pragmatic representations rather than beliefs and desires mediate sensory input and motor output. Less controversially, he claims that, even when beliefs and desires are involved in the production of action, pragmatic representations are nevertheless involved.

Nanay (2013a), then, defines the model depicting the traditional route to action as the view that action is determined by propositional attitudes, desires, and beliefs, which generate an intention to act in a particular manner, which in turn brings about the action. But this sequence, with its reliance on computation of the probabilities and outcomes of competing courses of action, is, he argues, comparatively rare; more common is the guidance of action by means of pragmatic representations, and even in those cases where computation and propositional syntax is present, there will still be a pragmatic representation which is the immediate precursor of the action. We can reformulate this slightly in terms of knowledge by description and knowledge by acquaintance. The Classical Model of Rationality explains action as the outcome of the interaction of desires (what one wants) and beliefs (how one can acquire it). In other words, knowledge by description, being propositional, consists in or gives rise to desires and beliefs which eventuate, via the formulation of an intention to act, in action:

Knowledge by description → desires and beliefs → action intention → action.

Non-propositional, perceptual knowledge directly presents the world and represents it in such a way as to make interaction with it possible. The particular knowledge it provides we may therefore depict as contingency-representation. Pragmatic representations emerge from this as a kind of contingency-representation that indicates the consequences of attempting to grasp, physically acquire, or otherwise deal materially with an entity in one's environment. But, in general, contingency-representation refers to the outcomes of previous action that is similar to that being contemplated at present, i.e., the representation of their reinforcing and punishing consequences, as well as the prospective outcomes of the current action:

Knowledge by acquaintance → *contingency-representation* → action.

It is this concept of contingency-representation which we are seeking. But first, Nanay's scheme requires further attention. We have seen that Nanay does not, at least initially, deny that some actions, especially complex ones (which he defines as those consisting of one or more basic actions) require the classic model of desires and beliefs to explain motivation. Rather, he asserts that *most* of the actions of adult humans and the overwhelming majority of those of animals and children do not require this. The action of moving a book out of the way as we seek to put our laptop down flat on the table is an example. Conscious belief is not necessary here, but might unconscious belief be? It is possible that whenever we engage in actions that are guided by pragmatic representations we must also have a belief of some sort, even if this is at a subliminal level. But this reasoning raises complexities of its own as it involves positing a whole complex of prior beliefs and other mental states. Nanay initially concludes that, although some, complex, actions require desires and beliefs most do not because they are relatively simple, even actions that require desires and beliefs also require pragmatic representations in order to bring them about.

Whatever aspect of the contingencies of reinforcement and punishment must be represented in order that an agent can carry out utility-maximizing actions in the circumstances. They make actions actions rather than simply bodily movements. Contingency-representations depict the consequences of an action rather than a behavior. They thus refer to the physical and social reinforcers/punishers that will result from an action *and* the emotional outcomes that will predictably eventuate therefrom. As a result they represent the reinforcing and punishing results of acting that are causally associated with the enhancement of the individual's survival, biological fitness, and social acceptance. Perceptual contingency-representations are therefore among the immediate pre-behavioral mental antecedents of action; although they are penetrated and influenced by those desires and beliefs that also depict the contingencies of reinforcement and punishment, they are more immediate precursors of action than these. They are the perceptual components of the immediate mental antecedents of action. But they are not the only such representations. Unlike Nanay, who seeks to exclude desires and beliefs as pragmatic representations, I do not deny a role to desires and beliefs as representations of the contingencies of reinforcement and punishment. Indeed, they shape the perceptual contingency-representations by virtue of the ways in which they depict the contingencies. Without such contingency-representations it is impossible for the agent to act appropriately in the circumstances it faces.

Like pragmatic representations, contingency-representations are (a) guides to bodily movements, (b) intentional (contentful) while not propositional (conceptual), and (c) able to be right or wrong. Nanay argues that (a) signifies that such bodily movements are actions rather than behaviors. They are mentally-directed rather than the result of selection by the contingencies of either survival (encountered in the course of phylogenetic progress) or operant selection (encountered during ontogenetic development). I should add the possibility that it is the absence of knowledge on our part as investigators of the processes of natural selection or the operant stimulus field required for these explanations that makes intentional interpretation inescapable. The scientific demonstration of mental direction remains empirically elusive and we employ it on the grounds of necessity and intellectual probity rather than because it can be validated or falsified. Only the discovery of the evidence necessary to the phylogenetic history or stimulus field in question can remove it.

Clarifying perceptual contingency-representation

The following discussion which compares and contrasts pragmatic representation and perceptual contingency-representation is not intended to provide a detailed critique of pragmatic representation, as a philosophical approach to explanation. It seeks only to understand better the nature of contingency-representation by pointing up its essential features using Nanay's conception as a yardstick for the development and positioning of the conception of contingency-representation, and the resulting emphasis concerns what a conception of contingency-representation needs in order to contribute to the explanation of human economic behavior. The conception of pragmatic representation provides an instructional template for that of perceptual contingency-representation as well as motivating an answer to the question of whether there is a need for the higher cognitive processes of desire and belief formation.

While pragmatic representation does not seek to account for the dependency of current action on past performance and the circumstances in which it has occurred, contingency-representation, by contrast, must find a place for the actor's perception of the consequences of her behavior. This is important because pragmatic representations, the perception of what an individual can physically accomplish vis-à-vis the physical world, are not conative; they do not motivate action. They inform the individual whether the action is physically feasible, whether she can physically produce it successfully. This is only a part of the pre-behavioral perceptions that humans – notably, in the current context, consumers – have. Insofar as contingency-representations are conceived as components of the immediate mental precursors of action, they are required to take perceptions of the contingencies into consideration. They therefore take note of the learning history the consumer has acquired, both the reinforcement history and the punishment history, and their interaction to produce action on this occasion.

There are, however, three aspects of pragmatic representation that render it unuseful in the development of a conception of contingency-representation: it does not take the appropriate consequences of action into consideration; it ignores the fact that perception is cognitively and conatively penetrated; and it actually precludes the necessity of psychological explanation as Intentional Behaviorism understands it.

It is inaccurate to portray pragmatic representation as failing to take past and projected contingencies into consideration, but the scope of contingency-awareness it entails is too limited for the explanation of consumer choice. Pragmatic representations, as we have seen, portray objects as having action properties: in order to perform the action of reaching out and picking up an object, an individual must be able to attribute to that object the action properties of a certain shape, size, weight, and so on. Otherwise, she will not be able to pick it up. The action properties represented can lead either to the successful operation of this task or to failure: they can be good or bad. However, this conception seems to be entirely about the mechanics of picking up the cup; pragmatic representations seem to be internally-oriented since they are about the (perceived) properties of the object that render behavior toward it effective or ineffective. The relative efficacy of the action is what pragmatic representations are concerned with. But what is required in the context of explaining social and economic behavior is a concept of the consumer's perceptions of the *outcomes* of such action. That is what the idea of contingency-representation must seek to supply. Contingency-representation cannot be simply a portrayal of the expected outcomes of acting in a particular way toward the object, which could be a product, brand, retail outlet: it must help define that portrayal interpreted in light of the consumer's learning history. The resulting action needs often to be rapid, and is, therefore, not adequately captured by the classic desire/belief model. As Nanay is at pains to point out, action of this kind relies on mental events that are most probably perceptual and which, I would add, are likely to involve emotional reactions to the contingencies of reinforcement and punishment. However, the perceptual determinants of behavior involved in the operation of contingency-representations may be instant or may involve the scrutiny of mental imagery in terms of its emotional impact. It may be necessary still to call on the idea of central cognitive processing in order to describe their function.

The question is where does cognitive processing fit? Just because, with Nanay, we seek an account of how consumers *actually* make decisions, does not imply that desires and beliefs do not influence these processes nor that they have no place in our modeling of how decisions are reached. Even an account of decision making as boundedly-rational involves goals and information, particularly in the form of performance-related indications from the environment. Admittedly, desires and beliefs and their interactions may play a less formal role than a full-blown decision theory based on the optimization of behavioral outcomes assumes (see Bermúdez, 2003); but desires/goals are still in force – satisficing is a kind of maximization (of utilitarian and informational reinforcement). The information that the environment provides is not only perceived: it enters also into decision procedures that influence how the consumer formulates perceptions and acts on them. This is fully consistent with Dretske's *indicators* (perceptions) and *representations* (beliefs).

Pragmatic representations are dominated by basic bodily movements which have immediate physical consequences. Typically they involve such considerations as "Can I pick this drinking glass up/reach the milk on the supermarket shelf, get this morsel of food into my mouth?" Now, although Nanay seeks to understand these operations in terms of their immediate perceptual antecedents, there is a readily available operant explanation for each of them. A person's learning history with respect to picking up glasses of this kind that are positioned in roughly this location, or stretching forth and grasping the milk in a standard supermarket configuration, or eating a sandwich at her desk is sufficient to predict her current activity in terms of instrumental conditioning. The behaviorist has no need of a concept of perception in these cases, being able to confine analysis to the observed behavior itself, the stimulus field in which it occurs, and its outcomes. If the behaviorist employs the term perception at all it is with the sense of sensation through the five modalities (since in behaviorism perception carries no implication of the translation of sensory information into a response by means of cognitive interpretation.) Else the behaviorist employs the idea of behavioral discrimination, an observable, rather than perception. Hence, the behavior can be explained in terms of the consumer's ability to discriminate weights, distances, bodily positions (e.g., of the mouth in relation to the sandwich) as is demonstrable by her actual behavior. The success of the operation is the index of ability to discriminate responses that have previously proved reinforcing from those that have not. If prediction and control of the behavior can be achieved by appeal to a stimulus field, then there is no need of a psychological explanation. The requirement to turn to intentional language, to explain in terms of perception, arises only if no such stimulus field is empirically available; in its absence it is essential to turn to intentional idioms, to speak of perception and perhaps other mental events. In order to propose an intentional interpretation of a behavioral episode for which there is no apparent stimulus field, one strategy is to propose such an interpretation for a similar behavioral episode for which such stimulus conditions can be identified and then to transfer this interpretation to the initial context. This is an accepted element in an Intentional Behaviorist approach (Foxall, 2016b).

Another standard component of Intentional Behaviorist methodology is the rule that there is no reason to ascribe intentionality to an activity for which a stimulus field satisfactorily provides an explanation in extensional terms. Such activity is not action; it is behavior. This raises an important implication for the application of Intentional Behaviorist explanatory procedures, and the word "satisfactorily" is the key. If we want to do more than predict (and possibly control) behavior for which a stimulus field is available, we may treat it or aspects of it as action and, accordingly, seek a psychological explanation for it. And this raises the possibility that opportunities for psychological explanations may be more prevalent than a simple approach in terms of prediction and control would allow. But the present point is that the bodily movements for which Nanay offers explanation in terms of pragmatic representations are generally explicable in operant terms, rendering a psychological explanation superfluous, at least on the basis of Intentional Behaviorist methodology. This is a key point for Intentional Behaviorism. Just because a behaviorist explanation is possible for part of an action sequence does not rule out a psychological explanation for other aspects thereof. Those who do not adopt Intentional Behaviorism are, of course, at liberty to seek a psychological explanation for any bodily movement by positing pragmatic representations or other mental operations, even if an operant interpretation is feasible. I stress only that this is not the psychological explanation pursued in Intentional Behaviorism, which understands the necessity of a psychological explanation to arise only when the theoretically-minimalist strategy of operant explanation has been exhausted.

Nanay (2013a) assumes that actions by definition have antecedent mental operations that guide, cause, or accompany them or which are necessarily ascribed in order to explain them (see, inter alia, Hornsby, 1981; Steward, 2012). He takes the immediate mental antecedents of action to be perceptual and to have at least two components: (a) a representation of the world or the immediate goal of the action, and (b) motivation to act. His focus is the representational component of the immediate mental antecedents of action, which he nominates *pragmatic representations*. Whether a pragmatic representation results in action depends on its being accompanied by the conative component of the immediate mental antecedents of action; i.e., action requires *both* components. These two components, the cognitive component and the conative component, respectively, are not the only elements required by a concept of the immediate mental antecedents of action. We turn now to the affective component, which is arguably (a) perceptual, and (b) a representation of the reinforcement and punishment previously contingent on the performance of similar actions to that now contemplated, and (c) a representation of the contingent consequences of action that are likely to eventuate should the contemplated action be performed. The focal domain of the action to which the analysis applies is the economic psychology of consumer choice, a pervasive human concern and therefore an exemplar of human activity.

This focus immediately suggests a difference of emphasis or level of analysis from that of Nanay, who is concerned only with basic actions, typified by bodily movements such as raising an arm, rather than complex actions such as pointing out a local landmark to a stranger which is topographically identical. The kinds of action with which I am concerned are, however, typically complex: buying the food and wine for a dinner party, driving a prestigious car to the office, or taking an exotic vacation. Of course, the execution of these consumer actions necessarily requires the performance of numerous basic actions, each of which entails immediate mental antecedents of action and, therefore, pragmatic representation. Pragmatic representations are integral but also incidental to the performance of consumer actions, actions that eventuate in a pattern of reinforcement that brings about a pattern of reward that influences the rate at which similar actions are performed in the future.

Notes

1 But note that the cognitive penetrability of perception is denied by some modular approaches to mental processes, typically that proposed by Fodor (1983), who understands perceptual input processes as modular, which entails their being informationally encapsulated from other perceptual processes as well as from central cognitive functions.

2 Two brain regions exhibit double-dissociation when each is shown to be uniquely implicated in the production of a particular behavior or cognitive function.

3 A more comprehensive account of the variety of uses of "modularity" in the philosophy of psychology is provided by Faucher and Tappolet (2008b). See also Prinz (2006).

4 The systems which Fodor (1983) designates modules have all nine characteristics: domain specificity, mandatory operation, limited central accessibility, fast processing, informational encapsulation, shallow outputs, fixed neural architecture, characteristic and specific breakdown patterns, and characteristic ontogenetic pace and sequencing. In fact, the criteria for modularity are not inflexible: Fodor points out that these characteristics need only to be represented in a system to an appreciable degree, i.e., most of them need to be found substantially, for modularity to be ascribed. Some modular features are more important than others: informational encapsulation is paramount.

5 See also Dretske (1981) for earlier work on the nature of belief and its explanatory significance.

6 For a critical view of Dretske's typology of representation, see Millikan (2004), particularly pp. 31–39.

7 For a recent exposition in terms of social and behavioral science generally, see Bermúdez (2003). For an exposition in terms of the social psychology of action, see Fishbein and Ajzen (2010). I have described and commented on the application of some of this logic to marketing and consumer research: see Foxall (1983, 1997a, 2005).

8 Not according to Skinner, it is hardly necessary to add, but certainly on closer inspection: see, for instance, Foxall (2016b).

9 Dretske (2001), in arguing that the mind is within the individual, observes that when we insert coins into a vending machine to obtain a product we are likely to explain the money inserted as the cause of this delivery. I obtained the chocolate bar because I inserted the designated amount; had I inserted only half of this, I should have received nothing. However, he also points out that we know that the properties of the coins inserted (shape, size, mass) are causally instrumental in obtaining the item: "The monetary value of these objects is causally irrelevant" (Dretske, 2001, p. 43) because the machine does not register the socio-legal and economic significance of the coins and would yield the chocolate even if metal slugs with the appropriate properties were used instead of legal tender. It is the workings of the machine and their response to the insertion of metal objects of particular physical proportions that causes the release of the product. Dretske claims that coins inserted into a vending machine symbolize intentionality and that these physical entities lead to the operation of the machine in providing a product. However, I would argue that beliefs and other categories of ascribed intentionality correspond, despite what Dretske (2001, p. 43) says, to the *value* of the coins inserted. Several combinations of coins can have the same effect (release of, say, a chocolate bar). In explaining behavior by reference to intentionality, I am in the position of someone who knows the combined values of the coins that have to be inserted prior to the chocolate bar's appearance, but who knows nothing about how the metal discs come to cause the machine to release the product. To equate the intentionality-explanation (the value of the coins) with the metallic discs is to cross a line. The discs have no intrinsic value vis-à-vis releasing the chocolate. We have even less idea how a desire for chocolate and a belief that placing certain coins in the machine causes its release bring about the neural mechanisms necessary for the discharge of this task. The best we can do is shape our intentional explanations to these neurophysiological and operant events we do know about.

10 Compare, however, Dretske (1995).

11 Since the discussion of perceptual contingency-representation continues in Chapter 4, the conclusions are reserved for that chapter.

12 My discussing Nanay's work at some length is in the spirit of celebrating his approach and the uses to which he puts it. I employ it largely as a source of critical guidance for the view I am advocating and to demonstrate how it differs from his wholly legitimate and well-reasoned argument for a perceptual approach to action.

13 While some psychologists and philosophers take intentionality to be the causation of behavior, others will not take this step but still accord intentionality a significant role in the explanation of action. The latter is the view taken here: on the one hand, it is not possible to speak of action in the extensional terms of theoretical minimalism, but it is also impossible for intentional entities to enter into an experimental analysis or, except as latent variables, into a correlational analysis. Although, for the sake of intelligible exposition, I shall speak *as though* intentions (desires, beliefs, emotions, perceptions, and decision making) were causally linked to action, my position is it is simply impossible to provide an explanation of actions for which no stimulus field is empirically available without resorting to intentional language. In such cases, intentional language is essential to the *explanation of action*, though the question of if and how it might be causally linked to it remains open.

14 For a discussion in the context of Intentional Behaviorism, see *Perspectives on Consumer choice: From Behavior to Action, From Action to Agency* (Foxall, 2016b, pp. 125–133).

4

REFINING PERCEPTUAL CONTINGENCY-REPRESENTATION

Abstract

The possibility is raised that the chief component of perceptual contingency-representation is consumers' emotional experience. This is discussed principally in the context of empirical research which has shown consumers' emotional responses to consumer-situations belonging to the contingency categories defined by the Behavioral Perspective Model to be predictable on the basis of the patterns of utilitarian and informational reinforcement and consumer behavior setting scope that define those situations. This empirical evidence strengthens the possibility that consumers' recall of past contingencies that shaped their behaviors and their mental understanding of present opportunities for reinforcement are encapsulated in their emotional experience. The concept of perceptual contingency-representation is further refined by comparison with that of pragmatic representation and the quest to identify the content of perceptions and beliefs through success semantics.

Emotion as perceptual contingency-representation

Understanding emotion

This chapter divides into two parts which may, at first glance, seem disparate though in fact they are both concerned with the clarification of the concept of perceptual contingency-representation introduced in Chapter 3. In discussing the construction of the intentional consumer-situation, this chapter considers emotions as contingency-representations. Emotion is a prime candidate for contingency-representation by virtue of its being perceptual, quasi-modular, linked to patterns of reinforcement, and experiential.[1] It is, moreover, systematically related to patterns of contingencies of reinforcement.[2] The second part of the chapter is concerned with the nature of perceptual experience, be it pragmatic representation or contingency-representation, in relation to Ramsey's ([1927] 1990) system of success semantics, which may sound esoteric at this point to anyone unfamiliar with it but which is again dedicated to the refinement of the definition of perceptual contingency-representation.

It is common to distinguish emotions from other forms of affect such as moods on the basis that emotions are intentional; the question then arises: what are emotions about; what is their content? For many philosophers, including Prinz, emotions are perceptions of those bodily states that monitor the individual's environmental conditions.[3] Prinz differentiates the *nominal* content of an emotion, which is a representation of the bodily state itself, from *real* content, which is whatever environmental element instigates the bodily state. For example, taking possession of my prestigious new car may cause a particular bodily state and the representation of this state eventuates in pleasure: the bodily state *is* the nominal content of my emotion, the physiological state that results from getting the car, while its real content is the car's arrival. My feeling my bodily state in these circumstances *is* my felt emotion. Now, if emotions are perceptions of bodily states that arise in relation to the opportunities and threats posed by an external environment, it should follow that emotions are "embodied appraisals" and this is precisely the conclusion Prinz reaches, allying himself with the James–Lange theory of emotion. In this way he claims to account for a wide range of emotions, from those acquired in the course of phylogenetic history to those that derive from the ontogenetic development of the individual.

Prinz (2004, 2008) proposes that emotions, since they can be considered as perceptions, are modular, though he has in the course of these two publications moved from a Fodorian conception of modularity by relinquishing the requirement that modules be informationally encapsulated (Prinz, 2006). Hence, he argues that

> A mental capacity is *quasi-modular* to the extent that it is:
> 1. Functionally specialized
> 2. Subject to characteristic breakdowns
> 3. Capable of automatic processing
> 4. Built up from a system of innate rules and representations
> 5. Stimulus-dependent
>
> *(Prinz, 2008, p. 139)*

Stimulus-dependency carries the implication that modules are restricted by their inputs and therefore not entirely influenced by central processes: "we cannot simply choose what we perceive ... but top-down influences can significantly affect what happens in perceptual systems. And this is an important departure form Fodor's idea of 'encapsulation'" (p. 140). While Fodor is adamant that modules are completely insulated from higher cognitive processing, Prinz is equally sure that modules are cognitively permeable and even amenable to inter-modular communication among a variety of forms of inter-modal accommodation.[4]

Basic emotions

That emotions have a biological foundation, even though we are unable to pin-point all specific emotions in relation to particular brain regions, indicates that emotions have been laid down in the course of natural selection. LeDoux's (1988) demonstration that emotion is correlated with particular brain areas such as the limbic system and especially the amygdala – and that phylogenetically prior species have similar brain circuits suggests a genetic basis for emotion. Emotions can be considered relatively short-lived responses to extrapersonal conditions (see Prinz, 2004, p. 107). As such, they can be considered as states rather than traits, but they are closely related to traits, e.g., of personality as well as to affective disorders, both of which are heritable.

Mehrabian (1980) argues that pleasure, arousal, and dominance are primary adaptations and Barrett et al. (2007) confirm Mehrabian and Russell's (1974) judgment that these three emotions are fundamental to the representation of emotion and also relate them to reinforcement and punishment (see also Barrett, 2005; Russell & Barrett, 1999). *Pleasure–displeasure* ranges from extreme pain or unhappiness to extreme happiness. It is assessed with self-report, e.g., on semantic differential scales, or through such behavioral indicators as smiles or laughter and other facial expressions judged to be positive or negative. *Arousal–nonarousal* ranges from sleep to frantic excitement and is assessed using verbal report or via such behavioral indicators as vocal activity (positive and negative), facial activity (positive and negative expressions), speech rate, and speech volume. *Dominance–submissiveness* ranges from feelings of being strongly influenced and controlled by one's environment to strong feelings of mastery and control over it. Its assessment usually takes the form of verbal reports using the semantic differential method. In behavioral terms, dominance is reflected in postural relaxation and the individual's manifest freedom to act in a variety of ways.

Toronchuk and Ellis (2013) set forth a model of emotions which stresses their phylogenetic origins. Their model proposes a primary emotional organizing system dealing with power, rank, dominance, and subordination as well as contributing to self-esteem in humans. They also make an interesting comment on valence, which is usually interpreted simply in terms of pleasure versus displeasure:

> Although the notion of valence (usually as approach/avoidance or pleasure/pain) is common in theories of emotion, we use the term as referencing reward and punishment, which most likely reflect internal states or makers.
>
> *(ibid, p. 1)*

They are, moreover, clear that the psychological traits experienced by us as emotions are the result of evolutionary pressures.[5] Their function is to enhance survival, as for example when reproductive needs give rise to bonding and desire that lead to mating and gene survival. The model put forward by Toronchuk and Ellis is based on a number of underlying propositions, several of which are germane to the current discussion. First, they argue that the reason emotional systems emerged in the course of evolution is related to their causal efficacy in modifying patterns of behavior. This is supportive of the idea that emotional experience is the ultimate source of reward and punishment of preceding behaviors. Second, emotional systems were selected on the basis of their enhancing survival, resulting in the evolution of primary emotional systems which then shaped cognition and secondary emotional systems. Third, the attachment systems and the dominance system evolved for socially connected humans, supplementing basic systems for survival and learning at the level of the group. Fourth, humans' subjective feelings are their experiences of emotional operating systems that underlay evolutionary and developmental events which do not entail awareness of their evolutionary origins.

Toronchuk and Ellis's (2013) model builds on Panksepp's (1998, 2005, 2007) seven core or primary emotional systems – SEEKING, RAGE, FEAR, LUST, CARE, PANIC, and PLAY – by adding to it DISGUST and POWER/DOMINANCE as core emotions. They also refer to the SEEKING system as the "pleasure/SEEKING system." Table 4.1 summarizes the linkages between human needs and the emotional systems which have evolved to satisfy them.

These emotional systems correspond at a general level to the three emotions adopted by Mehrabian and Russell (1974) (see Figure 4.1). The Pleasure/SEEKING and PLAY systems have a clear affinity with *pleasure*; the DISGUST, RAGE, FEAR, and LUST systems suggest *arousal*; and the PANIC/attachment, CARE, and POWER/dominance systems are associated with *dominance*. These considerations give confidence to the expectation that Mehrabian and Russell's typology and measures of emotion are relevant to the explanation of consumer choice. Before turning to the evidence generated by empirical research, however, it is instructive to look at the case of emotion being related to contingencies of reinforcement and punishment.

FIGURE 4.1 Primary emotions. Primary emotional systems as proposed by Panksepp (1998), augmented by Toronchuk and Ellis (2013), and related to the primary emotions of pleasure, arousal, and dominance proposed by Mehrabian and Russell (1974).

TABLE 4.1 Evolutionary needs, and the emotional systems that have evolved to meet them

Evolutionary needs met	Primary emotional system	Works with:	Functions
INDIVIDUAL NEEDS			
Basic functioning	E1: SEEKING system	E2–9	Situation evaluation, incentive salience, hedonic appraisal, facilitates learning
Basic survival	E2: DISGUST system (repulsion, avoidance)		Avoiding harmful foods, substances, environments
	E3: RAGE system	E4, E9	Defense: protection of organism, resources, and conspecifics, limiting of restraint on movement
	E4: FEAR system	E3, E9	Defense: flight, limiting of tissue damage
SOCIAL NEEDS			
Reproduction	E5: LUST system (sexual desire, satiation)	E6, E7	Ensuring procreation, enhancement of bonding
Group cohesion: bonding and development	E6: PANIC/ attachment (affiliation, separation distress)	E5, E7	Protection of vulnerable individuals; creates bonding through need for others
	E7: CARE system	E5, E6	Caring for others, particularly offspring
	E8: PLAY system	E6, E7	Bonding with conspecifics, development of basic adaptive and social skills, creativity
Group function: regulating conflict	E9: POWER/ dominance (rank, status, submission)	E3, E4, E5	Limiting aggression in social groups: allocating resources, especially sexual ones

Source: Toronchuk, J. A. & Ellis, G. F. R. (2013). Affective neuronal selection: The nature of the primordial emotion systems. *Frontiers in Psychology*, 3, 589. Reproduced by permission.

Emotion and contingency[6]

An account of behavior as influenced by its consequences which did not make this explicit link with emotion would still have to explain how patterns of reinforcement and punishment contingent on past behavior could influence current responding. Emotion seems to be the link that evolution has provided. Linking reports of emotion with patterns of contingency is a necessary first step in explaining the relationship between learning history and subsequent action.

Several authors have pointed out that emotions represent contingencies of reinforcement and punishment and that they are related not only to current behavior but also to cognitive processing which informs subsequent decision making. As Jones (2008, pp. 3–4) puts it,

> Emotions are clever design solutions to the problem of making fast decisions in response to significant practical problems posed by the natural and social worlds: we perceive a danger and fear immediately primes us to take protective action ... Emotions can, with experience and regulation, become reason-tracking mechanisms that enable an agent reliably to track the way her concerns are implicated in concrete choice situations.

Rolls's (1999, 2014) theory of emotion proposes that the way in which the brain facilitates the reward and punishment of behaviors through the generation of emotions provides a key to understanding the neuropsychology of behavior. He argues that the primary (biological) *goals* of behavior, rather than specific behaviors, are influenced by the genes which "selfishly" (Dawkins, 1976) regulate what will act as reinforcers and punishers in order to promote their own survival through the biological fitness of the organisms that are their vehicles. By operating in such a way as to *evaluate* rewards and punishers, the brain interfaces sensory inputs and action outputs. Behavior is thus the outcome of the procedure in which the brain *computes* the values of sensory stimuli and selects between reinforcers and ways of avoiding punishers. The behaviors on which reinforcers and punishers act are motivational and emotional behaviors: motivational behaviors usually result from intracranial stimulation whereas emotional behaviors result from stimuli that originate outside the brain. Sensory processing, that which relies on the identification of reinforcing and punishing stimuli via the sense modalities, enables the appropriate decoding and representation of the reward value of reinforcers once they have been identified.

Brain systems involved in motivation and emotion transfer reward and punishment signals to the action systems; the action systems tend to maximize the reward signals so obtained, and switch behavior from one reward to another following any reduction in the reward value of the former and as the possibility of punishment increases. Hence, "emotions are states produced by instrumental reinforcing stimuli" (Rolls, 1999, p. 61; see also Damasio, 1994).

Emotional response in behavioral perspective

The ability of consumers to identify their emotional experiences in response to verbal scenarios of consumer-situations displaying the various combinations of utilitarian and informational reinforcement, and open–closed consumer behavior setting scope proposed by the BPM Contingency Matrix (Figure 1.2(c)) has been demonstrated in a number of separate studies across several cultures, beginning with Foxall (1997a, 1997b.)[7] The research has measured three emotions, *pleasure, arousal,* and *dominance* (P, A, D, or PAD), as well as conation, employing the scales devised by Mehrabian and Russell (1974). The overall expectation has been that higher pleasure scores would be found for situations in which utilitarian reinforcement was higher rather than lower, higher arousal for those in which informational reinforcement was higher rather than lower, and higher dominance for situations marked by more open consumer behavior setting scope (for further detail, see Foxall, 1997b, 2011; Foxall et al., 2012). Behavioral propensity, readiness-to-act, or conation were expected to increase with both pleasure and the higher levels of setting openness.

Participants completed the scales for the assessment of the three emotions (yielding scores for P, A, and D) in response to verbal stimulus descriptions of eight consumer-situations defined functionally in terms of the BPM Contingency Matrix (Figure 2.3); they also assessed the amount of time they would prefer to remain in each of eight situations and the extent to which they would wish to socialize in each, yielding the behavioral preference variable which was disaggregated into approach and avoidance and summarized as their mean difference, "aminusa." (For details of the nature and administration of the measures of P, A, D, and the behavioral elements, see Mehrabian and Russell (1974), and for adjustments made in the research summarized here, see Foxall (1997a, 1997b) and Foxall and Soriano (2005).) The scenarios were constructed initially to illustrate the nature of the consumer-situations proposed by the BPM (Foxall, [1990] 2004) and subsequently refined and subjected to assessment by expert panels according to criteria for utilitarian and informational reinforcement and consumer behavior setting scope (Foxall, 1999). Stimulus scenarios for the consumer-situations investigated, as allocated by expert panels among the contingency categories identified by the BPM were employed, sometimes with slight modification, in the eight studies (see Foxall, 1997b, 1999).[8]

Figure 4.2 summarizes the hypotheses and the results.[9]

Emotion and contingency-sensitivity

According to Reinforcement Sensitivity Theory (RST), approach and avoidance behaviors are functions of environmental events that take the form of appetitive and aversive stimuli which are either accepted or rejected by the individual. Individual differences in sensitivity to these stimuli determine personality. The RST proposes two brain systems

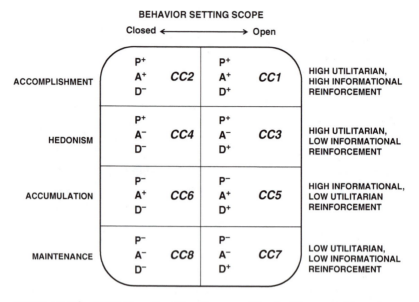

FIGURE 4.2 The BPM Emotion Contingency Matrix. The general hypotheses tested are that pleasure will increase with utilitarian reinforcement, arousal with informational reinforcement, and dominance with the openness of the consumer behavior setting. The research hypotheses predicted and the results indicate that (i) *pleasure* scores for contingency categories (CCs) 1, 2, 3, and 4 each exceed those of CCs 5, 6, 7, and 8; (ii) *arousal* scores for CCs 1, 2, 5, and 6 each exceed those of CCs 3, 4, 7, and 8; (iii) *dominance* scores for CCs 1, 3, 5, and 7 each exceed those for CCs 2, 4, 6, and 8. Moreover, (iv) approach–avoidance (aminusa) scores for CCs 1, 2, 3, and 4 each exceed those for CCs 5, 6, 7, and 8; and (v) approach–avoidance (aminusa) scores for CCs 1 and 3 each exceed those for CCs 2, 4, 5, 6, 7, and 8. *Aminusa* is simply a[pproach] *minus* a[voidance], the difference between the scores for these two aspects of behavior, presented as a composite summary variable for behavior or behavioral tendency.

that moderate these behaviors and their reinforcing and punishing consequences (Corr, 2008; Smillie, 2008; the following account is indebted to both of these sources).

Approach behaviors, which are sensitive to positively reinforcing stimuli, are mediated by a Behavioral Approach System (BAS) that incorporates the brain circuitry known to accompany the receipt of reinforcement. BAS is located in the basal ganglia and the mesocorticolimbic systems that deliver dopamine from the Ventral Tegmental Area (VTA) to the ventral striatum (notably, the nucleus accumbens) and mesocortical dopamine PFC (Smillie, 2008). Phasic dopaminergic activity intensifies as a result of unpredicted reward, is reduced in response to unpredicted non-reward, and is stable in the case of rewards that are fully predicted; on this basis, Schultz (2000; Schultz et al., 2008) argues that dopamine encodes reward prediction error (RPE). The implication is that BAS activation is aroused as a result of unpredicted reward and maintained by predicted reward. Positive affect is also engendered by BAS activation and the behavioral approach to the stimulus that causes it is motivated. These processes are related, moreover, to personality: people display individual differences in reinforcement sensitivity, the activity of the BAS, which manifests in a greater or lesser tendency to display the personality trait of extraversion or positive emotionality. In summary, reward sensitivity leads to positive emotion, approach behavior, and extraversion.

By contrast, punishment sensitivity leads to negative emotion, avoidance, and neuroticism. *Avoidance* involves sensitivity to aversive stimulation and threat. It is mediated by two biobehavioral emotion and motivation systems. The first, the Fight–Flight–Freeze System (FFFS) is activated in response to the threat of aversive stimuli and the emotional consequence is fear, and the motivation consequence that eventuates from this is defensive avoidance. The FFFS comprises the periaqueductal gray in the case of intense or promixal threat, and the medial hypothalamus, amygdala, and interior cingulate cortex in the case of distal threat. Stimuli of these kinds generate release of serotonin (5-HT) and noradrenalin (NA) which projects to all levels of the avoidance system. Consequential stimuli leading to conflict between goals (i.e., stimuli of mixed valence) activate the second biobehavioral emotional and motivation system connected to avoidance, the Behavioral Inhibition System (BIS). The emotional output of the BIS is anxiety, which is accompanied by risk assessment and caution, which are the hallmark of the behavior pattern known as defensive approach. The BIS consists of the septo-hippocampal system and amygdala and generates trait fearfulness (which is FFFS-mediated) and anxiety (which is BIS-mediated). Most approach–avoidance models refer, however, to punishment sensitivity and relate this to such personality dimensions as neuroticism or negative emotionality. Personality traits thus reflect individual differences in reactivity to consequential stimuli.

RST refers to all consequential stimuli as "reinforcement" and in its terminology reinforcement sensitivity is therefore a central explanatory tool. The following summary of the behavior–personality–emotion systems of RST, however, retain Skinnerian usages for the reasons explained earlier. In the case of positive reinforcement, it is the BAS which mediates approach to *all* appetitive stimuli, generating the hopeful emotion of "anticipatory pleasure." The attendant personality is marked by optimism, reward-orientation, impulsivity (mapping on to addiction and high-risk behaviors. In the case of negatively reinforced behavior (escape, avoidance), the FFFS mediates actions to *all* aversive stimuli: it involves the "get me out of here" emotion of fear (not anxiety). Finally, in the case of punishment, the BIS, dedicated to the resolution of goal conflict, generates the "watch for danger" emotion of anxiety, leading to the inhibition of prepotent conflicting behavior, engagement of risk assessment procedures, and scanning of memory and the environment to help resolve current goal conflict. The BIS aids the resolution of conflict by increasing the negative valence of stimuli until conflict resolution occurs in favor of either approach or avoidance. The procedures leading to this are rumination and worry.

The associated personality is marked by worry-proneness, anxiety, rumination, generalized anxiety, and obsessive-compulsive disorder (OCD).

Since each of the kinds of consumer-situation proposed by the BPM Contingency Matrix entails behaviors that meet with both reinforcement and punishment, it follows that both the BAS and BIS will be relevant to each of the contingency categories functionally adumbrated. In addition, the FFFS is likely to be implicated in the explanation of several of the categories of behavior specified by the contingency categories of the matrix. The possible ways in which the BAS, BIS, and FFFS systems explicate behaviors and emotions are set out in Table 4.2 (Corr, 2008), and the following discussion relates each of these to the contingency categories specified in the matrix, beginning with the performance of approach behaviors for which reinforcement is unattainable.

Figure 4.3 summarizes how these considerations may apply to the contingency patterns that comprise the BPM Contingency Matrix, and the consumer-situations and behaviors that are suggested by them. An initial observation is that, just as the Continuum of Consumer Behavior Settings (Figure 1.1) is a restricted range of the comprehensive continuum of behavior settings in which humans may find themselves, so the range of emotion-eliciting behavior settings that are relevant to the explanation of consumer choice is likely to be restricted compared with that which

TABLE 4.2 Emotions/states and behaviors associated with: (a) the avoidance of (FFFS) and approach (BIS) to aversive stimuli, and (b) the approach to appetitive stimuli

	Stimulus conditions	*Emotion/state*	*Behaviors*
Aversive stimuli			
Avoid (FFFS)	Avoidable	Fear	Phobic avoidance, escape, flight
	Unavoidable	Panic	Fight (defensive aggression), freeze
Approach (BIS)	Avoidable	Anxiety	Behavioral inhibition, risk assessment
	Unavoidable	Depression	Behavioral suppression
Appetitive stimuli			
Approach (BAS)	Attainable	Hope, anticipatory pleasure	Exploration, sub-goal scaffolding
	Unattainable	Frustration, anger	Fight (predatory aggression), displacement activity

Source: Corr, P. J. (2008). *The Reinforcement Sensitivity Theory of Personality.* Cambridge: Cambridge University Press. Reproduced by permission.

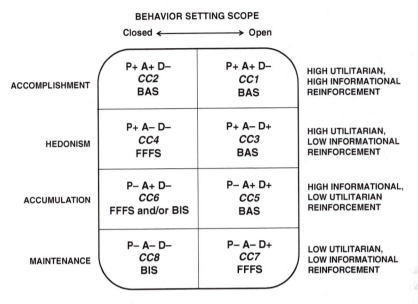

BEHAVIOR SETTING SCOPE

Closed ←——————→ Open

	Closed	Open	
ACCOMPLISHMENT	P+ A+ D– CC2 BAS	P+ A+ D– CC1 BAS	HIGH UTILITARIAN, HIGH INFORMATIONAL REINFORCEMENT
HEDONISM	P+ A– D– CC4 FFFS	P+ A– D+ CC3 BAS	HIGH UTILITARIAN, LOW INFORMATIONAL REINFORCEMENT
ACCUMULATION	P– A+ D– CC6 FFFS and/or BIS	P– A+ D+ CC5 BAS	HIGH INFORMATIONAL, LOW UTILITARIAN REINFORCEMENT
MAINTENANCE	P– A– D– CC8 BIS	P– A– D+ CC7 FFFS	LOW UTILITARIAN, LOW INFORMATIONAL REINFORCEMENT

FIGURE 4.3 **Contingency-sensitivity and emotion.** In Reinforcement Sensitivity Theory (RST), as in radical behaviorism, previously-encountered post-behavioral environmental stimuli are responsible for the regulation of behavior. The contingency-sensitivity theory emphasizes, however, that the reinforcing and punishing consequences of behavior engender emotional experiences that are the ultimate rewarding and punishing outcomes of action. In RST, BAS is the behavioral approach/activation system which indicates approach to appetitive stimuli (such behavior is positively reinforced). FFFS indicates the avoidance of or escape from aversive stimuli (such behavior is negatively reinforced). The BIS indicates approach to aversive stimuli (such behavior is punished).

Corr considers in Table 4.2. So, Figure 4.3 must be interpreted with circumspection in the realm of consumer action.

It must also be borne in mind that the following descriptions of consumer behaviors suggested by Figures 4.2 and 4.3 are based on gross averaging. All consumer choice involves some reinforcement and some punishment. There will therefore be a considerable degree of BAS-activated behavior and emotion in all of the consumer-situations denoted by the matrix; and there will be some BIS-activated punishment of behavior and/or the consumer. The figure seeks to set out a general idea of the behaviors and emotions as they relate to contingencies of reinforcement and punishment. Emotional feelings and contingency-sensitivity reflect individual differences: not all of the consumers whose behaviors are under the control of/ associated with a particular pattern of contingency (a specific CC) as defined in the BPM Contingency Matrix will experience identical patterns of emotion, of course. We are averaging and generalizing on the basis of the summarized BPM/PAD research. This is an instance where the extra-laboratorial exploration of behavior is inevitable, but psychometrics provides an acceptable alternative to experimentation. Hence, Figures 4.2 and 4.3 do not attempt a one-on-one mapping of contingencies and emotional/behavioral responses but suggest how most consumers are likely to respond to particular patterns of contingency.

The first consideration is the BAS and its association with positive reinforcement. The overall classification of the CCs contained in the BPM Contingency Matrix in terms of the explanatory categories of RST are as follows. CCs 1, 2, 3, and 5 are explicable in terms of the BAS. In the case of CCs 1, 3, and 5, at least three of the four emotional and behavioral measures indicate that these CCs each score higher than their corresponding closed-setting CC on behavioral propensity. Pleasure means for each of CCs 1, 3, 5, and 7 are greater than each of CCs 2, 4, 6, and 8. In the case of CC2, three of the four measures are also positive and greater than those for the other closed settings and CC8 in the case of P and A and two of those for Dominance. Approach and Aminusa are much higher for CC2 than for the remaining closed settings and greater than for the open settings with the exception of CC1.

In all of these CCs, positive reinforcement is attainable. Corr denotes another kind of situation in which reinforcement is not attainable. This kind of situation is not covered by the BPM Contingency Matrix since all of its CCs are concerned with behavior that is *reinforced*. The effect of a situation in which *no* reinforcement is attainable is to suppress behavior and to result in the emotional consequences of frustration, anger, and depression.

We might consider the thwarted behavior that this entails to be a separate category (to be added to the BPM Contingency Matrix) *or* we might argue that all of the behaviors denoted by the BPM Contingency Matrix can at times lead to these outcomes when reinforcement is simply not forthcoming. Reinforcement can be interrupted or removed in any circumstances, and emotional rewards may pall. This kind of situation, which is much more negative than CC8, is possibly a context for addictive behavior – when *liking* is no more but *craving* is continual.

Second, we turn to the FFFS and its association with negative reinforcement and behavioral suppression. FFFS is concerned with aversive stimulation. Aversive stimulation is either avoidable, in which case actions to avert it are negatively reinforced, or unavoidable, in which case the behaviors that result in it are punished. Four of the CCs involve behavior that is under the control of the FFFS. Two are under the control of the BIS. In each case, one of the kinds of behavior is avoidable, the other unavoidable.

In the case of CC4, *inescapable entertainment*, this is an instance of negative reinforcement; the enforced reception of entertaining stimuli is a respite from the boredom of a long flight or an unanswered telephone call, and is a kind of imposed displacement activity, not necessarily highly valued in itself and possibly a sign of resignation. Of course, there are air travellers who just love the inflight movies and for these passengers this entertainment represents genuine entertainment and pleasure. But CC4 activities may more generally take the form of assuagements for something else that must be endured if it is consumed at all. But it is important to bear in mind that the BPM Contingency Matrix is a *functional* taxonomy of consumer behaviors – if a passenger loves the inflight movie her behavior does not belong to CC4 but to CC3.

Although panic is probably too strong a descriptor of the emotional state involved here, boredom, frustration, discomposure, and distress may not be. The unavoidable circumstances in which the entertainment is delivered may make its experience a matter of emotional punishment. The behavior may not reduce (one may have little option but to listen and watch) but the person suffers. (If a consumer hangs up the phone because she can bear the imposed music no longer, that is behavioral punishment too.) "Freezing" is also an exaggeration in general in these circumstances but enforced resignation of this kind may be a kind of freezing, perhaps.

CC7 behaviors are maintained by negative reinforcement even though they occur in relatively open settings; typically, those involving routine shopping. Behaviors occurring in this category of consumer-situations are maintained by low levels of both utilitarian and informational reinforcement, and result in low levels of pleasure and arousal, but the consumer does feel reasonably in control of the situation. Fear is undoubtedly not the correct feeling tone: the approach behavior of doing routine shopping is *in itself* maintained by positive reinforcement: the consumer might escape/avoid having to do this kind of shopping if that were possible but since it is not possible to go without these products the routine behavior is escape from/avoidance of these life-threatening consequences. On any given occasion the task is avoidable but at some stage it has to be undertaken. The typical consumer may, however, be fighting rather than embracing the experience. Again, we must remind ourselves of the functional nature of the classification suggested by the BPM Contingency Matrix. It would be a misallocation to place every routine food consumer in CC7 and explain her behavior in this way. Some consumers may obtain higher levels of utilitarian and informational reinforcement and feel freer than this analysis suggests. On the basis of individual differences in learning history, temperament, personality, and so on we might place their routine food shopping behavior in CC1 for instance.[10]

Finally, we come to the BIS and its association with approach to aversive stimuli, and punishment. Some behavior that is negatively reinforced or punished may be under the control of the FFFS and/or the BIS. CC6 contains consumer-situations where behavior is to a degree negatively reinforced even though it continues to receive positive reinforcement too. This is because the proceeds accrued thus far under the collecting schemes entailed here would be lost or depleted if the process of collecting were not continued. Half a partwork encyclopedia is of restricted value, less than half that of the entire work. Continuing to collect in the face of mounting costs is negatively reinforced. There is a predictable degree of anxiety connected with the prospect of ceasing to collect; perhaps it also implies a negative judgment on the value of having collected thus far. Risk assessment is therefore predictable as a process of conflict resolution, caution, leading to a suspension of the behavior of ceasing to collect. Anxiety is thus avoided. If continuing in the scheme becomes too expensive, the collecting behavior may be terminated: it has been punished (and it is the BIS that is the relevant system).

In CC8, however, there is no prospect of avoiding punishment (as emotionally experienced, not in the sense of a reduction or cessation of behavior) if the positively reinforcing outcomes of attaining a good are to be realized. Taxes must be paid on consumer durables or, in countries like the UK that legally impose a licensing system, to operate a television set; forms must be completed to obtain a passport. These unavoidable procedures may lead to frustration, anger, even depression, and behavioral suppression (e.g., buying a laptop that is less than ideal for one's purposes just because it is cheaper). This is a form of punishment because the act of purchasing the more expensive computer that provides the more desired outcomes is stymied. It is also likely to result in emotional punishment, frustration, and possibly anger.

Filling out an application form for a passport may be tedious in itself but it is nevertheless the unavoidable route to pleasurable foreign travel and vacations. There is some anticipated pleasure involved, therefore, in the painstakingly dull requirements of accurately providing personal information, photographs, signatures, and so on. And there is probably a resolution of the conflict by undertaking these tasks stoically while thinking of the benefits of conforming. Some of the respondents in the empirical research reported high levels of pleasure in relation to this activity. Indeed, qualitative research with some of them revealed that they were anticipating the travel, vacations, or other pleasurable experiences for which obtaining a passport was more of a detail than a chore: for them, these behaviors, though required by third-party fiat, were not cognitively classified as onerous so much as a gateway to enjoyment. They are probably closer to behaviors usually assigned to CC2 or even CC1 rather than CC7.

There is one other possibility that Corr mentions and which he lists under appetitive stimuli that are unattainable. This would represent the limiting case of consumer behavior and it does not appear in the BPM Contingency Matrix as a category in itself since this schema defines consumer-situations and their typical behaviors predominantly in terms of reinforcement rather than punishment. There are two ways of regarding it. First, it may refer to a form of consumer behavior that is not reinforced at all, ever, under any circumstances. This would be exemplified by the self-administration of a drug which no longer has any pleasurable consequences for the addict who nevertheless craves it. Pleasure is, importantly, not even available from the negatively reinforcing alleviation of withdrawal symptoms since even consumption of the substance or process that is the source of the addiction leads only to further craving and relentless search for new opportunities. It answers to Berridge and Robinson's (2003) idea of *wanting* in the absence of *liking*. (See Berridge, 2007; Berridge & Kringelbach, 2015; Berridge & Robinson, 1993, 1995, 1998, 2012. For discussion of the process of addiction and its behavioral and neurophysiological correlates, see Koob, 2013; Koob & Le Moal, 2001, 2006; Koob, Arends & Le Moal, 2014. For discussion in the context of consumer choice, see Foxall, 2016a.) The emotional outcome is not simply frustration and anger but also shame (loss of self-esteem); the behavior in question comprises severe displacement activity as the search for the drug or behavioral opportunities becomes so relentless that it takes over the addict's life. Second, at a far less severe level, behavior of this kind may at some stage be a concomitant of all the consumer behaviors depicted in the various contexts of cognitive consumer-situation to CC8. All consumer behavior is punished as well as reinforced (Alhadeff, 1985), at some point and for a limited time. The situated consumer behaviors proposed by the BPM Contingency Matrix are *types* of consumption: but not every isolated act of consumption is highly reinforced even in the case of CC1 activities. The law of diminishing returns or Herrnstein's melioration process means that high levels of pleasure and arousal can decline as consumption continues (Herrnstein & Vaughan, 1980).

Perceptual contingency-representation and the nature of action

Success semantics

Prediction plays a vital role in the substantiation of an intentional interpretation and the formulation of its suitability as the basis of cognitive interpretation. The desires and beliefs that we ascribe to an intentional system to predict its behavior must, Dennett (1987) argues, be those that the system "ought" to have, given its history and current position. The same goes for perceptual contingency-representations, including emotion experiences. Dennett proposes that the prediction of action is the key criterion by which to judge his intentional systems theory account, which corresponds to the intentional interpretation in Intentional Behaviorism.

But prediction in these circumstances is likely to be somewhat vague and gross (Foxall, 2016b). We can have a general idea of the learning history of the system (from the application of the contextual stance), its internal disposition (from the design stance), and the components of its current behavior setting especially insofar as they are likely to motivate its activities. As such, it is likely that we can make only very broad predictions of what the system will do, predictions moreover that would be difficult to falsify. It is easy to make gross assumptions about what a system's behavior is leading it toward but these are commonsense attributions that scarcely deserve the attention of psychological science. Useful as these predictions are as orientating frameworks for the explanation of the system's behavior, they must be supplemented by a more rigorous methodology for intentional ascription. Success semantics suggests a useful approach.

Originally advanced by Ramsey ([1927] 1990) and critically evaluated by, among others, Bermúdez (2003), Dokic & Engel (2001, 2004), Dretske (1988), and Nanay (2013a, 2013b), success semantics proposes that a belief's content is determined by the success conditions of actions to which the belief leads. As Bermúdez (2003, pp. 54–55) summarizes it, Ramsey's claim entails "first, that we need to approach the truth conditions of beliefs through their utility conditions and, second, that these utility conditions should be understood in terms of the satisfaction of desires."

The satisfaction conditions of a desire have been met when the action to which the desire led is terminated, presumably because it has been reinforced to the point of satiety. Success semantics, therefore, stresses that the ascription of desires and beliefs must be constrained by understanding what conditions would satisfy the desires and what utility the beliefs would have in the satisfaction of the desires through the promotion of particular actions. This is necessary to the formulation of more specific and, above all, testable predictions.[11] Success semantics is, therefore, consonant with standard scientific method in that it permits the examination of such predictions in light of the outcomes of actions that are publicly observable. It is in this context that this section examines some of the ramifications of success semantics, notably in connection with Nanay's arguments that it applies to perceptions rather than beliefs and that perceptions ought to replace the desires x beliefs model in the philosophy of action and, presumably therefore, theoretical psychology.

The success semantics framework enables us to clarify the nature of contingency-representation by further comparing it with that of pragmatic representation. For, Nanay (2013b) suggests that success semantics applies not to beliefs but to some simpler, perceptual mental states that are the immediate precursors of action. Recall that, as representations which mediate sensory input and motor output, pragmatic representations make it possible to carry out actions such as picking up a pen from the table. More accurately, they are "the representational components of the immediate mental antecedents of action" (p. 3). As perceptions, they have representational content, that is, their content is a portrait of the world in which we act. Lacking linguistic syntax, they are not propositions; in fact, they are expressed neither in the form of propositional attitudes nor a language of thought. But they can be right or wrong, and their degree of accuracy inheres in their capacity to guide actions well or badly. In the case of my picking up a pen from the table in front of me, my pragmatic representations embody such properties as the spatial position of the pen, its size, weight, and so on: all factors that make it more or less probable that my actions of reaching out and grasping will succeed in relocating the pen appropriately. In Nanay's terminology, these properties are action-properties, in the successful attribution of which inheres an important function of pragmatic representations (p. 4).

This section examines some implications of Nanay's proposal that pragmatic representations' being perceptions renders their content amenable to determination by means of success semantics. It proposes that in similar fashion success semantics applies also to contingency-representations. Specifically, since perceptions are not empirically available for scientific analysis, their content can be revealed only in the form of beliefs, desires, and other propositional attitudes derived from them, that the knowledge by acquaintance in which perceptual experience inheres is publicly knowable only by their expression as knowledge by description. There is, therefore, a need to distinguish the "stated" content of pragmatic representations, which depends on the consideration of logical inference, from their "manifest" content, which flows from the success conditions of actions derived from such beliefs and, by extension, from their underlying perceptual experience. The beliefs and perceptions whose content is being tested must be stated prior to the performance of the actions based upon them. This is the stated content. The success conditions of the actions determines the manifest content of beliefs and perceptions which correctly prefigure the actions. If the stated content is identical to the manifest content, then the beliefs and perceptions bearing this content are true.

The "A priori statement of mental antecedents" section briefly describes Ramsey's success semantics and "The generation of testable beliefs and perceptions" section (both later in this chapter) describes Nanay's argument that the content of pragmatic representations can be determined in accordance with them. However, acceptance of Nanay's reasoning that pragmatic representations but not beliefs are susceptible to analysis in terms of success semantics still leaves open the implications of this argument for the nature of pragmatic representation. Therefore, I argue that perceptual pragmatic representations are logical inferences that are not empirically available for scientific analysis, that this necessitates a distinction between stated and manifest content, and that determining the manifest content of pragmatic representations is dependent upon their translation into beliefs that provide their stated content.

Ramsey's claim

To say that a mental event has content is to acknowledge that it is about something and to explain the content of a mental event is to explicate the relationship between the mental event and whatever it is about. But how do we know the content of a mental event? We have noted in passing Ramsey's argument that the content of a belief is a function of the success conditions of an action performed in accordance with it (see also Nanay, 2013b, p. 151; Sahlin, 1990, Chapter 2). Formally, Ramsey proposes that the content of a belief is fixed by the success conditions of actions based on the belief; hence,

> any set of actions for whose utility p is a necessary and sufficient condition might be called a belief that p, and so would be true if p, i.e. if they are useful.
>
> *(Ramsey, [1927] 1990, p. 40)*

For example, "that it is raining [p]" is the content of a belief that is true if it is useful; say, if, holding this belief, I open my umbrella and hold it above my head. The success conditions of this belief are determined by the usefulness of the action it gives rise to.[12] This supposes that I also have an appropriate desire, such as to keep dry. As Whyte (1990, p. 150; see also Whyte 1993, p. 84) puts it,

> A belief's truth-condition is that which guarantees the fulfilment of any desire by the action which, combined with that desire, it would cause.

Nanay picks up on two objections to Ramsey's claim raised by Whyte. First, that an action's outcome relies on *several* of one's beliefs; we cannot isolate one belief the truth of which could be fixed by a particular action coupled with a particular desire.

The success of such an action would depend on several beliefs. So, in my example, keeping dry depends on the belief that it is raining, plus the belief that using this umbrella will keep me dry, plus the belief that falling rain is prevented from reaching my head by the intervention of the fabric of the umbrella, plus the belief that water is wet … and so forth. Whyte's second objection is that the truth of all our *relevant* beliefs cannot guarantee the successful performance of an action because there may be all manner of *unforeseen circumstances* that intervene to prevent it. This can be removed by arguing that we also have the belief that there are no impediments to the completion of the action. Whyte calls these no-impediment beliefs.

But we may still be motivated to perform an action even if we do not have absolute no-impediment beliefs: we may simply hold that it is *probable* that we shall succeed. Our mental state does not guarantee success; it merely says that success is likely. This, Nanay suggests, is a better way of understanding no-impediment beliefs but he claims that, in the process, it renders Ramsey's idea of success semantics vacuous. He notes, however, that Ramsey does not claim that the content of *all* beliefs could be determined in terms of the successful outcome of some actions based on them. It is from this that Nanay's reinterpretation of Ramsey's proposals derives. He notes that they apply only to very simple beliefs, and certainly not to "those beliefs which are expressed in words … or other symbols, consciously asserted" (Ramsey 1990, p. 40). Nanay (2013b, p. 156) interprets this to mean "that the content of some simple mental states could be explained in this manner: the content of *some of* an agent's mental states is fixed by the success conditions of her actions. On this basis, he proposes that principles that are similar to but not the same as Ramsey's ideas can apply to relatively simple mental events such as the pragmatic representations with which he is concerned. Hence, Nanay's refinement of Ramsey's conception: the kinds of mental antecedents whose truth conditions are provided by the success of the actions to which they lead comprise non-propositional knowledge by acquaintance which would include perceptions such as pragmatic representations.

Pragmatic representation and success semantics

Nanay's (2013a) conceptualization of pragmatic representations is closely bound up with his understanding of the nature of actions themselves. He first espouses the commonplace that what differentiates actions from other bodily movements is that actions are triggered by mental events.[13] He goes on to point out that, whatever these antecedent mental states may be, they must represent the properties of the perceptual object that are necessary for the action. That is, they are representational. All actions, intentional or nonintentional, are therefore preceded by pragmatic representations. Before we can designate actions as intentional or autonomous, we need to be able to define what it is that makes them actions, something that can be done only in terms of their immediate mental precursors, pragmatic representations. So,

> Pragmatic representations are genuine mental representations: they represent objects as having a number of properties that are relevant for performing the

action. As a result, pragmatic representations can be correct or incorrect. If they are correct, they are more likely to guide our actions well; if they are incorrect, they are more likely to guide our actions badly.

(Nanay, 2013b, pp. 157–158)

Crucially, they are not beliefs, for, if they were, they would be sensitive to other beliefs – but they are not. They are (based on) knowledge by acquaintance rather than knowledge by description.

Nanay's understanding of success semantics deviates in two ways from Whyte's. First, Nanay (2013b) maintains that success semantics is relevant to no more than a subset of mental events, namely, pragmatic representations. Second, the accuracy of these mental states gives no assurance of the success of any action. A first approximation of his position is that the accuracy of a pragmatic representation increases the probability of the successful performance of the action of which this pragmatic representation is the immediate precursor. The content of the perceptual pragmatic representation is therefore expressed probabilistically rather than deterministically. Hence, even an accurate pragmatic representation does not ensure a successful outcome; rather, if the pragmatic representation is correct, then the *probability* of, say, my correctly picking up and holding the pen and writing with it (if these are my desires) will increase. The accuracy of my pragmatic representation increases the likelihood of my succeeding in the action which it immediately antecedes.

The import of this reasoning is that success semantics apply only to some mental events, namely, pragmatic representations. The more correct a pragmatic representation is, the greater the likelihood that an action of which this pragmatic representation is the immediate precursor will be successful. The correctness of the pragmatic representation increases the probability that the action of which it is the immediate antecedent will succeed.

But Nanay further points out that this resolution can be viewed in either a weak sense of probability raising and a strong sense of probability raising. In the weak sense in which such probability raising can occur, *any* mental event can increase the probability of success, as long as there are no additional mental entities that can impede the successful performance of actions that would be consistent with the pragmatic representation.[14] In this case, which is that of the original success semantics, we can conclude that even a *belief* is such a mental event as long as we assume that there is nothing else of a contradictory nature going on in the mind, nothing that would override the belief and thwart the action. But we cannot make such an assumption and a success semantics based on this weak portrayal would be very limited if not useless.

In the strong view, a mental state raises the probability of success of whatever action is based directly upon it irrespective of what else is happening in the actor's mind. By this, I understand Nanay to mean that whatever else might be going on in the actor's mind must be of such a nature that it cannot interfere with the mental event that is the focus of our analysis, that whose accuracy enters into the determination of the success of an action to which it directly leads. Nanay adopts this strong view, arguing that it is the case for pragmatic representations: "The correctness of a pragmatic representation, R, is C if and only if C raises the probability (strong sense) of the success of the action R is the immediate antecedent of" (2013b, pp. 160–161.) But, since there are *several* actions the success of which is raised, in this strong sense, by a pragmatic representation, Nanay further refines his proposal by arguing that C is the correctness condition of the pragmatic representation, R, if and only if C increases the probability (in the strong sense) of the success of the action of which R is the immediate precursor *and* this action is not the proper part of any other action the probability of whose success is raised by R.

We may ask, for example: If the immediate mental precursor of the action of picking up the pen in front of me is R, what is the content of R? The correctness of R is the factor that increases the probability that the action of picking up the pen will be successful. It does so, however, only in the weak sense, since, if I have the wrong notion of how to pick up a pen, my action will not succeed. R's accuracy increases the probability of my picking up the pen in the strong sense, but it increases that of my holding it or of writing with it only in the weak sense. This is because there is a single action, the probability of the successful completion of which R is likely to increase. If I have the wrong notion of how to hold the pen or to write with it, the probability of my successful execution of these actions is unaffected by the accuracy of R.

Nanay is transparent with respect to the limited sphere of applicability of his exposition. Having pointed out that there can be no suggestion that the success of the action is guaranteed, he reminds us that, in any case, his claim is pertinent to a single sort of mental event, namely, pragmatic representations. But he argues that by imposing these limitations on the original success semantics he can overcome Whyte's objections. First, by basing his claim singularly on the success condition, C, of the mental event that immediately precedes the action, that is, the appropriate pragmatic representation, R, he avoids the charge that any other mental events that may be in the actor's mind could interfere with the efficacy of this representation. Second, he avoids the charge that the success of an action might be subject to unforeseen circumstances; since a pragmatic representation does not assure the success of the action but simply increases its probability of occurrence, there is no suggestion that Whyte's no-impediment beliefs, with all their implications, are necessary. Unforeseen circumstances are not a problem.[15]

The empirical availability of pragmatic representations

Although Nanay's reasoning redresses several objections to the idea of success semantics, especially in the understanding that this claim of Ramsey applies to perceptions rather than beliefs, it raises a problem of its own in relation to the availability of perceptions such as pragmatic representations for the public empirical investigation that is the hallmark of scientific methodology. This problem has three elements: the distinction between perceptions and beliefs, the empirical reliance on third-personal knowledge of one's own and others' perceptions as a basis for success semantics, and the necessity of formulating both stated and manifest content of mental precursors of action.

Distinguishing perceptions from beliefs

While accepting Nanay's argument that success semantics applies to perceptual pragmatic representations, I would maintain that beliefs (and other propositional attitudes such as desires) still play an important role in the process of ascertaining the content of pragmatic representations by reference to the success of the actions based upon them. I shall illustrate principally in connection with beliefs, however, since these are the propositional attitudes with which Nanay contrasts pragmatic representations and which he seeks to displace as the foci of success semantics.

While perceptions entail knowledge by acquaintance, beliefs take the form of knowledge by description (Russell, 1912.) Knowledge by acquaintance emerges through direct experience, as in my sensing the warm water on my face even before I realize that there is a summer shower; knowledge by description, however, relies on propositional statements such as my announcement that it is raining. In the first case, my knowledge is non-propositional: I just know how things are; in the latter, it is propositional: all within hearing, including myself, now know that *p*.

For all that knowledge by acquaintance is non-propositional, it is genuine knowledge: it is through knowing by acquaintance that we understand at all what consciousness is. Knowledge by acquaintance is prerequisite to knowledge by description and propositional knowledge would be impossible without it. It is knowledge by acquaintance which, by providing implicit understanding of the phenomena of consciousness, legitimizes our using mental language to make our own and others' behavior intelligible, to the extent that the limitations of our introspection permit. Knowledge by acquaintance is, therefore, prior to knowledge by description. Even if I am a research biologist, my knowledge of photosynthesis is by description; but, whoever I am, my knowledge of my elation is by acquaintance. As McGinn (2004, p. 8) puts it, "No propositional knowledge would be possible unless we know some things in a non-propositional way." (See also Foxall, 2016b.)

I propose, therefore, that Russell's distinction is sufficient to distinguish non-propositional perceptions like pragmatic representations from propositional knowledge as exemplified by beliefs, and that knowledge by acquaintance is logically prior to knowledge by description.

Empirical availability

Perceptual experience is an abstract entity which, even if it be real and conscious to the person whose experience it is, has no third-personal availability. This is an acknowledgment of the status of perceptual experience as *autophenomenal* rather than *heterophenomenological*. Heterophenomenology is a procedure for obtaining a third-personal account of the first-personal (hence, subjective and private) thoughts and feelings which are an individual's personal responses to environmental cues (Dennett, 1991). This attempt to translate subjective experience into a public form that can be employed in scientific analysis comprises the following sequence: (a) conscious experiences, (b) beliefs about these conscious experiences, (c) verbal expressions of these beliefs, and (d) the spoken and/or written utterances that make the subject's knowledge by description of her experience publicly available. Conscious experience exists only as knowledge by acquaintance, the "raw data" of the individual's phenomenological responses and the point of heterophenom-enology is to generate from this data that can be employed by trained interpreters in the quest for an account by which hypotheses about the individual's actions can be tested and explanation thereof proffered. While (a) consists of knowl-edge by acquaintance, (b) is the individual's knowledge by description thereof, which then becomes verbalized (c), and is finally transformed into the knowledge by description of the investigator (d), which forms the primary (third-personal, public, amenable to scientific inquiry) data required for heterophenomenological analysis.

The import of this is that perceptual experience itself remains an empirically unavailable (except to the person whose experience it is) entity that cannot enter directly into scientific analysis. It is an abstraction derived from a statement of belief. As such, it belongs, heterophenomenologically, to (a) conscious or unconscious experience, which is knowable, if at all, through the expression of (b) beliefs about this experience and (c) verbal expression thereof. Although pragmatic representa-tion is therefore a logical necessity for understanding and defining action, exactly as contingency-representation is, neither is an empirically discernable entity for scientific analysis.

This is a matter of revealing the nature of perceptual experiences such as contingency-representations, even when they are conscious, which they are not necessarily: they are not empirically available for scientific analysis. They cannot be made available publicly in the third-personal manner which science requires. They consist in knowledge by acquaintance and their communication to ourselves and others requires their translation into knowledge by description. Knowledge by acquaintance is, moreover, prerequisite to knowledge by description: perception is necessarily prior to belief (McGinn, 2004).

Stated and manifest content

Making empirical sense of pragmatic representation requires us to make a distinc-tion between two kinds of content, which we may call stated *and* manifest. The *stated* content of the perception is expressed by the belief that derives from the per-ception, while its *manifest* content is that which is revealed by the success conditions of the actions derived from the belief and hence the perception. Where perception is unconscious and not therefore capable of giving rise to articulated beliefs, it may be inferred logically from the nature of the action in which it is theoretically implicated.

We must distinguish between the *stated* content of perceptions (be they pragmatic representations or contingency-representations or whatever), i.e., what they refer to when they are verbalized, and their *manifest* content, which is that which is established by the success conditions of the actions to which they give rise. So my perception may be that it is raining and this may be expressed verbally as the belief that it is raining. So I take an umbrella when I go for my morning walk and as a result I do not get wet.

Admittedly, if we are to use success semantics to evaluate pragmatic representations or, more to our intentions, contingency-representations, we must conceptualize them as perceptions rather than beliefs. But we can only know their stated content by their conceptual expression as beliefs. When we use the stated content in order to determine its manifest content by the applications of Ramsey's success semantics, we are determining the manifest content of the perception rather than the belief.

Contingency-representation revisited

The indispensability of belief

Making empirical sense of pragmatic representation requires also an acknowledgment that the stated content of perceptual representations can be ascertained either by deriving beliefs from them (when the perceptions are conscious and can be publicly articulated) or from a logical analysis of the kinds of perception that would be necessary for the performance of particular tasks. As Nanay points out, correctly I believe, the method of success semantics applies to perceptions rather than beliefs; we are dependent upon either the heterophenomenological method and/or a logical deduction from the nature of actions in order to determine the nature of the perceptions we assume in order to complete our scientific analysis.

This reasoning does not necessarily contradict Nanay's conclusion about the susceptibility of perceptions, but not beliefs, to analysis in terms of the success of the actions to which they give rise. But the avoidance of conflict requires that we accept that perception is a logical precursor of action and acknowledge that we need to establish the stated content of pragmatic representations through analysis of beliefs presumed to derive from them and/or a logical regression from the nature of actions to their perceptual requirements. It does, however, clarify the nature of pragmatic representations, contingency-representations, and other conceptions of perceptual experience. They are inferences, concepts employed to aid explanation but not able in their own right to enter into a scientific analysis. They are inferred on the basis of individuals' verbal (or other behavioral) responses to environmental stimuli and/or a logical analysis of the perceptual operations that would be necessary for the discharge of a particular action.

Nanay's claims for pragmatic representations apply, therefore, equally to contingency-representations. Contingency-representations are conceived as (i) being part of the immediate mental antecedents of action; they are perceptual, based on knowledge by acquaintance; and they are probabilistic rather than absolute in their effect on action. Hence, they also overcome Whyte's objections: (i) indicates that there is no interference from knowledge by description; (ii) implies they are the kind of mental event that Ramsey and Nanay claim are covered by success semantics (i.e., they are not beliefs); and (iii) means that they are not determinative but increase the probability that an action based on R will be successful.

Reported emotional experiences to patterns of contingency are particularly amenable to treatment in this regard. We can consider consumers' responses to Mehrabian and Russell's (1974) inventories of pleasure, arousal, and dominance to result in perceptions of past or present contingencies of reinforcement and punishment. If the immediate mental precursor of the action of purchasing Brand A is R, then the content of R, of whatever factor, increases the probability that the action of making this purchase will be successful in terms of generating the physical and social utilitarian and informational reinforcement that I seek to maximize and thereby the sum total of pleasure, arousal, and dominance that is the ultimate reward thereof.

A priori statement of mental antecedents

If Ramsey's success semantics claim is to guide the explanation of action through the ascription of appropriate beliefs or perceptions, it must be possible to identify a priori the beliefs or perceptions that will be examined for the truth of their contents by comparison with the ensuing success conditions of the actions to which they lead. The necessary sequence is (i) statements of relevant beliefs and perceptions, and identification of their stated content, (ii) identification of the resultant actions, and the derivation from them of the perceptions and beliefs that would be true guides to the actions, and (iii) evaluation of the correspondence between the stated content of the initiating belief and perception and the manifest content of beliefs and perceptions that would be consonant with the success conditions of the action. Although our assumption is that beliefs follow from perceptions (as knowledge by description follows from knowledge by acquaintance), in logically arriving at the pragmatic representations that must *precede* action by representing the action-properties of, say, the pen that is to be lifted, we must reverse this sequence. The only mental antecedents of action we can know for this purpose – which are empirically available for scientific analysis – are beliefs from which we infer pragmatic representations based on the action-properties of the item to be lifted. We can ascertain them only by *asking* the individual what she believes. But how do these beliefs become available?

The generation of testable beliefs and perceptions

Suppose I say to a friend as I look out of the window, "I think that it is raining outside." My belief is empirically available to my friend on account of its taking the form of a public utterance. We can only ascertain the truth value of my belief "that it is raining outside" if we have some way of, subsequently, determining whether actions based on this proposition are successful. So my action of using my umbrella can be adjudged successful in the context of my desire to keep dry if I do in fact remain dry. This successful outcome satisfies my desire based on the content of the belief to the effect that rain is presently falling. From my original statement to my friend we can logically derive the existence of not only the belief that it is raining but also a perception which has identical content: before I can state my belief, I must perceive that it is raining outside, since knowledge by acquaintance is assumed to precede knowledge by description. On this logic, that there must be a perception is unassailable. But my perception is not empirically available since it is private to my personal experience: if I make a verbal statement to the effect that I perceive that it is raining, my utterance takes the form of a proposition rather than a percept and is thereby to be classified as a belief rather than a perception.

It follows from Ramsey's success semantics claim that the belief must be available prior to the action. But where do beliefs come from? If they are observations about what the individual would need to know in order to, say, lift a pen, then their content is inferred from the very actions the success of which provide that content. But this smacks of circularity. The beliefs from which we (i) derive perceptions and (ii) test by reference to subsequent actions must come from the individual's independent action in the form of verbal statements about what would be required to lift the pen. The same is the case for perceptions such as pragmatic representations. Where do they come from? Whence the individual's perceptions of the size, weight, and distance of the pen?

In the case of pragmatic representations, if they are to enter into the scientific arena, it is possible to ascertain the relevant perceptions only if they consciously enter into belief statements; this requires that the perceptions themselves be available to consciousness and translatable into empirically available public statements of belief. Can this be done? Such statements can consist only in verbalizations like "I believe I can reach/grasp/pick up this pen given its action-properties." From this we can deduce the perception of the corresponding action-properties and personal capabilities. But if an individual attempts to lift a pen can we not take for granted her belief that she is capable thereof and deduce pragmatic representations of the appropriate action-properties. But this does not seem satisfactory: it is an a posteriori judgment of the content of her mentality, based only on examination of the action to which it led. In the absence of verbally expressed conscious awareness on the part of the lifter of her perceptions and beliefs, we have no means of checking out what is the content of the mental precursors of action.

In the case of contingency-representations, we have access to the individual's ratings of the consumer-situation in terms of PAD and behavioral preference from which to form a perception with stated content. In fact, as they stand, in the form of psychometric ratings, they embody a *belief* which we assume has identical content with the underlying perception necessary to the formation of this belief (insofar as knowledge by description is predicated upon knowledge by acquaintance). We can accept the psychometric data provided by the PAD scales as a priori beliefs that logically have a perceptual basis and check on the appropriateness of their content by nonverbal means of ascertaining the consumer's emotional response to actually encountered consumer-situations. In connection with the consumer's desires we can make the underlying assumption that she is seeking to maximize pleasure, arousal, and dominance on the basis of the reasoning put forward by Rolls, Damasio, and others and the empirical evidence which shows a correspondence between these basic emotions and the pattern of reinforcement and behavior setting scope identified by the BPM/PAD researches.

Notes

1 But probably not cognitive. Prinz argues that "cognitions are states containing representations that are under [direct] organismic control" (2003, p. 49) and that "we call a state cognitive just in case it includes representations that are under the control of structures in executive systems, which, in mammals, are found in the prefrontal cortex" (p. 47). It is clear from this that he does not consider emotions to be cognitive. For another view, see for example Moore and Oaksford (2002). As to emotions being phenomenal, Prinz (2002a, p. 137) points out that "emotions are characteristically conscious" – they usually entail feeling. The important point is not that emotions are always felt but that they are capable of being felt.

2 The journal *Dialectica* published a special issue on emotion and perception in 2015. See the introduction by Döring and Lutz, and papers by Brady; Deonna and Teroni; Döring; Dokic and Lemaire; Helm; Lacewing; Lutz; Schroeter, Schroeter and Jones.

3 For a contrary view, see Whiting (2012).

4 He claims "overwhelming evidence" for this view and cites McGurk and MacDonald (1976) in support.

5 The evolutionary context of emotion draws attention to its inhering in subjective feelings which regulate behavior in ways that enhance the survival and biological fitness of the organism. Moreover, evolutionary logic suggests that the behaviorally contingent reinforcement and punishment which influences learning history to guide further behavioral choices in similar contexts does so by generating appropriate felt emotions. It is difficult otherwise to comprehend why strong and insistent emotional responses evolved. However, while emotional feelings correlate with neurophysiological processes which exercise a causal influence, we must be careful to maintain separation of the phenomenological experience of emotion from its causation (what Searle (2000) calls "biological naturalism"; see also Barrett et al. (2007)). The sub-personal neurophysiological processing does not on this view equate with the experience of emotional feelings, though it is of course essential to it. The content of emotion viewed as its subjective experience is equally important. Although emotion, seen as knowledge by acquaintance, will not come about in the absence of either the appropriate neural firings or contextualized behavior, it is of itself neither of these. Emotion, the capacity for which has evolved in the course of natural selection, can surely not instance further behavior unless it is felt.

6 Broader aspects of the relationship between emotional experience and contingencies of reinforcement and punishment are discussed at greater length in Foxall (2016a, 2016b) in terms of Rolls's theory and Damasio's somatic marker hypothesis.

7 See also Foxall and Greenley (1998, 1999, 2000 and Foxall and Yani-de-Soriano (2005). For reviews and theoretical extensions, see Foxall (1997c, 2005, 2011), Foxall et al. (2012), and Yani-de-Soriano, Foxall and Newman (2013).

8 The consumer-situation scenarios employed in the first four studies (Foxall, 1997b) and, with modification, in subsequent research are as follows:

Study 1

CC	Consumer-situation	Description
1	Luxury shopping	You are wandering from department to department in a store such as Harrods, looking for an expensive treat for yourself which you feel you deserve and which you can well afford.
2	Gambling in casino	You are playing roulette in an exclusive casino. Many people around you are gambling and enjoying themselves.
3	Watching TV	You are watching a fast-moving entertainment program on TV: a sports program, a quiz show, a soap – whatever you often watch. You use your remote control to switch channels to see similar shows.
4	Inflight entertainment	You are on a transatlantic flight, travelling economy class. You are reading an interesting book. The flight attendants close the blinds, subdue the lighting, and announce that a movie is about to be shown.
5	Saving up	You are saving up to buy a major item. Each week you deposit cash in your savings account. You have just received notice of the amount of interest to be added to your account.
6	Frequent flier scheme	You have just bought a number of items which you chose specifically because they confer frequent-flier points. You make a note of how close you are to achieving your goal of a free flight.
7	Grocery shopping	You are doing your weekly grocery shopping in a large supermarket.
8	Paying taxes	You are comparing the ex-VAT price with what you must actually pay for a consumer durable such as a home computer.

Study 2

CC	Consumer-situation	Description
1	Ritz	You have just checked in at the Ritz where you will be staying for a break. You can well afford to do this.
2	DIY	You are undertaking a DIY project such as fitting bookshelves or converting an attic into an extra bedroom. DIY jobs like this are something you are good at and have done several times before.
3	Sports event	You are watching your favorite sporting event at the stadium/track/poolside.
4	Buskers	You are listening to buskers while queuing for the cinema.
5	Christmas club	You are checking how much you have paid into a Christmas club to which you belong.
6	Loyalty points	You are accumulating "loyalty points" by shopping at a given supermarket.
7	Newspaper	On your way to work, you call into the newsagent's to buy a newspaper, as you do every day.
8	Bank queue	You are queuing at the bank to pay in a check.

Study 3

CC	Consumer-situation	Description
1	Exotic holiday	You are taking a holiday – say, a Mediterranean cruise or a stay in Hawaii.
2	Training course	You are on a training course in connection with your job or to acquire a new skill (for work or pleasure). This involves attending classes and practical sessions.
3	Drink in pub	You are having a drink in the pub or a coffee in a cafe with friends.
4	Hanging on the phone	While holding on the phone, you are listening to background music.
5	Paying into bank account	You are depositing some money in your savings account (as you do every month). You check the interest that has built up.
6	Garage smart card	You are checking how many points you have accumulated on your garage smart card (points that are exchangeable for gifts).
7	Sandwich	You are buying or making a sandwich for lunch.
8	Waiting in air terminal	You are waiting in an air terminal for your flight to be called. You understand you will be there for some time.

Study 4

CC	Consumer-situation	Description
1	Porsche	You are showing off your new Porsche to your relatives and friends.
2	Hobby course	You are on an educational course in connection with your favorite hobby, attending lectures and practical classes (learning how to improve your skills and enjoyment).
3	Party	You are at a party. Your favorite music is playing. Around you, people are talking in a lively manner.
4	Cinema	At the cinema, you are sitting through the travelogues and advertisements while waiting for the main feature film you came to see.
5	Part-work magazine	You are having your first look through the latest issue of a part-work magazine that you buy every month (one that builds into an encyclopedia or manual on something you are interested in).
6	Insurance renewal	You are writing to your insurance company to renew your house/contents insurance for another year.
7	Petrol	At your local garage, you are filling your car up with petrol.
8	Passport forms	You are filling in the forms for a passport, which you need for a planned holiday abroad. You are making sure the form and the photos are countersigned, etc.

Source: Foxall (1997b).

The hypotheses presented in the text are all supported by the results which are aggregated over the eight studies in the following table:

Means and standard deviations for the independent and dependent variables by contingency category (CC) ($N = 7479$)

CC	Pleasure	Arousal	Dominance	Approach	Avoidance	Aminusa
1	47.39	41.49	39.86	14.48	4.82	9.49
	(5.73)	(12.48)	(7.52)	(5.29)	(4.39)	(7.39)
2	43.30	40.20	29.40	13.14	5.80	7.22
	(7.02)	(6.74)	(8.91)	(5.42)	(5.03)	(8.26)
3	44.04	31.69	36.34	11.93	5.98	5.96
	(7.67)	(8.14)	(7.38)	(3.64)	(4.82)	(7.39)
4	34.51	26.78	25.73	5.88	9.86	−3.88
	(10.72)	(7.30)	(7.39)	(3.73)	(5.57)	(8.01)
5	37.05	37.93	36.37	7.08	8.60	−1.50
	(98.67)	(6.69)	(7.23)	(3.79)	(5.33)	(7.54)
6	33.82	35.67	29.44	6.83	8.92	−2.18
	(8.38)	(8.08)	(6.95)	(3.78)	(5.42)	(8.70)
7	32.53	27.56	35.41	7.53	8.15	−.47
	(7.85)	(6.97)	(7.06)	(3.77)	(5.14)	(7.66)
8	25.31	27.14	24.77	6.04	10.16	−4.13
	(8.78)	(6.81)	(7.54)	(3.67)	(5.40)	(7.85)

Source: Foxall et al. (2012).

9 The paradigm shown in the following figure also summarizes the results of the eight studies. The hypothesized patterns of emotional response to each of the consumer-situations devised to illustrate the eight contingency categories of the BPM Contingency Matrix were evidenced by the empirical investigations (Foxall, 2011; Foxall et al., 2012). As explained in the Introduction, the Behavioral Perspective Model elaborates the three-term contingency in which a discriminative stimuli increases the probability (:) of a behavioral response that entails ($\rightarrow$) reinforcing (S^r) and punishing (S^p) consequences. In the BPM, the consumer-situation, comprising a consumer behavior setting (CBhS) that is composed of discriminative stimuli and motivating operations in interaction with the consumer's learning history (LH) is the immediate precursor of an operant class of consumer behavior defined by the pattern of reinforcement (and punishment) to which it leads. In this paradigm, which is concerned with the explanation of consumer action, the reinforcing and punishing stimuli which shape and maintain operant consumer behavior are understood to elicit, through classical conditioning, the pattern of emotion which is the ultimate reward of consumer action. Pattern of emotion then modifies the consumer's learning history, influencing the consumer-situation that prefigures subsequent action.

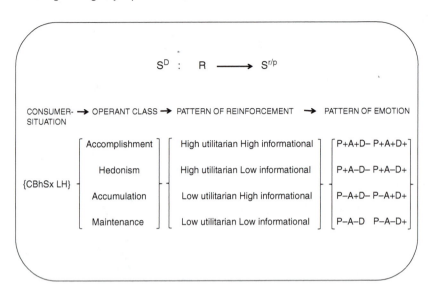

Emotional reward and pattern of contingency.

Key: CBhS = consumer behavior setting; LH = learning history; P = pleasure; A = arousal; D = dominance.

10 One of the reasons why Corr's use of "fear" and "panic" may not apply to the examples of consumer choice we have been considering is that the continuum of closed–open consumer behavior settings represents a restricted span of the entire closed–open continuum of settings available to humans. Therefore, we would not expect to find the most extreme emotions (especially those of extremely negative valence) that Corr includes in his Table 1.2 (2008, p. 26). Whatever the situation in which she is located, the consumer is always more in control of circumstances than would be the case for an individual whose situation is to be found toward the left extreme of the continuum shown in Figure 1.1.

11 Note that Bermúdez takes issue with Ramsey's conceptualization of success semantics, however, principally insofar as Ramsey does not allow that beliefs are functions from desires to actions. Having defined a belief as a set of actions, he would now be saying that actions are a function from desires to actions.

12 True beliefs, then, are "functions from desires to actions that will cause believers to behave in ways that will satisfy their desires" (Bermúdez, 2003, p. 65). The content of a belief consists in its "utility condition," i.e., the condition that would need to be brought about in order that the desires associated with it would be satisfied. "In brief, true beliefs cause actions that satisfy desires" (p. 68). If I believe "that p," then p is the utility condition of my belief.

13 In the idiom of Intentional Behaviorism, we might express this in terms of the bodily movements being actions if no stimulus field is available for their explanation, leading us to conclude that they are the result of mental events.

14 In this, he is following Blackburn (2005).

15 Nanay raises new objections of his own, however, suggesting for instance that it might be objected that pragmatic representations occur so infrequently that the range of applicability of success semantics is severely curtailed by his reformulation. However, pragmatic representations are very commonplace since actions are ubiquitous. Moreover, the analysis is not limited to humans; insofar as many animals perform actions, they must have pragmatic representations (cf. Steward, 2012).

5

THE INTENTIONAL CONSUMER-SITUATION

Abstract

The second stage of the Intentional Behaviorist research strategy, intentional interpretation, involves the construction of an intentional consumer-situation based on the desires, beliefs, emotions, and perceptions which an idealized, utility-maximizing consumer would evince. For the first time, this mentation is examined in psychoanalytical terms so that the akratic component of consumer choice can be explored in terms of a-rationality as well as rationality and irrationality. The possibility is explored that much consumer action occurs in response to neurotic beliefs rather than beliefs-proper and that it is therefore a pre-rational or a-rational means of responding to perceptions of environmental stimuli. The full gamut of contingency-representation is explored, including desires and beliefs as well as perceptions and emotions.

Psychological explanation I: Intentional interpretation

The intentional consumer-situation comprises (a) the contingency-representations that inform the consumer's action with respect to a set of contingencies of reinforcement that govern current and future choice, in light of (b) the consumer's likely perceptions of her consumption history, and (c) the beliefs which result from contemplation of that history and the probabilities of the reinforcing and punishing outcomes of further action. It takes the form of an account of the intentionality that would be appropriate to an idealized, utility-maximizing consumer whose learning history is inferred from the average for the consumer group to which she belongs who is faced with the current contingencies of reinforcement and punishment, and whose behavior is observed. Moreover, it (a) comprises an account in terms of the emotional perceptual experience that the consumer is likely to have; (b) is a reconstruction of her subjective recollection of her history of reinforcement and punishment, first, in general and, second, in terms of consumption experience both generally and in relation to the kinds of purchase and consumption activity under review; and (c) is an account of the belief structure the consumer is likely to have in order to undertake the observed actions and to support the emotional ascriptions made to her in (a).

Psychoanalytical tools for intentional interpretation

Primary and secondary mentation

In a closely argued series of studies, Brakel (2009, 2010, 2013) presents a philosophical critique of psychoanalysis. The emphasis is not exclusively on the therapeutic efficacy of psychoanalysis but on psychoanalytic concepts as a source of both theory of mind and explanation in psychology (Brakel, 2015a).[1] Of special relevance to the present discussion, she argues that several conditions must be met before rationality can be ascribed: reality testing, the achievement of consonance, the avoidance of contradiction, and the proper use of indexicals (Brakel, 2010). The first requires that a belief cannot be held by rational agents who are conscious of evidence that (seriously) contradicts the belief. It follows that a rational agent must be in a position to appraise the evidence for the beliefs she holds independently of her wishes and desires. In the face of evidence that demonstrates the falsity of a belief, then a rational agent can be expected to abandon it. This process of evaluation is known as "reality testing" and it requires recognition of the truth and falsity of propositions.

An important distinction, particularly significant in Sigmund Freud's (1900) analysis of dreams, is that between primary and secondary mentation.[2] Primary mentation is pre-rational or a-rational and relies on a perceived rather than a reasoned understanding of the world and how it works; it is typical of younger children and some animals. Secondary mentation is the rational and logical understanding of these matters which informs everyday living. In Freud's (1895) characterization, the primary process is marked by (a) unconscious operation, (b) appearing early in development, and (c) obeying procedures that are different from those of secondary process.[3] Primary process is associated with the id impulses, the single goal of which is pleasure: when it predominates (a) ideas are not synthesized, (b) affects may be displaced, (c) opposites do not exclude one another, and (d) condensation occurs (A. Freud, 1937, pp. 7, 59; see also Brakel & Shevrin, 2003, p. 527). The separation of the ego from the id in the course of development is a central component of its evolution from primary to secondary process (A. Freud, 1937, p. 59). These secondary processes rigorously govern the ways in which ideas are combined: ideas are now judged according to reality and, beyond that, by the ethical principles imposed by the superego. "They are exposed to criticism and rejection and have to submit to every kind of modification" (ibid, p. 7). The pleasure principle has given way to the reality principle: "With the introduction of the reality principle one species of thought-activity was split off; it was kept free from reality testing and remained subordinated to the pleasure principle alone. This activity is *phantasying*" (Freud, [1858] 1911, p. 222). Yet, the ego is not necessarily supreme, even in otherwise rational adults, as "[t]he instinctual impulses continue to ... make hostile incursions into the ego, in the hope of overthrowing it by a surprise attack." Freud (1895) also argued that primary mentation lacks some subtleties: it tends not to express negation, degrees of certainty, and is blind to past and future. Secondary mentation, by contrast, can represent tenses other than the present, and is a means of testing reality.

Commenting on Freud's distinction between primary and secondary mentation, Ainslie (1989, p. 12) comments, "the impulsiveness of the former stemmed from an overvaluation of immediate results. Over time, a more farsighted principle arose from the pleasure principle via learning." In support, he quotes Freud to the effect that: "The substitution of the reality for the pleasure principle implies no deposing of the pleasure principle, but only a safeguarding of it. A momentary pleasure, uncertain in its results, is given up, but only in order to gain along the new path an assured pleasure at a later time" (Freud, 1911, p. 223). And, Ainslie goes on to make an acute observation that promotes genuine interdisciplinary integration: at the heart of the pleasure and reality principles lie different ways of discounting future rewards. The id and the ego exert independent motivational influences on behavior via the pleasure and reality principles, respectively; their interaction is supplemented by that of the superego, a function of classical conditioning, which is capable of exercising an even greater inhibitory influence on the pleasure principle than the ego. Ainslie finds that less separates behaviorist and psychoanalytic conceptions of the motivational competition between pleasure and reality than their various exponents have assumed. But he argues that Freud's idea that potentially unpleasant stimuli can be removed from current mental consideration (through the displacement of affect) may be restated more simply in terms of the individual's steeply discounting more delayed rewards.

These considerations raise the possibility that the desires and beliefs that form important components of the contingency-representations that compose the intentional consumer-situation can be conceived in psychoanalytic terms. It is also necessary to examine whether these aspects of an intentional interpretation are consistent with the cognitive structures and processes that provide the cognitive interpretation aspect of the Intentional Behaviorism research strategy.[4]

Psychological rationality in psychoanalytical perspective

Of particular importance in the present context, primary process excludes the possibility of rationality-based reality testing. As Brakel (2009, p. 56) points out, "Primary process is not rational, does not operate with standard everyday logic, and is not guided by the reality principle.... It is a-rational and guided by the pleasure principle." She goes on to argue that primary process mentation does not permit the formulation of hypotheses and their testing against evidence, the correction of beliefs in light of the evidence, or the abandonment of beliefs that have been disconfirmed by evidence. It follows that primary process thinkers cannot attain the cognitive requirements for the proper holding of beliefs which she defines as the capacity to differentiate beliefs on the basis of their accordance with conditions in the world. This makes it difficult to ascertain the contents of primary process mentation. Hence the first reason for the epistemological opacity of primary process mentation is that thinkers dominated by this style experience difficulty in knowing anything at all.[5]

In connection with the achievement of consonance, rational agents strive to maintain consonance between beliefs and sometimes also between desires. This not only refers to how the world is organized (this flower I am looking at cannot be both entirely red and entirely blue) but also to what I want (my desire to go to the lecture this evening and my desire to stay home and watch TV this evening need to be accommodated in some way), and to what I am (my ectomorphic self-image cannot be reconciled with my obesity). In other words, rationality must adhere to the law of non-contradiction. My assertion that I am writing this on a MacBook Pro cannot be held simultaneously with an assertion that I am not using a MacBook Pro to write this. Rationality, that is, must recognize the law of the excluded middle.[6] With respect to the proper use of indexicals, rational agents can distinguish self from others, here from there, the present from the past and future – and do so properly (presumably in accord with social norms). So rationality also rests upon the foundation of oneself and one's assertions temporally, positionally, and interpersonally.

An important concomitant of these implications of primary process mentation arises from humans' capacity to dissemble, to translate the incomplete conclusions of primary process thinking into propositions that resemble those of secondary mentation. Because humans are natural cognizers, they tend to transform primary process mentation into the categories of secondary process thought. This again obscures the nature of primary process mentation as it is prone to become understood in terms of rational secondary thinking processes, which requires the reinterpretation of primary thought into the forms and organization of secondary processing (see Brakel, 2010, pp. 57, 59). Brakel points out, however, that primary process thinking, though a-rational, is representational or contentful (pp. 59–60).

If these are requirements of rationality, in what does irrationality inhere? It is more than the absence of these elements. It is, Brakel notes, (a) rational thought that has gone awry, that emphatically flouts these principles of commonplace logic; (b) rational logic that is marshaled in the pursuit of irrational and detrimental goals; (c) *a*-rational thinking employed in the pursuit of irrational goals; or (d) a mixture of these. Irrationality is shown, for instance, by an individual who knows full well that she is perfectly safe when trying to go to sleep in the dark but is nevertheless afraid of turning out the light when in bed. Such a belief flies in the face of reality testing: it is irrational; in fact, it is a neurotic belief. It also reflects what Brakel refers to as *a-rational mentation* (pp. 56–57). A-rationality is not rationality that has become askew in the ways just mentioned: it is a *lack of rationality*, which Brakel suggests may also be seen as the "not-yet rational" (p. 57). This designation reflects Freud's (1900) conceptualization of primary and secondary styles of mentation in which secondary mentation consists in the ordinary everyday rational logic we take for granted in the discourse of non-infant humans, while primary mentation is the predecessor of this found in infants and nonhuman animals. It is a sort of *pre-rational* state of understanding the world.

On the negative side, primary mentation *lacks any conception of tense*: it is unconstrained by considerations of past or future; its concern is with a "tenseless, unexamined present." Further, its procedures and conclusions are not subject to testing against reality. It follows that, within this perspective, mutually inconsistent ideas can be held simultaneously without any felt contradiction. These three components of primary mentation will loom large in the subsequent discussion of severely akratic choice. On the positive side, primary mentation involves condensation and displacement, which entail associative connections. Condensation entails the representation of a multiplicity of items by a single entity, while displacement is the converse of this: an entity is represented by an associated item which comes to replace it. Primary process mentation is essentially based on a-rationality and is evident in several contexts such as dreams, children's everyday thoughts, a-rational categorizations, e.g., those based on superficial similarity, classical conditioning,[7] and psychosis.

Beliefs-proper, fantasies, and neurotic beliefs

Beliefs are generally taken to be cognitive states in the form of propositional attitudes. Brakel, however, calls attention to two kinds of propositional attitude which vary according to their amenability to truth-testing, both of which may nevertheless influence action.[8]

Hence, *beliefs-proper* are cognitive attitudes that are "reality tested, truth-directed, and regulated by their truth conditions" (Brakel, 2009, p. 105). That is, they are retained or abandoned on the basis of evidence that the world conforms or fails to conform to the belief. My belief, formed on a Saturday afternoon, that the radio is tuned to *Jazz Line-Up* is grounded in the fact that I can hear Bill Evans playing and Tony Bennett singing *But Beautiful*. This is the program that is always available at this time and to which I usually listen. This belief is, therefore, a true belief-proper, given the accumulated evidence at my disposal. However, if it transpires that this track is one being played for comparative purposes on an entirely different program dedicated to classical music, then my belief becomes a false belief-proper. My hearing the presenter explicate the comparison as he moves on to a classical piece eliminates the false belief to the effect that the program is *Jazz Line-Up*.

By contrast, *neurotic beliefs* resemble fantasies more than beliefs-proper. Fantasies, like neurotic beliefs, are propositional attitudes that belong to primary process mentation; both the fantasy and the neurotic belief have content that is "not regulated by truth considerations, and not subject to reality-testing" (ibid, p. 106). But what is crucial to understanding the nature of neurotic beliefs and how they influence action is that neurotic beliefs *seem* like secondary processes, and are maintained by "counterfeit "evidence" that is based not on genuine reality testing but on psychic-reality-based grounds that are mistaken by the reality testing mechanism for the kind of legitimate actuality-based evidence that underpins beliefs-proper. Neurotic beliefs are therefore entertained as genuine beliefs, though they are impervious to real-world evidence. Any such evidence presenting itself is ignored by the neurotic who does not, therefore, need to abandon the neurotic beliefs nor see them as anything other than beliefs-proper. Whereas beliefs-proper are amenable to falsification in the face of genuine evidence that contradicts them, neurotic-beliefs are impervious to it; rather, they are substantiated within the psychic reality adopted by the individual in place of the real world by phony evidence based on unwarranted conjecture.

In summary, then, beliefs-proper are "reality tested and truth directed," while neurotic beliefs are "primary process in organization, prior to truth considerations, and not reality-tested." In these matters, neurotic beliefs resemble fantasies (Brakel, 2001, pp. 363–364), highly resistant to revision in light of the kinds of factual evidence that would in other contexts lead to cognitive dissonance followed by the correction of erroneous beliefs-proper. This process of correction is inhibited in the case of the person whose ideas rest on fantasizing in that the subjective experience of neurotic beliefs is identical to that of beliefs-proper: as a result, individuals can readily adduce apparent evidence to support their neurotic beliefs which tends to render them unyielding in the face of genuine reality testing (Brakel, 2001). Neurotic beliefs are therefore more than fantasies: in addition to a fantasy element, neurotic beliefs also contain fallacious knowledge masquerading as "evidence" that reinforces the fantasy. But the "evidence" is not the outcome of testing a proposition against the state of the objectively-available real world: it is based on the use of subjectively-experienced psychic-reality to support an erroneous proposition. The problem is that the gathering and accommodation of this "evidence" hijacks the very secondary mentation processes which genuine reality testing recruits and thereby acquires the veneer of intellectual probity. Hence, a fantasy is a primary process phenomenon that has not reached the stage of reality testing while a neurotic-belief has acquired a veneer of the genuine logicality which is based on secondary, information processing-based mentation.

I shall illustrate the ascribed belief system of the akrates by reference to the phenomenon of the so-called "near-miss" in slot machine gambling in which a combination of symbols that falls short of that designated for a win but which visually resembles the winning combination is taken as evidence of play that only narrowly fails to achieve a winning outcome. In fact, it is no more closely related to a win in terms of the probabilities of success than are three totally unrelated symbols but is interpreted nonetheless as a "near-miss." (The following is not a comprehensive exposition of this phenomenon; rather, it forms part of a continuing commentary: for further detail, see Foxall, 2016a; Foxall & Sigurdsson, 2012, 2016).

A slot machine player, A, who scores two identical symbols, three of which are required to win a large cash prize, may entertain the belief-proper that this is clearly not a winning outcome, on the reality-tested evidence that no payout has ever followed an outcome other than three matching symbols or, if she is a novice player, that the rules clearly state what is required to win. A can also have the belief-proper that two symbols is no closer to winning than any other non-winning combination of symbols since A understands the laws of probability sufficiently to draw this factual conclusion. Another player, B, may, however, entertain the erroneous belief-proper that scoring two identical symbols is "nearly a win" or, as the common phrase has it, a "near-miss." If B comes to understand the laws of probability, she will abandon this erroneous belief-proper in favor of one that is akin to that of A. However, B may fantasize that she is going to win a large amount of money on the slots and seek "evidence" for this by subjectively interpreting her performance as evidence of developing skill in playing. The notion of a near-miss that heralds an imminent jackpot through B's improvement in playing is a fantasy that is transformed into a neurotic belief by the acceptance of the two-identical-symbols outcome "evidence" supportive of the fantastic notion that winning games of pure chance depends on acquisition of prowess. The neurotic belief comprises B's fantasy and her succumbing to the "evidence" of making progress that derives entirely from the fanciful accommodation of perceived events to a conjectured inner psychic-reality that has no objective connection with the world. Fantasies, which are founded on primary process mentation, can contradict one another or even be internally self-contradictory. Neurotic beliefs, however, also entail a degree of secondary process mentation in the form of a consideration of false evidence that has the logical form of genuine reality testing against the way the world works but which flies in the face of adopting real-world evidence.

Fantasies are not reality-tested; they are a-temporal, taking place in a tenseless present; and they may embody contradictions. None of these is true of beliefs-proper, which are subject to revision in light of genuine evidence; are properly framed in time and space, taking account of prior occurrences and potential future consequences; and cannot be held alongside contrary beliefs. Reality testing entails important elements of secondary process mentation, such as (i) matching the actual state of the world (as the unassailable criterion of truth) with the condition of the world as represented in a propositional attitude, (ii) ascribing truth and non-truth conditions, and (iii) categorizing the nature of the propositional attitude one is holding. These cognitive capabilities are not required for fantasizing but are found at least to a degree in pretending and imagining, and are essential to supposing, hypothesizing, and entertaining beliefs-proper (Brakel, 2009).

Additional propositional attitudes for intentional interpretation

We are familiar by now with beliefs-proper and neurotic beliefs and their essential differences. Beliefs-proper are propositional attitudes that are based on reality testing (so that any factual disconfirmation of the proposition requires that it can no longer be held), temporal consonance (so that there must be continuity of understanding among past, present, and future), and non-contradiction (so that the proposition cannot be held alongside other propositions which are contrary to it; nor can a proposition contain two or more parts which are contradictory of one another). *Fantasizing*, we have seen, is not subject to reality testing, temporal consonance, or non-contradiction. And neurotic beliefs are propositional attitudes that begin with fantasizing and are sustained by false evidence that is taken at face value. But these are not the only propositional attitudes relevant to the construction of the intentional consumer-situation in a treatment which emphasizes the possibility of an akratic component to consumer choice. Others to which Brakel (2001) accords attention are *pretending, imagining, supposing*, and *hypothesizing*. All of these are of relevance to the construction of the intentional consumer-situation and the question of whether a cognitive theory of intellectual functioning is required in order to justify or refute this intentional interpretation.

Pretending and *imagining* require the ability to ascertain whether the truth conditions of propositions have been met, making it possible to assess whether the proposition can be viewed as true or false. Pretending to be Mark Antony while one is an actor in *Antony and Cleopatra* is dependent on the prior understanding of what it is to act out a role, to suspend disbelief for a time, and to be aware that in fact one is John Doe, an actor, who is imagining being a Roman general of a bygone age and pretending to behave as the play's author, director, and audience expect one to in a specific time and place. All of these pretenses are readily dropped when the actor returns to his regular haunts and non-professional roles. In fantasizing, by contrast, the individual lacks the capacity to assess truth and falsity and temporal alignment is beyond her competence; rather, contradiction may actually be encouraged. In the case of pretending and imagining reality testing is voluntarily, temporarily, and consciously suspended, but this is necessarily not the case in fantasizing.

Supposing and *hypothesizing* are central components of cognitive rehearsal that require high levels of understanding of the distinction between truth and falsity, the temporal relationships among proposed scenarios, including the longer-range consequences of one's action, and the need for logical (non-contradictory) integrity among the various drafts of proposed plans for the future. Supposed futures need to be quarantined from the realities of one's present position in order to avoid confusion of the situation as it currently is and the imagined alternative situations among which one may choose. Cognitive rehearsal also demands the capacity to formulate and mentally test hypotheses. Although the rehearser is fully able to test reality as and when it becomes necessary, she can postpone this procedure while the contemplation of scenarios is in progress. But these operations of suspended critical faculties and judgment are subject to individual differences in cognitive level as well as cognitive style:

> With hypothesizing some proposition to be true, there is not only the presupposition that the hypothesizer has intact capabilities for assessing truth and falsity and reality testing but also that he/she has a serious interest in the truth status of the proposition in question. The hypothesizer is concerned with getting things right about the proposition and its relation to affairs of the world. He/she has perhaps performed some reality testing operations already.

And, the hypothesizer will likely be interested in the outcome of other, more definitive tests.

(Brakel, 2001, pp. 370–371)

In short, while fantasizing is a matter of primary process mentation, pretending and imagining, supposing, hypothesizing, and of course the entertaining of beliefs-proper are all integrally based upon secondary mental processing, frequently of a high level.

Creating the intentional consumer-situation

The intentional consumer-situation comprises those desires, beliefs, emotions, and perceptions that relate to the consumer's prior experience of contingencies of rein-forcement and present patterns of reinforcement and punishment, together with the action propensities they portend. It follows that desires, beliefs, emotions, and perceptions are *all* contingency-representations. As will become increasingly appar-ent from the following analysis, part of the task of reconstructing the consumer's intentional consumer-situation on the basis of what we know of her actions is to determine how these components of the intentional consumer-situation, these var-ious modes of contingency-representation, interrelate to produce or account for the consumer's actions.

The analysis of the intentional consumer-situation has four steps, beginning with (Step 1) the identification of activity that is not under the control of a stimulus field, i.e., that is action rather than behavior; followed by (Step 2) the assignment to the consumer of *desires* on the basis of what we know about her utility func-tion; then (Step 3) the identification of the *perceptual contingency-representations* that establish the *emotional reactions* to past and present patterns of reinforcement and punishment; and finally (Step 4) the construction of the *beliefs* that the consumer would have on the basis of her learning history and current stimulus field, beliefs that render the observed actions and the emotional contingency-representations jointly intelligible, and which promote the explanation of the actions.

Step 1: The identification of action

The intentional interpretation, first, has to specify the observed behavior that is not under the control of a stimulus field, the *target activity* that is to be treated as con-sumer action. In the present case, the activity we have to explain is the *persistent* slot machine gambling of players whose performances lead to two identical symbols rather than the three required for a win which would yield a financial reward. The lack of an operant interpretation is due to the consequences of the gambling having precisely the opposite effect to that predicted by operant psychology, namely, that the punishment provided by losing (gaining two identical symbols when three are required) actually leads to increased play (*pleasure* depends on failing). We have to answer the questions: What is the consumer maximizing? What intentionality can be ascribed to her in order to render this behavior intelligible (given that there is no stimulus field to provide an operant interpretation).

Before discussing in greater detail the beliefs that are relevant to the interpretation of akratic action particularly as it characterizes gambling, it may be useful to make some preliminary remarks about the nature of gambling itself. We may wonder whether there is not something a-rational about engaging in commercially-provided gambling at all if the intention is to gain any money thereby let alone a large sum. The odds are stacked against the gambler, either because they are legitimately set to favor the house, as in casino games, or because so many other competing bettors are also involved, as in national and international lotteries. There must be a degree of fantasizing on the part of the person who seriously expects to make a fortune in this way. Some gamblers play for short periods as a pleasurable leisure activity which is soon terminated whether the gambler is winning or losing; many such gamblers set aside a specific, relatively small kitty before approaching the gambling venue and play only until it is exhausted; this is the sum they are willing to pay for the pleasure of taking part in the venue's business; they are under no illusion that they are about to acquire a life-changing sum of money by staking a small sum. For such consumers, gambling is a pleasure rather than a problem. But not all gambling is of this sort: it is neither so-limited by pecuniary and temporal factors nor constrained by a circumscribed expectation of pleasure or an informed view of the actual probabilities of winning a large amount. The possibility looms large, therefore, that gambling based on the expectation of serious financial gain is actually a form of consumer action based on fantasy. While such fantasy may play a part in all gambling to an extent, it is particularly prevalent to varying degrees in pathological and problem gambling.

Pathological gambling is understood as a "chronic inability to refrain from gambling to an extent that causes serious disruption to core life aspects such as career, health and family." Problem gamblers are "people whose gambling behavior is at least a *nuisance* to them, and is so along the same dimensions as are used to operationalize [pathological gambling]." Finally, disordered gambling "denotes the inclusive disjunction of the two ideas above, i.e., gambling that is either [pathological gambling] or problem gambling" (Ross et al., 2008, pp. 32–34, emphasis in original; see also Petry, 2005).[9]

Disordered gamblers' fantasies are not always apparent, however, even to themselves. Most gamblers, like most consumers, are rationalizers in that they seek reasoned foundations for what they do or have done, reduce cognitive dissonance by basing their actions on evidence or what appears as evidence of how the world works, and try to act in consonance with norms that they feel justified in regarding as generally accepted. The cognitive activities that accompany their life-disrupting gambling have the same *form* as the cognitive activities by which an affluent consumer whose life is not so-disarranged selects this rather than that model of a TV or laptop computer, but they are based on a disparate logic. Disordered gamblers' fantasies include both the wishes that motivate them, wishes based on the baseless idea that they are likely to become rich by gambling excessively, and the notion that continuing to gamble in the face of prolonged loss-making play will bring success. Of course, neither of these fantasies is unconnected with positive human outcomes: the media stories of "first-time-lucky" punters and the "gutsy persistence" of the doggedly-determined players who reap a fortune are evidence that large payoffs are *possible*. Neither reveals the fact that the risks involved make such successes extremely *improbable*, however. Yet they give some global justification to those who would try, an overarching dream that sustains their efforts. What are of interest to us here, however, are the personal beliefs that motivate further play when everything is going wrong, the propositional attitudes that nourish continued action despite a sequence of punishing losses.

The surprising finding that ought to be of interest to the theoretical minimalist who relies on radical behaviorism to explicate consumer activity is that the behavior of disordered gamblers is not necessarily deterred by losses. In fact, there are instances in which the experience of a loss leads to increased gambling. In slot machine gambling, for instance, scoring two identical symbols rather than the three necessary for a win not only recruits similar neurophysiological responses to those that accompany winning but actually increases the rate at which many gamblers play exactly as an outright win would. But a "near-miss" is a loss, a fail. The enhanced gambling that it inspires goes against the basic principle of operant psychology to the effect that, while reinforcement (winning, in this case, as signified by the appearance of three identical symbols) will lead to an increase in the rate of behaving, punishment (loss, in this case, signified by the appearance of any combination of symbols other than three identical bells or pineapples or whatever) will result in a lower rate of behavior, that is, less play. Yet the well-documented near-miss phenomenon flies in the face of this commonplace finding of behavioral psychology.[10]

An explanation based on consumer behavior analysis which is within the realm of radical behaviorism is found in informational reinforcement. Many slot machines are configured to present exciting sounds and visual recognitions that a near-miss has been scored and these may perform the functions of informational reinforcement, encouraging the notion that some sort of achievement has occurred through scoring two identical symbols. This may be the case[11] but the conclusion that repeated play in response to near-misses is a function of informational reinforcement requires further explication. For example, we have to propose how these arbitrary sources of reinforcement arise and what the cognitive, affective, and perceptual bases of their influencing action may be. It is difficult to understand how these accouterments of a near-miss could be taken to signify some kind of victory without resort to considerations of collective intentionality, contingency-representation, and neurotic beliefs. Particular instances of sounds and visual stimuli could signify a near-miss, meaning a quasi-win, only if they were understood by the members of a social group to have this significance. Their influence on action could then be explained by virtue of their socially instituted power to confer social status and esteem as sources of informational reinforcement, i.e., as jointly constructed stimuli that would motivate further action. Individuals, working together, would have determined the contingencies of reinforcement (and punishment) that would shape and maintain a particular pattern of behavior. Both the sight of two identical symbols and the sounds and visual stimuli accompanying them would then be part of the contingencies represented perceptually and affectively to the player in such a way that they would act as prompts to further play. The explanation, in other words, draws on the logically necessary but empirically-elusive conception of perceptual contingency-representation. We must buttress this explanation with knowledge of the cognitive basis of contingency-representation, the desires and beliefs that comprise, along with contingency-representation, the intentional consumer-situation.

Step 2: The ascription of conation

Step 2, the statement of the consumer's *desires*, follows clearly from the extensional BPM research program: the consumer seeks to maximize utilitarian and informational reinforcement. This is clearly a consideration of economic rationality. Of this we need say little other than that the consumer is assumed to optimize the amount of utilitarian and informational reinforcement received by dint of a particular pattern of consumption and, thereby, the levels of pleasure, arousal, and dominance that are its ultimate reward. The intentional interpretation of consumer action entails the specification of the goal or desire toward the fulfillment of which the target activity is directed. We assume the consumer maximizes a combination of utilitarian and informational reinforcement. But there is no or very little utilitarian reinforcement in the form of actually winning money. If we assume the consumer's behavior is reinforced by means of informational consequences in the form of performance feedback, we must recognize that this is erroneous since it applies to situations in which the consumer's behavior results in failure. The informational reinforcement provided by the sounds and sights given off by the machine are not actually rewards but are *interpreted* as such. Since informational reinforcement is dependent on social and individual judgment about what is a reward, we can ascribe a degree of agency to the consumer who decides personally what is rewarding (in much the same way that individuals may collectively determine what will count as a reinforcer). There may be social support for this as others who are playing or observing comment enthusiastically that "That was a near-win!"

Turning to psychological rationality, we note that Brakel distinguishes *cognitive attitudes* in which the content of the attitude is looked upon as having come about from *conative attitudes* in which the content is to be brought about. This is essentially saying that cognitive attitudes, beliefs, have a mind-to-world direction of fit, i.e., they denote (at least subjectively to the individual who holds them) how the world is, while conative attitudes such as desires and wishes have a world-to-mind direction of fit, i.e., they denote how the world should be. However, whereas beliefs-proper portray the world "truly and correctly," other cognitive propositional attitudes such as fantasizing, imagining, pretending, and supposing do not. Brakel proposes a similar constitutive aim analysis for desire. She points out that in order to be a desire a conative attitude must contribute to *readiness-to-act*. If I "hope" to drink less alcohol, my hoping may take either of two forms. I might simply picture myself as a person who drinks little, *wishing* for this eventuality but doing nothing about it. If, however, I *desire* to drink less, then it is within my capabilities to *do* something about this, to arrange my life so that drinking alcohol is a diminished activity on my part. In the first case, I take no action toward changing the prevailing state of affairs: I may fantasize what it would be like to be a nondrinker or controlled drinker and this fantasizing constitutes the fulfillment of the wish, the "wish-fulfillment." While desires manifest in a readiness-to-act that is testable by real-world happenings, the function of wishes is to generate fantasy (Brakel, 2009, Chapter 8).

In Ramsey's terms, a conative attitude that is correctly classified as a desire entails preparedness for action in a way that contributes to the desire's reaching the success conditions of its content; in Brakel's terms, it is a *readiness-to-act* (p. 144). Wishes, by contrast, fulfill their content through the formation of fantasies, rather than through readiness-to-act in the real world. Desires involve a present-time readiness-to-act, whereas intentions are a weaker propensity to act at some future time if nothing more pressing comes along, and "if I feel like it."

Step 3: The ascription of perceptual contingency-representation

Next is the construction of an account of the consumer's perceptual experience that is consistent with this behavior pattern. This is accomplished by reconstructing the content of the contingency-representations that the consumer would require in order to perform the target action. This is conducted, initially, in *cognitive terms*, and takes the form of an intentionally-characterized statement of the contingencies of reinforcement and punishment that are consistent with the maintenance of this action.[12] In the present case, this step requires the specification of the cognitively-based, if eccentric, *perception* that the SSR is greater than the LLR at t_1, which flies in the face of the objective perception that the reverse is the case but that the attainment of the LLR requires patience. The contingency-representation so arrived at in cognitive/belief terms is reconstructed *in emotional terms*: a statement of the emotions that maintenance of the target action would rely upon.

In line with the conclusions reached in Chapter 4, if these emotional contingency-representations are intended to serve as predictions of action, it would be necessary to construct them not on the basis of the target action but through an independent source of action such as the consumer's verbal responses of pleasure, arousal, and dominance to scenarios describing the contingencies of reinforcement and punishment. In the current example, however, the emphasis is on the post hoc construction of an intentional interpretation that would be tested primarily in terms of its being borne out by a subsequent cognitive interpretation (to which we turn in Chapter 6).

The reconstruction of the consumer's *pattern of emotions* is concerned with the nature of the perceptual contingency-representations through which the consumer has direct knowledge of the contingencies. If the SSR is taken at t_1, then the levels of emotion that are germane to the decision taken just prior to this time $(t_1 - x)$ are, in relation to the current contingencies,

$$\{P_{SSR} \ A_{SSR} \ D_{SSR}\}\{\text{all extremely high}\},$$

while the levels of emotionally expressed expectations of the future contingencies at t_2 are

$$\{P_{LLR} \ A_{LLR} \ D_{LLR}\}\{\text{all vanishingly small}\}.$$

The levels of the emotions felt with respect to the current contingencies, those present at t_1, are not simply "extremely high"; they are highly exaggerated at that moment – the result not simply of desiring but of craving. The levels the emotions projected forward to the imagined consumption of the LLR after a patient wait are vanishingly small to the point of being completely *dis*counted. As a result, the consumer maximizes utilitarian and informational reinforcement at t_1 by maximizing each of the three emotions as a result of the contemplation of the SSR in contrast to the LLR. In other words, if the SSR is chosen, then the (brief) decision process that precedes this must evoke very high levels of pleasure, arousal, and dominance in relation to the *representation* of the SSR that enters into this decision sequence and relatively low levels of these emotions in the case of the consumer's *representation* of the LLR. This emotional prefiguring of the contingencies is responsible for the consumer's action in selecting the SSR. The actual high levels of all three emotions encountered as a result of this action are the rewards of the action and are maximized because of the pleasure of having an immediate reward (utilitarian reinforcement), the arousal evoked by personal feedback that one is succeeding (informational reinforcement), and the dominance of being in control of the situation (which is based now on an awareness of the openness of the consumer behavior setting: the consumer is aware that she had two choices and exercised personal control of the situation by making the one that provided the highest levels of immediate reinforcement available at t_1). These emotions are likely to enhance the consumer's feeling of self-esteem or pride, especially the feeling of having been in charge of her destiny. This feeling *might*, however, be assuaged by knowledge that a larger source of reward has been evaded in favor of the immediacy of the SSR, that she has not exercised self-control, or that she is weak-willed.

If, however, the LLR is selected at t_2, this must be attributable to high levels of evoked pleasure, arousal, and dominance experienced by contemplating, just prior to t_1, the LLR *representation*, and much lower levels of pleasure, arousal, and dominance evoked by the contemplation of the SSR. The decision to await the LLR and forgo the SSR maximizes informational reinforcement at t_1 since it provides feedback on the consumer's acting in such a way as to reap increased utilitarian and informational reinforcement at t_2; as such, this source of informational reinforcement is responsible for feelings of arousal. Can the consumer also be said to be maximizing utilitarian reinforcement at t_1, however, since nothing material has been received? It is more likely that the *anticipation* of the enhanced utilitarian reinforcement that is now expected at t_2

acts as further informational reinforcement; this source of informational reinforcement would be responsible for both further arousal and, given that its content is anticipated utilitarian reinforcement, pleasure. Dominance is also high as the decision to await the LLR is made, just prior to t_1, at t_1 as the decision is translated into the action of waiting, and beyond t_1 as the waiting, which encapsulates the consumer's self-control, continues. These emotions are likely to result in a high level of self-esteem.

This reasoning is germane to the construction of the intentional consumer-situation: we have assumed on the basis of the empirical extensional BPM research program that the consumer is maximizing utilitarian and informational reinforcement and, thereby, the ultimate emotional reward of pleasure, arousal, and dominance. On that basis we have interpreted her actions (choice of either the SSR or the LLR) on the basis of the pattern of reinforcement and punishment that such action would result in. There is a downside to this outcome, however. We have surmised that the consumer maximizes utilitarian and informational reinforcement and pleasure, arousal, and dominance whether her action was to choose the SSR or the LLR. Whatever the logic behind the argument that this is so, it provides only a further *description* of the observed actions that fails to differentiate between them or indeed *explain* them. Even if we were able to substantiate that the consumer actually had the required feelings prior to, during, and after t_1, we would not be able to differentiate on the basis of this evidence the action of a consumer who chose the SSR and another who selected the LLR.

One way to overcome this impasse is to make a further analysis of the intentional consumer-situation in each case and to employ the results thereof to derive testable hypotheses. This consists in working out the beliefs that would logically accompany the observed actions, influencing the selective nature of the perceptual awareness encapsulated in the emotion-based contingency-representations ascribed to the consumer. These beliefs must be of a kind that renders the ascribed pattern of emotion intelligible in light of the nature of the observed action.

Step 4: The ascription of cognition

The perceptions, desires, and beliefs that comprise the intentional interpretation are highly predictive of akrates' persisting in the behavior pattern of continued gambling even though it eventuates in aversive rather than rewarding outcomes. The beliefs that can be ascribed in making sense of an observed action are either beliefs-proper or neurotic beliefs. Insofar as perception is cognitively penetrated, we must look for the beliefs that underpin the perception that, at least at t_1, the SSR is in some sense greater than the LLR. The final stage, therefore, is the construction of an account of the *outcomes* of the consumer's cognitive processing beliefs as they are operative in the intentional consumer-situation.[13]

Recall that beliefs-proper are amenable to testing against reality and are abandoned if they do not conform to this standard; neurotic beliefs, on the other hand, *appear* to be rationally based on how the world is but are based in fact on counterfeit notions of reality while remaining obdurate in the face of evidence. The cognition that penetrates the perceptions of the addict consists of neurotic beliefs that shore up her notion that the SSR is superior to the LLR by reconciling it with the view that only what happens *now* is real, that there is no past or future to be taken into consideration. Candidates for such beliefs are well documented in the literature of addiction,[14] and include:

> *The gambler's fallacy.* "Because I have had a series of losses, I must, by the law of averages, be due a large win." The gambler's fallacy is the illusion that the game functions in such a way that a series of losing plays stands to be mitigated by a large win. The illusion is that the odds are about to change in the gambler's favor. Actually the risk conditions remain identical from play to play no matter how many plays are performed but the neurotic belief that encourages more play as a result of sustained losing is made to seem rational by the probability-defying logic of the fallacy.
>
> *The near-miss effect.* The illusion here is that, because the gambler scored two identical symbols (when three such are required for a win), she almost won. However, the appearance of two rather than three identical tokens in the score window of a slot machine is actually evidence of a loss, as surely as is that of three disparate tokens. It is, nonetheless, interpreted as evidence that the player is gaining skill in competing and as a signal that a win is imminent. These false impressions are dramatized by the informational reinforcement that accompanies them in the form of attention-grabbing sights and sounds generated by the gambling machine, and by the closure of the consumer behavior setting.
>
> *The skill acquisition fantasy.* This is illustrated by the notion that the achievement of two identical symbols demonstrates that the gambler is enhancing her skill at playing the game. Near-misses, plus the occasional genuine win, are all taken as evidence of increasing performance skill and thus provide the impression that the neurotic near-miss belief of primary mentation is actually a belief-proper that belongs to secondary mentation. The neurotic notion of a near-miss is thus transformed into an apparently rational reason to continue playing. The near-miss evokes similar neurophysiological responses to those that accompany an actual win, the same emotional reaction. Supported by the cognitive illusion of some sort of win in these circumstances, sustained by informational reinforcement, these emotional and cognitive effects can easily result in the neurotic belief that one is making progress.
>
> *The entrapment fallacy.* The gambler reasons that, "My previous gambling represents such an investment that I cannot stop now or I will lose the assets I have built up." Another neurotic belief encourages the feeling of entrapment: having spent so much on trying to win, the player feels obligated to remain in the game in order to justify her "investment" and to recoup the losses incurred by previous play. This is a version of the sunk costs fallacy in economics, which justifies continued outlays on a project the outcomes of which are highly uncertain or even known to entail loss on the grounds that the investment to date must not be lost.

These neurotic beliefs are not perceptual; they arise from mental consideration of what is happening. But these beliefs and the bases on which they were constructed are never reality-tested: the pathological gambler never asks (or at least does not ask while playing) whether the strategy she is pursuing is actually leading to more wins. Such beliefs are never allowed to achieve consonance with either reality or other beliefs. They are, in particular, never challenged by contradictory beliefs such as those that relate to the laws of probability. Crucially, they avoid the proper use of indexicals: as I continue to play, I fail to acknowledge that I am the same person who will incur any deleterious consequences of my present action. They, and the intellectual processes that brought them about, can also be seen as means of avoiding those contradictory beliefs, of ignoring intellectually demanding considerations (such as the concept of risk), or of evading the conclusions that would lead to cessation of continued play and the pleasures that accompany it.

How, then, can the cognitive processes of the akrates be incorporated into a theory of consumer choice? Are the beliefs the akrates holds rational, irrational, a-rational, neurotic? There is certainly a mixture of the apparently rational and the nonrational in the beliefs of the akrates. But the beliefs and actions of the person who simply selects the SSR over the LLR on the basis that the SSR is perceived as greater than the LLR are *a-rational*, for the actions are influenced by beliefs that are never truth-tested, which fail to achieve consonance with other beliefs and experience, and which are impervious to the proper use of indexicals. In the case of the individual who bolsters fantasies of winning under these circumstances with spurious evidence, her beliefs are *neurotic*.

Consider two consumers who are prone to the fallacies we have listed. The first displays a-rationality and she acts impulsively: her perception that the SSR has greater utility than the LLR is of itself not necessarily immediately *economically* or *socially* irrational when one considers that consumers maximize a bundle of utilitarian *and* informational reinforcement when they purchase/consume. There may be social status to be gained from early acquisition and consumption, group membership may depend on it, and prestige flow accordingly. Private or personal benefits may accrue from decisions that yield an SSR even though they are made in full knowledge of the LLR available in the future. The sense of being in control of one's destiny, being able to "decide for oneself," even though the results are suboptimal, may generate self-esteem and an accompanying feeling of pride, even if short-lived. But they are benefits that are in addition to the utilitarian reinforcement that derives from the functional benefits of acquiring and using the item. However, the selection of the SSR is not rational *in psychological terms* since it is tense-restricted if not tense-free (for what is temporal discounting if not an attempt to live in a tense-free world?), and it certainly is not rational when tested against reality – for the longer-term outcomes of this selection are deleterious to the individual in both utilitarian and informational terms. Waiting for the LLR could have conferred greater functional benefits and enhanced social status and personal esteem. Such action is, for these reasons, not rational in psychological terms, but neither is it irrational: it is not based on an outright effort to avoid and act contrarily to principles of rationality. It is *a*-rational.

We may note in passing, and in anticipation of the discussion in Chapter 6, how well the essence of a-rationality is caught in this example as *pre*-rationality, i.e., arising from a deficit in the cognitive skills required to make rational judgments, a lack of the *mindware* necessary to form sound evaluations. This suggests reliance on the three negative aspects of a-rationality to which Brakel has drawn attention: an inability to reason in ways that can conceive the import of past contingencies (e.g., drawing on an accurate consideration of one's learning history) or future contingencies (e.g., foresight of the outcomes of one's current actions); a failure to understand what the consequences of one's actions will be in reality (e.g., the recognition that, "I may not win and will end the evening with nothing"); and a consequent capacity to entertain contradictory notions without recognition of the inconsistency inherent in that stance ("My luck is about to turn!" "The odds have changed in my favor." "My performance is improving." And so on).

The sustained selection of the SSR brings us, however, to the question of neurotic beliefs, which pertain not to the immediate choice of one SSR but to the reasons one has for *persisting* in a course of action that objectively has negative consequences. This *sustained* behavior pattern is not a matter of perception but is based on the neurotic *belief* that the SSR confers greater benefit. The suboptimal selection of the SSR is maintained by an erroneous belief system which insulates it from reality. The belief system is therefore, from a psychological point of view, neurotic.

The second consumer, however, is considered to evince neurotic behavior in the sense that her actions can be understood only through the ascription of neurotic beliefs, i.e., fantasies *plus* defective evidence based on psychic-reality testing. We have seen that neurotic beliefs resemble fantasies more than beliefs-proper: they are elements of primary process mentation; they both have content that is not delimited by truth considerations; and they are not subjected to testing against the criteria of conformity to reality. The difference is that neurotic beliefs *assume the appearance of* secondary process mentation: they are insulated from real-world evidence; they are maintained by false "evidence" that is treated as genuine; and they are considered as though they were genuine beliefs. Contrary evidence is ignored by the neurotic, who avoids any pressure to abandon neurotic beliefs by sustaining their appearance as beliefs-proper.

The kinds of neurotic beliefs that are particularly relevant to such activities as pathological gambling are those we have considered: the gambler's fallacy, the near-miss fallacy, the skill acquisition fantasy, and the entrapment fallacy. Such beliefs are not shaped by how the gambling system actually works, for they do not come into contact with truth considerations and are not examined in the light of reality. One reason why they are effective, however, is that they *take the form* of reasoned propositions that are in touch with reality. They assume the trappings of secondary mentation and the conclusions to which they lead are, therefore, plausible in the context of a-rationality and believable as surely as if they constituted beliefs-proper. Moreover, they perform a protective shield for the neurotic addict who can rely on them in order to ignore, misinterpret, or reject genuine information about how the gambling system works: the neurotic beliefs are sustained in this process and entertained as proper beliefs that actually describe the world.

Table 5.1 summarizes.

TABLE 5.1 Primary and secondary mentation in the explanation of pathological gambling

Primary processes (a-rational mentation)	Secondary processes (rational mentation)	Observations of pathological gambling
Without tenses: confined to a tenseless and unexamined present	*Tensed*: based on an understanding of past, present, and future and the sense of temporal continuity this entails	The SSR is perceived as greater than the LLR simply because it is instantly available. There is no apparent understanding of the import of a superior reward if it is delayed. The present is perceived without context.
No reality testing: a-rational thought consists in propositional attitudes the representations of which are not sensitive to regulation based on considerations of truth	*Reality-tested*: beliefs take the form of propositional attitudes which are sensitive to external conditions	Beliefs such as the gambler's fallacy, the near-miss effect, skill acquisition, and entrapment have no basis in reality but they can attract the apparent support of pseudo-reasons that give the impression that they reflect how the world works.
Lack of unified selfhood: originates from a level of development at which a stable self is yet to come into being and with it the capacity to grasp continuity in experience	*Stable selfhood*: originates from the experientially continuous viewpoint of a single self or agent	There is no recognition that the same self that acts now will incur the consequences of the action.
Lack standard logic and therefore tolerant of contradictions	*Evince intolerance of contradictions*: a system of judgment based on reality testing can identify lack of consonance in arguments	Beliefs such as the gambler's fallacy, the near-miss effect, skill acquisition, and entrapment are not challenged by the evidence from the consumer's learning history that none of them fits reality. Because these ideas are not logically founded, they can coexist with the individual's experience of unfulfilled desires.

Notes

1 This section is indebted to Brakel's analysis of primary and secondary mentation, beliefs-proper, and, particularly, her innovative definition of neurotic beliefs in her paper, "Phantasies, neurotic beliefs, and beliefs-proper" (2001). A revised version of this paper appears in Chapter 7 of Brakel (2009). See also Brakel (2015b) and, for a range of views on philosophical psychoanalysis, Boag et al. (2015a, 2015b).

2 Freud alluded to primary and secondary psychical processes as early as the *Project for a Scientific Psychology* ([1895] 1964, pp. 324–327), the latter being a state regulated by considerations of reality that emanate from inhibitory activities of the ego. In *The Interpretation of Dreams* ([1900] 1953), he enlarged upon this, noting that, while primary process mentation is present from the earliest stages of human development, secondary process mentation accrues in the course of a lifetime, gradually inhibiting and taking precedence over the primary (see, especially, pp. 602–603). The primary processes do not, however, disappear, and are capable, if fulfilled, of interfering with the "purposive ideas of secondary thinking" (p. 604), thereby producing unpleasure rather than pleasure. The consequent repression of primary processes consists in a transformation of affect; but the primary process thinking is not expunged and may reassert itself.

3 For a concise and cogent summary of the Freudian psychoanalytical system, see Segal (1979, pp. 11–25).

4 This is a somewhat conservative attitude with respect to psychoanalysis for I am not at the present presupposing that the mental structure proposed by Freud is the cognitive interpretation that provides the standpoint from which the intentional interpretation is based on his categorization of beliefs: that would be to overstate the role of psychoanalytic theory in the explication of consumer choice. Moreover, the categories of belief and their psychological functions are too closely allied with the Freudian mental apparatus for the latter to act as a critical perspective for the evaluation of the former. Far better to employ the psychoanalytic framework of beliefs, especially as it is contemporaneously interpreted and extended by a writer such as Brakel, and to evaluate its use by reference to the theories of cognitive structure and function that have hitherto been adopted in the Intentional Behaviorism program.

5 Brakel and Shevrin (2003) argue that Freud's theory of primary and secondary mentation is a dual-process theory that prefigures those of later cognitive scientists. In fact, one can depict some aspects of Freudian theory as reflecting tripartite mental operations in which the *id* corresponds to The Autonomous Set of Systems (TASS) of Stanovich's (2009) framework, the *ego* to the algorithmic mind, and the *superego* to the reflective mind. There are important differences, however, between primary and secondary mentation, on the one hand, and the S1 (automatic) and S2 (analytical) systems, on the other. Brakel and Shevrin (2003) argue that System 1, the automatic mind, which in the tri-process theory encompasses the TASS, is neither rational nor irrational – it is a-rational. However, Stanovich and West (2003a) point out that, as sub-personal systems, neither S1 nor S2 (the analytic mind comprising, in their system, the algorithmic and reflective minds) can be characterized as inherently rational or irrational: instrumental rationality is a matter for the organismic (personal) level of exposition. S2 can operate on rules that are socially prevalent but the following of which does not contribute to logical rationality. We might resolve this by saying that S1 and S2 can lead to *behavior* (a personal-level construct) that is rational, irrational, or a-rational.

6 The law of the excluded middle holds that, for any proposition, either that proposition or its inverse must be true. For example, for the proposition *Jones is mortal* it must be true that *either* Jones is mortal *or* that Jones is not mortal. It cannot be the case that Jones is mortal and Jones is not mortal (the excluded middle position) can be true. The point is that contradictory statements cannot both be logically held to be true, something that occurs in the case of a-rationality where one may, for instance, dream that one is both the President of the United States and a non-American citizen.

7 Hence, a conditioned response is neither rational nor irrational but is an a-rational response to an arbitrary stimulus. Brakel says the generalization of the response to other stimuli requires that these stimuli be similar in some way to the original but in fact even temporal contiguity will is sufficient. Note also that similar considerations apply to operant conditioning, which is also an a-rational process: the transfer of function necessary to demonstrate operant conditioning – in which a stimulus which previously acted as a reinforcer acts, in subsequent training, as a punisher – is especially a-rational.

8 Brakel also mentions religious or social beliefs but says little of them because they are not amenable to reality testing. They are, therefore, omitted from the following discussion.

9 Section 312.31 of the fifth edition of the *Diagnostic and Statistical Manual of Mental Disorders* (American Psychiatric Association, 2013) speaks of "gambling disorder" rather than pathological gambling.

10 There is of course no such thing as a near-miss, a fact that is often emphasized by placing this expression in inverted commas. Rather than drop the term, which has become a commonplace description of the phenomenon, but in order to avoid the tedium of repeatedly encountering the scare quotes I shall abandon them. But we all need to remind ourselves that the term has no counterpart in the reality of games of chance.

11 Discussion of the interpretation of the role of these "bells and whistles" in the encouragement of further gambling can be found elsewhere: Foxall (2016a) and Foxall and Sigurdsson (2012) offer several possible understandings. The latter has been reprinted (Foxall & Sigurdsson, 2016).

12 This cognitive component of the contingency-representation is necessary just as there is a cognitive component of the pragmatic representation. However, for the reasons presented in Chapter 2, the concept of pragmatic representation will not do for this purpose.

13 These are clearly cognitive in constitution though they are treated separately from the *cognitive processing* from which they emerge and which forms the third stage of Intentional Behaviorism, the cognitive interpretation.

14 I have recently reviewed the literature on disordered gambling, particularly that involved in the near-miss phenomenon (Foxall, 2016a) and will not rehearse here all of the references to this field or to the prevalence of these beliefs. Please see, for elaboration of this section, my *Addiction as Consumer Choice: Exploring the Cognitive Dimension*, as well as Foxall and Sigurdsson (2012, 2016).

6

COGNITIVE FOUNDATIONS OF THE INTENTIONAL CONSUMER-SITUATION

Abstract

The intentional consumer-situation pursued in Chapter 5 posits an idealized consumer whose behavior can be readily understood in terms of her maximizing utilitarian and informational reinforcement. This is capable of generating a plausible intentional interpretation of consumer choice in intentional terms but it needs to be cashed out by reference to our understanding of the cognitive structure and functions that would be required to sustain the actions it suggests will follow from this supposed intentionality. This is pursued principally by reference to micro-cognitive psychology in the form of a discussion of the tripartite model of cognition proposed by Stanovich (2009), especially in its understanding of rationality and irrationality as elements which determine the desires and beliefs that influence action. An important question raised in this chapter is whether this level of cognitive theorizing is necessary in order to sustain the intentional consumer-situation that proceeded in terms of conative, and cognitive, as well as perceptual and emotional contingency-representations. Might it be possible to dispense with this cognitive apparatus and to restrict our explanations of consumption to perceptual contingency-representation?

Psychological explanation II: Cognitive interpretation

The final stage in the Intentional Behaviorism research strategy is the critical examination of the Intentional Interpretation in terms of proven depictions of cognitive structure and functioning. Three areas of cognitive psychology relevant to this task have been proposed: the micro-cognitive level, which links personal level intentionality and action to sub-personal, neurophysiological, events; the macro-cognitive level, which relates the personal level of exposition to super-personal humanly-devised contingencies of reinforcement and punishment that are founded and maintained on the basis of collective intentionality; and the meso-cognitive level that deals with the logic of the intra-personal interaction of competing interests that relate to the achievement of goals that have different temporal horizons. The aim of this stage is to ensure that the desires, beliefs, emotions, and perceptions ascribed in the course of treating the consumer as an idealized, utility-maximizing system are borne out by a broader sphere of intellectual inquiry. This is discussed in terms of the tripartite model (Stanovich, 2009) to account for the emergence and indulgence of neurotic beliefs, the capacity of picoeconomic analysis (Ainslie, 1992) to show how short- and long-range interests within the agent may interact to bring about suboptimal actions, and the prevalence of collectively-intentional desires and beliefs to influence perception of the longer-term consequences of present actions.

Chapter 5 examined cognition in terms of the *outputs* of intellectual processing, i.e., desires and beliefs as they appear in the intentional interpretation. In this chapter, the emphasis is on the underlying cognitive *processing* that determines the shape and impact of these desires and beliefs. In doing this, an important objective is to inquire into the status of the Classical Model. Is the development of perceptual contingency-representation with which we have been concerned a necessary complement of the conceptual analysis that underlies this model, or does the perceptual depose and replace the conceptual? Another objective in moving from intentional interpretation to cognitive interpretation is to evaluate the former in relation to its consonance with theories of cognitive structure and processing. These two themes are closely linked: for if the cognitive interpretation level of analysis is unnecessary, it can scarcely provide a rationale for the intentional interpretation.

Pragmatic mental imagery

Nanay (2013a, Section 4.4) argues that even complex decisions may not require desires and beliefs because all sorts of extraneous factors can affect the outcome of decisions. There is plentiful evidence, he notes, that contextual factors from the tidiness of one's room to the manipulation of affect by the provision of a small piece of candy can influence decision-making procedures and outcomes. He reviews some of these and concludes that the research program founded on the classic model is degenerate and consequently in decline. But we must point out that these factors, while undeniably real, do not mean that decision making does not occur in a fairly formal manner on occasion. They do not of themselves indicate that decision making does not occur, that it is not based on desires and beliefs; at best, they suggest that formal systems of rational decision making may need to be adjusted in line with actual decision processes. Decision making is especially apparent when there is a conflict between two major lifestyles that needs to be resolved one way or the other with profound effects either way. Hence, situations that are amenable to bundling, for instance, where whole swathes of cumulated consequences of doing A over a long period of future behavior and whole swathes of cumulated consequences of doing not-A over the same period are brought forward in time, weighed, compared, and a decision made based on them. Perhaps choosing the SSR on a single occasion and thereby precluding the choice of the LLR does, indeed, not need desires and beliefs for its explanation. But serious decision making that leads to a change in lifestyle is not so easily accounted for. Further, we do not know that unconscious desires and beliefs are not reflected in our pragmatic representations. To the extent that the important element in a pragmatic representation is the contingency-representation that embodies the individual's learning history it involves some level of desires and beliefs. That we can rely on a pragmatic representation is the result of our having worked through the desires and beliefs of our decision making in detail and repeatedly. I shall return to the critique of Nanay's approach but in the meantime it is useful to round out his argument that perception rather than cognition is sufficient to explain action by considering his idea of pragmatic mental imagery.

Nanay, therefore, sets forth an alternative depiction of decision making in which *imagination* plays a key role. By imagining alternative future scenarios, the individual compares them by conjecturing how it would *feel* to be acting within each putative situation. The outcome of this process is a preference for one or other course of action and this is the course that is to be followed. He notes the similarity of Evans's (2007) proposal, which is based on thought experiments that comparatively evaluated alternative scenarios. But Evans's idea is normatively concerned with decision making while Nanay says he is concerned with the actual manner in which decisions are arrived at. While Evans's approach is rational and reliable, based on hypothetical thinking which belongs to Type 2 processing, Nanay argues that his is neither of these.

The sort of imaginative episode to which Nanay refers has two aspects: imagining oneself behaving in a situation that is itself imaginatively designed on the basis of the outcome of one's decision. This "imagining from the inside" may involve either (i) projecting oneself into the experiences of another person, X, such that X is present but the imagining individual may not be or (ii) projecting oneself into X's situation so that the imagining is about oneself but X is not present. Nanay's scheme of decision making features the second kind of imagining and X is not someone else but one's future self. However, many of the details of these scenarios are not – cannot be? – known at this stage; they are supplied by one's imagination. Moreover, imagining oneself in X's situation can mean either being oneself in that situation or being X in that situation. That is, I may simply project my present self into that situation or imagine myself as a future person in that context. Neither of these possibilities necessarily yields reliable information. The only self that matters when it comes to making the decision is the future self since one's present self will never encounter that situation. But this requires knowing how one will change in the meantime to bring about that future self and there is again a lack of information on which to base the imagination of this future self. The problem with taking a decision-making approach can be summed up thus:

> there are three points where imagination plays a role in the decision-making process. You imagine what you imagine to be your future self, being in a

situation that you imagine to be the outcome of your decision. As none of these three episodes of imagination can be considered reliable, decision-making is extremely unlikely to yield the optimal outcome reliably.

(Nanay, 2013a, p. 98)

We might pause for a moment to raise the question of how this plays out in the case of what is normally thought of as a fairly complex process of mental reasoning rather than imagining such as bundling. The individual undertaking this exercise must indeed imagine both the utilitarian sources of reinforcement entailed, which is relatively easy, and the informational reinforcement one will gain or lose and the aversive consequences that may ensue as a result of shorter-term and longer-term decisions. But can this be accomplished in the complete absence of mental processing that results in *evaluations* of these imagined courses of actions and their outcomes?

Some relatively trivial decisions, like where to go locally for a decent cup of coffee, might reach an optimal outcome but complex decisions usually do not. The desires and beliefs model assumes rationality of reliability and seeks reasons why we may depart from this ideal. By contrast, Nanay begins with actual decision making along with its lack of reliability and rationality as paradigmatic. It is imagining ourselves in future situations – rather than our underlying desires and beliefs – that is subject to all of the interferences that were mentioned above: from the cleanliness of our surroundings to our easily manipulated feelings. Nanay claims for the progressiveness of his proposed research program based on imagination that it opens up novel sources of investigation that account for how we actually make decisions and how this account differs from the Classical Model.

Again let us pause momentarily to ask ourselves whether the outcomes of the imaginative process are not primarily emotional and conative. Such imaginative processing is the representation of the reinforcing and punishing outcomes of behaving in a particular manner in terms of pleasure, arousal, and dominance, as well as in terms of behavioral disposition.

An oft-noted tendency in decision making is to overestimate some probabilities of outcome and underestimate others. Nanay claims that what is more imaginable is overestimated:

> we have good reason to replace the belief-desire model of decision-making with a model where imagination plays a crucial role. And this would push the belief-desire model even further away from the monopoly it once held in thinking about the mind.
>
> *(pp. 100–101)*

Prominent among *action-properties*, properties of a perceptual object that must be represented in order that the agent can execute an action with regard to that object, must, as I have argued, entail contingency-representations that encapsulate the consumer's perception of the opportunities and threats offered by the current consumer-situation in light of her learning history. This learning history has a neurophysiological substrate in the form of a somatic marker that is reactivated by either (a) fresh acquaintance with the contingencies of reinforcement that generated the somatic marker or (b) descriptions of those contingencies. Somatic markers produce feelings of pleasure, arousal, and dominance as appropriate. They also engender the action tendencies established in the course of exposure to those contingencies.

How does this idea of imaginative contemplation of the outcomes of alternative courses of action square with the tripartite theory of mental structure and functioning that was briefly described in Chapter 2? And which framework is better fitted to the production of the kinds of contingency-representations that the intentional interpretation identified as necessary to the construction of an intentional consumer-situation?

The rationale of tripartite theory

Stanovich and West (2011a) argues that the successful functioning of the override function that belongs to Type 2 systems (the rational mind comprising the algorithmic and reflective minds in Figure 6.1) relies on both procedural and declarative knowledge. Taking Type 1 responding (The Autonomous Set of Systems (TASS) of the autonomous mind in Figure 6.1) offline is probably procedural but developing

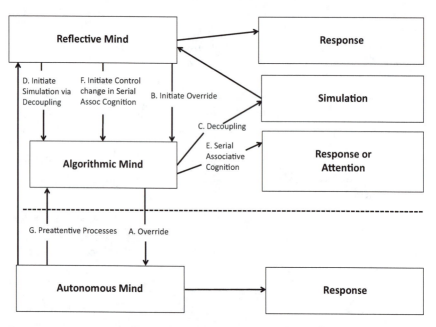

FIGURE 6.1 A more complete model of the tripartite structure.

Note: Above the dotted line is shown the S2 systems that form the analytic mind; below, the S1 systems (TASS) that form the autonomous mind. For explication, please see the text.

Source: Stanovich, K. E. (2011). *Rationality and the Reflective Mind*. Oxford: Oxford University Press, p. 62. Reproduced by kind permission of Oxford University Press, USA.

an alternative through cognitive synthesizing depends on the use of stored knowledge. In the process of simulation declarative knowledge and linguistically-coded strategic rules transform a decoupled representation. Each of the levels in the tripartite model needs access to knowledge if it is to undertake its tasks: the reflective mind draws upon beliefs, goals, and general knowledge; the algorithmic mind upon strategies and production systems; and the autonomous mind upon encapsulated knowledge base and tightly compiled learned information.

The *reflective mind* needs access to general information but it also relies on access to the opinions, beliefs, and goals that have been arrived at through a process of reflection and deliberation. The *algorithmic mind* needs to access the "micro-strategies for cognitive operations and production system rules for sequencing behaviors and thoughts." The *autonomous mind* has access to (a) encapsulated knowledge acquired in the course of a phylogenetic history and (b) information acquired through ontogenetic development "that has become tightly compiled and automatically activated because of overlearning and practice" (Stanovich & West, 2011b, p. 95).

These are only the sources of information required exclusively by each mind. In addition, the algorithmic mind and the reflective mind receive information from the "computations of the autonomous mind." (Hence, the autonomous mind computes: it is a metacognitive system.) These are the preattentive processes shown in the tripartite model (Figure 6.1). One of the knowledge structures available for retrieval, especially to the reflective mind, is *crystallized intelligence* (i.e., "Gc," intelligence-as-knowledge). Fluid intelligence (i.e., "Gf," intelligence-as-process) is implicit in the model as the general computational power of the algorithmic mind, notably the capacity to sustain cognitive decoupling.

Sources of rationality

Stanovich and West (2011b) argue that each of the two elements of the Gc/Gf theory omits important facets of rationality. Gf is related to rationality insofar as it is a function of the capacity of the algorithmic mind to perform and maintain decoupling. Override and simulation depend on the presence of Gf. However, the abilities involved in initiating override (arrow B in Figure 6.1) and to initiate simulation (arrow D) are aspects of the reflective mind that are not part of the assessment provided by intelligence tests. Intelligence testing therefore fails to consider these facets of rationality. Such abilities are assessed in the context of cognitive style or thinking disposition. Stanovich refers to tests of these intellectual features as "typical" performance rather than the "maximal" performance assessed by intelligence tests.[1] In the case of Gc, rational thought requires certain kinds of knowledge: crystallized intelligence. But it is not knowledge that intelligence tests assess. The kinds of knowledge required for rational thought include: probabilistic reasoning, causal reasoning, and scientific reasoning. It is *specialized* knowledge rather than the generalized knowledge IQ tests are concerned with.

The mentation ascribed in the intentional interpretation must have some basis in the cognitive operations we can ascribe to the individual. But, insofar as consumer choice is akratic, they represent a maladaptive operation of the analytic mind, an irrational or a-rational bias. How can this occur? There are a number of sources of individual difference that can account for the greater or lesser formation and holding of neurotic beliefs.

Sources of individual difference in rationality

There are at least three sources of individual difference in rationality. First, there are individual differences in cognitive style. Cognitive style, which is proposed as a major component of the reflective mind, is the manner of decision making, problem solving, and creativity evinced by an individual, the way in which she gathers and uses information gathering, and deliberates. It is also a determinant of the sorts of solution a decision maker seeks and applies. Cognitive style is conceived as being orthogonal to cognitive ability (and, therefore, intelligence, level, or capacity). While some decision makers are cautious in their approach to decision making and problem solving, employing tried-and-tested methods, a high degree of efficiency and rule-conformity, others exhibit more radical solutions, and are more likely to modify or even break with the accepted ways of working. The former may produce fewer potential solutions but a higher proportion of them are practicable and have a chance of succeeding; the latter are more likely to generate numerous approaches to solving a problem, even if a lot of them prove unworkable (Kirton, 2003). These are differences in *style*; neither approach is intrinsically superior to the other but each fits a particular set of circumstances. Cognitive style influences the manner is which the reflective mind operates, the kinds of external threats and opportunities it will "allow" automatic mind to pursue, those it will intervene to block and supersede.

Second, there are individual differences in what Stanovich (2009, p. 12) refers to as dysrationalia, the tendency of "intelligent people taking injudicious actions or holding unjustified beliefs." The fact that he specifies that the people he is speaking of have a high cognitive level indicates that this is principally a problem of cognitive style. One way dysrationalia manifests is in *cognitive miserliness*: in solving a problem, one may be faced with a choice between two sorts of mental process, one of which entails giving in to the automatic mind while the other entails engaging the algorithmic mind. The first option is relatively easy but the second means adopting a more computationally demanding and therefore cognitively costly procedure. The automatic temptation can be to select the less computationally demanding of these two kinds of mental processing. This puts a block on fully disjunctive reasoning; in other words, it precludes consideration of the entire range of possibilities before a conclusion is decided upon. Another problem of dysrationalia in the form of cognitive miserliness is showing *my-side bias*, which means approach a problem from one's personal perspective, as a result of which the decision maker works with an incomplete view of the nature of the problem and its solution. Cognitive miserliness involves a problem of process, a preference for selecting and using the cognitively more economical (at least in the short term) of two modes of intellectual functioning.

Stanovich (2009) speaks also of a source of dysrationalia that constitutes a problem of content: people exhibit *mindware gaps*, that is, they do not possess the specific knowledge, rules, and strategies required to think rationally. Mindware refers to things that need to be retrieved from memory to solve problems such as the ability to understand logic, risk, and scientific inference. This reflects more a problem of cognitive level than style. Many aspects of mindware require the ability to think at a high and abstract level and this entails on the part of some humans an inability to learn the principles involved. Simply choosing not to engage with the modes of thought necessary to conceptualize problems at a highly abstract level reflects a miserly approach to intellectualizing, a style of reasoning that results from surrendering to the pathways of automatic mind. But being unable to acquire the tools necessary for reasoning is a problem of level, which affects the content of mental operations.

Finally, there are individual differences in neurophysiological balance. General imbalance between impulsive system and executive system leads to steep temporal discounting; this is again linked to neurophysiological issues: hyperactivity of limbic and paralimbic systems compare with the hypoactivity of the PFC.[2] One of the reasons the analytic mind fails to inaugurate override and to instigate cognitive rehearsal and judgment can be that the neurophysiological effects of near-missing are those that should accompany winning, not losing. These neurophysiological outcomes are rewarding in themselves and encourage excessive behavior patterns. This is at the heart of what Stanovich and West (2003a) say about Brakel and Shevrin's idea that the primary processes and secondary processes are respectively equivalent to S1 and S2. S1 is neither rational nor irrational (a-rational?) and S2 is not entirely rational either.

Rationality revisited

Levels of analysis

The nature of rationality is a question of what level of exposition one adopts. At the personal level, *instrumental rationality* is a property of the individual (or, perhaps more precisely, the individual's behavior) and consists in behavior that strives toward utility maximization bounded by the goals, beliefs, and resources (e.g., Stanovich & West, 2003b).[3] Stanovich and West (2003b) contrast this with *adaptive optimization*, which is a strategy of maximization pursued at the level of the genes. They point out that Dawkins (e.g., 1976, 1982) distinguishes optimization processes of the replicators (genes) from instrumental rationality that involve the utility maximization of the vehicle (the organism that carries the genes). The key conclusion is that evolutionary adaptation does not necessarily lead to instrumental rationality, which is concerned with the goals of the organism as a whole.

Hence, while the S1 system is the repository of content-specific modules that are directed toward satisfying the interests of the genes in phylogenetic history (e.g., desire for sweet foods), S2 involves content-independent reasoning, on a long leash, in order to accommodate novelty and uncertainty (e.g., whether a previously unencountered sweet food might be minimally detrimental to health even in large amounts). Individuals differ in the effectiveness of their System 2 in overriding the demands of S1. Overriding of this kind can be rational for the organism as a whole (i.e., at the personal level of exposition) but not necessarily for the genes. This is the basis of the distinction between evolutionary rationality, which is concerned with the interests of the sub-personal replicators, and instrumental rationality, which is concerned with the wellbeing of the personal-level organism. This is the source of Stanovich and West's (2003b) criticism of evolutionary psychologists who concentrate solely on the former.

Mindware

Knowledge required for rational thought is that which can be brought to bear on the task of transforming decoupled representations – it is *mindware* (Perkins, 1995). Mindware that can be drawn upon in the course of cognitive simulation results partially from prior learning and this has the implication that the ability to imagine ways of improving on the responses that the TASS would bring about will differ from person to person. Information or rules that overcome TASS-inspired responses must have been previously learned. If mindware does not exist for the purpose of overcoming TASS responses, the failure is that of not having acquired the right mindware rather than with the TASS override system – a distinction that Stanovich and West present as the start of a taxonomy of causes of cognitive failure.

Cognitive miserliness

Three of the rationality problems refer to *cognitive miserliness*. The first, *response automaticity*, is a source of cognitive economizing that leads the individual to immediately select a solution to a problem that has become habituated in the autonomous mind, a handy approach that has worked in the past. The individual automatically selects a response formulated by the autonomous mind (this entails no Type 2 activity, and is therefore a shallow reaction, requiring least cognitive engagement, the most miserly option: not an override failure). It is worth noting here that this pattern of response becomes more probable through operant conditioning as familiar patterns of behavior are increasingly supported by characteristic patterns of behavior and as emotionally-based modularity encourages automaticity of response to frequently encountered stimulus fields.

The second, *serial associative cognition with focal bias*, over-economizes on Type 2 processing, and fails to engender a comprehensive simulation of alternative actions or to engage fully in disjunctive reasoning. Type 2 processing typically involves cognitive simulation that takes place once decoupling has been resolutely achieved. In this context, it is possible to propose alternative futures to oneself which can then be comprehensively examined in a style marked by slow serial cognition. However, while hypothetical thinking of this kind always involves the analytic mind, some Type 2 processes are not of this kind (Stanovish, 2009, pp. 62–63).

The third, *override failure*, is the least miserly option because cognitive decoupling is undertaken. Type 2 activity attempts to inhibit Type 1 processes but fails. Cognitive decoupling occurs but cannot overcome the Type 1 activity. This is characteristic of impulsivity (akrasia, breakdown of will, or the conflict of competing short-range and long-range interests (Ainslie, 1992) in which the short-range triumphs). Although the expected operations of the analytic mind occur, they are insufficient to overcome the promptings of the activities of the autonomous mind: even though the reflective mind initiates override and decoupling and, even though the algo-rithmic mind brings the process of decoupling in some degree, this is not capable of preventing the autonomous mind carrying through its computation processes and inaugurating the usual response(s). This can account for the failure of the rea-soning processes of the analytic mind, which make clear the advantages of patience and self-control, considerations that are not allowed to inhibit impulsivity. It also accounts for the recalcitrance that enables emotional and other perceptual reactions to outweigh rational judgment: far from demonstrating that such perceptions are cognition-free, this understanding only adds to the conclusion that they are cogni-tively penetrated.

Mindware problems

The next two kinds of rational thinking error relate to *mindware problems*. The first, *mindware gaps*, refers to the absence of the rules and strategies required for ratio-nal thought. Knowledge of how to reason with respect to probability, or causality, logically, and according to the insights of scientific method (e.g., the inclusion of alternative hypotheses and their comparative evaluation), and access to reasoned folk psychology is necessary in order to avoid irrational thinking and conclusions. Simulation depends highly on these procedures. Problem gambling is especially associated with missing mindware – awareness of the implications of probability and the nature of risk, as well as the skills required to cope with these in practical situations. Note that some of these reflect cognitive level and cognitive omission but several involve cognitive style – e.g., consideration of competing paradigms in scientific reasoning, an intellectual procedure which is more probable for innova-tors than adaptors. The second, *mindware contamination*, is the problem of *mis*infor-mation which can lead to irrational reasoning and the drawing of unsupported conclusions. The gambler's fallacy is an obvious example.

A psychoanalytic dimension

Turning now to a considering of psychological rationality in psychoanalytical terms, we note Brakel's argument that human developmental may be portrayed as a two-stage process in which fantasizing is the initial stage in "the development of propositional attitudes with truly representational, referring mental content"

(2001, p. 371). This development is presumably by virtue of the acquisition of what Stanovich calls mindware and the ability to overcome cognitive miserliness. Brakel (2002), we have seen, points out that fantasizing has no need of reality testing, temporal integrity, or consonance. It is a-rational, i.e., prior to these mental processes. None of this is true of the other propositional attitudes which Brakel (2009) identifies and we met in Chapter 5 (and which are summarized for reference, along with fantasizing and neurotic beliefs, in Table 6.1), which are rational in that they are reality-testable, temporally cohesive, and non-contradictory. Even pretending and imagining belong to the second stage of development which entails the capacity to distinguish between situations that actually exist and those that exist only as

TABLE 6.1 Characteristics of mental processes/propositional attitudes in relation to world-reality and psychic-reality testing

Mental process/ propositional attitude	Style of reality testing
Belief-proper	World-reality testing, temporal consonance, non-contradiction. Objective (or inter-subjective) empirical appraisal with replicability and potential falsification of results. Psychic-reality testing plays no part in the establishment and evaluation of beliefs-proper.
Fantasizing	Fantasizing is founded upon primary process mentation which eschews world-reality testing, temporal consonance, and avoidance of internal and external contradictions. Its parameters are provided by psychic-reality, the world as it is subjectively fancied, distorted and recreated, by untrammelled conjecturing. As such, it is the source of fantastic notions about how the world should and does work which are impervious to real-world testing and its conclusions.
Hypothesizing	Hypothesizing is actually a central component of world-reality testing. There is a conscious awareness that the hypothesizer is seeking to establish the viability of propositions, if acted upon, in real-world circumstances. Beyond the contemplative components of supposing, hypothesizing is focused on the establishment of whether a course of action measures up to the truth conditions of how the world works. Secondary process mentation is integral to hypothesizing.
Imagining	Portraying and examining events that have, as yet, no or little real-world significance for the individual but which may be included in her repertoire of actions. Requires ability to suspend incredulity in order to undertake thought experiments that may bear little or no correspondence to world-reality but which can provide lessons that will be instrumental in evaluating alternatives and selecting effective action. World-reality testing is temporarily suspended but not abandoned; it remains the ultimate authority for action. Secondary process mentation is, once more, central.

TABLE 6.1 (*cont.*)

Mental process / propositional attitude	Style of reality testing
Neurotic beliefs	The psychic-reality of fantasy gives rise not only to conjectured notions but also to the means of comparing them to reality. However, it is an internally-conceived reality that engenders false "evidence" to support its quasi-propositions. A fantasy *plus* this spurious evidence constitute a neurotic belief. However, to the person holding it, this neurotic belief appears to be a belief-proper and is equally likely to evoke action consistent with it.
Pretending	Acting as though something is the case while being aware that it is not. Ability to suspend incredulity in order to take on a role that is entirely supposititious but that is instrumental in achieving short-term goals (e.g., having fun) and/or clarifying options for future action. In the latter case, world-reality testing may be consciously on hold but will provide the ultimate means of judging how to act. Secondary process mentation is, therefore, at the heart of pretending.
Supposing	More than imagining in general, more abstract terms, supposing involves active involvement in a possible future situation and the consequences of so acting. It involves the capacity to quarantine the supposed reality from what actually obtains in the individual's life. World-reality testing remains supreme. Secondary process mentation is the essence of supposing.

mental artifacts. This secondary processing allows the individual to compare and contrast these two kinds of situation whilst maintaining their separation in place and time. Avoiding the immediately available S1-inspired responses and formulating courses of action which promise longer-term advantageous consequences rests on the capacity to make and maintain this kind of distinction. Earlier chapters emphasized the reliance of normal social and psychological functioning on an ability to distinguish among extensional and intentional sentences in relation to their capacity for reality testing against criteria provided by the real world. Here, I emphasize the necessity of being able to appreciate the kinds of truth value that various intentional sentences, expressed as propositional attitudes, have. Hence, it is also important that those who imagine and pretend can be aware that what they are indulging in mentally is not the devising and holding of beliefs-proper but a form of cognitive rehearsal that will at some stage have to make contact with situations that actually obtain and/or can be brought about through action. Failure to accomplish this switch, to decouple from the world in which one lives in order to mentally pursue and evaluate alternative courses of action and then to return to the real world in which one acts, invites the enactment of maladaptive rather than successful action. And such a pattern of responding invites the label of psychological a-rationality. As Brakel (2001, pp. 371–372) puts it,

The awareness that one is supposing X to be true rather than having the belief-proper that X is true is a necessary condition for supposition. It allows the supposer, a thinker fully capable of ordinary reality testing, to circumvent the usual tests of the matches between world and propositional truth conditions and, due to some goal more pressing than truth assessment, provisionally ascribe truth to an untested proposition. Hypothesizing requires at least as much cognitive sophistication as does supposing. This is so with respect to differentiating the various propositional attitude types and with respect to matching truth conditions of propositions with states of affairs in the world. Unlike all the other propositional attitude types examined, only hypothesizing shares with holding beliefs-proper the goal of aiming at the truth. When a proposition is hypothesized-true from the hypothesizer's viewpoint, however, more tests need to be applied before the proposition can be held as a belief-proper and believed-true.

Action revisited

These ideas link closely with the themes that have been pursued in this book. When we seek to answer the question what action is, we must take into account these capacities for the creative imagination of the contingencies of reinforcement and punishment but we must also recognize the capacity inherent in action to determine what contingencies one will *create* rather than merely accept, what contingencies one will be subject to, with what contingencies one will with others collectively fashion the social world that will shape human activity. It is conscious awareness of the short-range and long-range interests that are strategically active within one's psyche and that the choice between them is up to the individual concerned. All of these considerations, which stem from macro- and meso- as well as micro-cognitive psychology (Foxall, 2016a), are inherent in the concept of contingency-representation. This rational picture of the consumer whose thoughts and actions are consonant with mature secondary process mentation is not at the heart of the extreme consumer activities with which we are concerned. It is subject to the proclivities wrought by problems of cognitive miserliness and mindware gaps. It is less costly from a cognitive point of view to choose conscious or unconscious fantasizing rather than pretending, imagining, supposing, or best of all hypothesizing as the prelude to the rational pursuit of beliefs-proper. It is also the case that there are divisive individual differences in the mindware contents and skills that this pursuit demands. Above all, the subjective evaluation of one's fantasies as propositional attitudes that are beliefs-proper is inimical to decision making that is in line with one's long-term interests.

Brakel (2001, p. 374) also points out that "beliefs-proper, unlike phantasies, must be separable from desires and wishes." The continued existence of beliefs-proper depends on how the world is arranged, irrespective of what an individual wishes were the case. Beliefs-proper are concerned with the actual probabilities of winning a game of chance, for instance. They may be erroneous, as when a player believes there is a one in ten chance of winning when in fact the gambling machine is engineered to pay out on only one in a hundred plays. The point about beliefs-proper is that they are corrigible on the basis of comparison of their content with the prevailing contingencies. Fantasies, on the other hand, can coexist with wishes. A gambler's fantasy that, having suffered a protracted series of losses, she is due a large payout is consistent with her desire or wish to win a large sum of money, even though it is not consonant with the actual probabilities governing the game. The gambler who maintains contact with the real-world probabilities on which a game is predicated must possess a certain resilience which enables the maintenance of rationality in the face of strong desire. As Brakel (ibid) puts it,

> To be capable of having those cognitive propositional states (i.e., beliefs-proper) that are entirely separate from conative prepositional states (i.e., wishes and desires), it is required that secondary process mediated reality testing has developed sufficient stability that it will be maintained even under the pressures of primary process wishes to override it.

In the terminology of tripartite cognitive theory, the individual requires the cognitive abilities to maintain a detached view of present and future contingencies that allows a rational appraisal of the situation that governs the chance of winning; this in turn depends on the capacity to engender decoupling from the scenario presented by the TASS to the effect that a win has become highly probable. This is likely based on a contingency-representation that is based on high levels of PAD as a result of being in the gambling situation (defined by the utilitarian and informational reinforcement presently available, the scope of the setting, and her relevant learning history). This emotional response must be tempered by a representation of the actual chances of winning or losing, and of the wider consequences of the more probable of these outcomes, namely loss. These must be evaluated cognitively but also emotionally as the rational depiction of the loss first of a serious amount of money and subsequently possibly of friends, home, spouse, employment, and so on are contemplated. These need not all be examined thoroughly in terms of rational decision-making processes; the relevant beliefs may already exist and these can guide the rapid evaluation of the situation in terms of PAD, leading to a consistent action tendency. These emotional representations of the current and future situations are contingency-representations.

Neurotic beliefs often act together with wishes/desires – are in fact subject to them. Sometimes there seems to be a wish to obliterate an unsuccessful past and this is coupled with the neurotic belief that there is a higher probability of success now, somehow *because of* previous failure. There may also be a neurotic tendency to blame oneself for having lost, coupled with the wished-for possibility of making amends by winning in the future, thereby gaining self-esteem, emotional (P+A+D+) reward, prefigured by a contingency-representation of this pattern of emotion. The wish and the neurotic belief are self-reinforcing conative influences. This brings us nicely to action.

As compared to fantasies, beliefs-proper must be reality-tested, which entails that three requirements be met (see Brakel, 2001, p. 376). First, beliefs-proper must be truth-assessed by reference to the state of the world (reality testing). Second, they must be correctly typed as a belief-proper. Now this is interesting in that it means that the actor must know her way around the propositional attitudes and be able to classify beliefs-proper correctly. The import of this is, as I have proposed in an earlier exposition (Foxall, 2016b), that the intensionality is necessary for agency. Fantasies may be experienced as fantasies or not, i.e., one may be consciously aware that one is fantasizing or not have this awareness. At this point, I should like to raise the question of whether, in the latter case, one can be said to be an agent when acting on the fantasy. Is the fact that, in this case, one's actions are not constrained by reality sufficient to withhold the ascription of agency? This is an issue to which we shall return. Third, beliefs-proper must be capable of being judged independently of desires or wishes.

Neurotic beliefs are not beliefs-proper but "fantasies +" the addition sign signifying that the "evidence" for the fantasy is based not on real-world derived criteria for belief but on "psychic-reality testing" in which fantasized reasons are adduced for the belief. Nevertheless, this information is used as a basis for action just as surely as if it had been generated through genuine reality-testing procedures (Brakel, 2001, p. 376). Crucially, the content of neurotic beliefs is similar to that of primary process-based fantasies and, on a subjective level, they are experienced as beliefs-proper. The difference is that beliefs-proper are founded on genuine empirical knowledge of the world (this is a pragmatic criterion) while neurotic beliefs are assumed to have been supported by a line of reasoning that actually has no empirical basis. The individual has come to recognize that convention requires that reasons have to be given for one's beliefs, especially if they are to be acted upon. But she fails to realize the nature of the reasoning that has to be employed: that it requires testing beliefs against objective reality as opposed to subjective (psychic) surmise even though this has the form of a rational argument. That pathological gamblers can find so many "reasons" for their behavior (near-miss, skill, entrapment, etc.) suggests they are capable of appreciating the necessary *form* of a logical argument: what they lack is the mindware to appreciate the *actual* form of a genuine argument in which there is proper correspondence between the content of the belief and the nature of the world. Or, if they can detect the form of a proper argument, they may lack the intellectual skills to put one together – possibly because of the emotional context of their actions.

The pathological gambler's neurotic beliefs become problematic when they influence her actions, leading to the psychological irrationality that is a symptom of addiction. Especially if she is unaware that the fantasies on the basis of which her actions occur belong to this kind of propositional attitude, the result is likely to be actions that are severely punished by the contingencies.

This raises the question of whether we can properly speak of activity that is inspired by neurotic beliefs as *action*. If by action is meant consciously purposive activity, then presumably the answer is affirmative, and this is especially so if we specify that transitive activity is meant (i.e., activity$_T$). If by action one means activity caused by or a function of one's desires and beliefs or other propositional attitudes or that can be explained only by reference to propositional attitudes,[4] then the response is again positive: we are undoubtedly speaking of action. A related question is whether we are justified in ascribing agency to the individual who acts on the basis of neurotic beliefs. Action implies an attribution of causation, or minimally the inability to render their activity intelligible without employing the language of intentionality. But if the essence of agency is the capacity to appreciate the intensionality of sentences – to type sentences as beliefs-proper or fantasies/neurotic beliefs – then are we justified in referring to the person who acts on neurotic beliefs as an agent? The import of so referring is surely that the individual is responsible for the actions she takes on the basis of holding such beliefs. On this basis, neurotic belief-inspired action is attributable to a kind of agent, not someone who acts simply under a misapprehension but who either is incapable of distinguishing fantasy from beliefs-proper or unwilling to do so. That the beliefs on which her actions are founded are misrepresentations does not render them agent-less in one sense for she is still acting consciously on the knowledge acquired through a process of testing mental propositions, albeit fantastical ones. But insofar as she is incapable of detecting the fantasized basis of her beliefs and the spurious nature of the psychic-reality testing by which they are supported – or unwilling to do so – she cannot be accounted a fully rational agent. To be capable of reasoning intensionally is a prerequisite of such comprehensive psychological rationality. The one who is *incapable* of so reasoning is not acting with psychological *ir*rationality, i.e., a willful turning aside from the standards of rationality, but acts a-rationally, i.e., in a pre-rational manner.

I have noted that addiction defies a single-sentence definition but that it is likely to include (i) the preference reversal in terms of which akrasia may be (perhaps somewhat loosely) understood, possibly to the extent of (ii) demonstrating economic irrationality to a degree that leads to (iii) the loss of important components of one's lifestyle such as friends, spouse, home, and job; finally, the maladaptive behavior involved may be (iv) exacerbated by neurophysiological excess (see, for instance, Foxall, 2016a; Ross et al., 2008). To these characteristics of addiction we can now add the possibility that it is also likely to be psychological a-rationality insofar as it is based on neurotic beliefs (fantasies +), aided and abetted by wishes/desires, none of which are reality-tested, temporally insensitive other than to a tenseless present, and self-contradictory or inconsonant with other beliefs. This is to say that it involves a degree of primary process mentation that is insufficiently countered by genuine secondary processing to make possible a pattern of action that is reliably related to the world of actuality. This somewhat extreme situation is a far cry from the consumer actions that compose most of the Continuum of Consumer Choice but insofar as consumer action can be described as more or less akratic, defined in terms of preference reversal, it may enter into the explanation of a considerable range of consumption activities.

We can now summarize in greater depth the requirements for the ascription of beliefs-proper (Brakel, 2001, p. 377). Our distinguishing beliefs-proper, though not fantasies, from wishes and desires goes hand in hand with the establishment of what Brakel calls a "special relationship between beliefs-proper and actions." Both rely on the two elements of reality testing: (i) "matching propositional truth conditions with world conditions" and (ii) "properly ascribing mental content to its cognitive state type" (ibid). Brakel also reiterates that (iii) the holding or relinquishment of beliefs-proper must be carried out independently of wishes/desires, and points out that, (iv) because they are bound by these three conditions, beliefs-proper are peculiarly related to actions. Incidentally, much of what Brakel says about beliefs-proper applies also to veridical perceptions.

Although dream-beliefs, neurotic beliefs, and "the unconscious contents of the multilevel, multidetermined, complex central phantasies contributing to those neurotic beliefs are all quite different from beliefs-proper," they are all experienced and acted upon as though they were beliefs-proper.

Humans have a tendency to assume that their conscious cognitive states (perceptions, beliefs, memory, imaginations, etc.) are less influenced by their conative states than is the case. They are also apt to mis-categorize waking fantasy states (including the fantasy+ states that have been described here as neurotic beliefs) as beliefs-proper. This is important because beliefs-proper alone among the propositional attitudes have a strong influence on the selection and determination of actions which are effective encounters with the world. Therefore, when humans commit the category mistake of attributing beliefhood-proper to fantasies and neurotic beliefs, the actions they perform in the expectation of their being fully effective are all the more likely to result in suboptimal outcomes.

Cognitive rehearsal requires the mental ability to decouple from world-reality testing in order to explore possibilities for future action and their probable outcomes, to compare and contrast these, and to select the one that promises most to fulfill the decision maker's goals. It also requires the intellectual capacity to maintain this decoupling as the scenarios contemplated become more complex, more similar in some respects to the decision maker's actual situation in the world, pressing demands to make a decision or choose an action or simply to *do something*.

The necessity of cognitive interpretation

The dependence of the conative, cognitive, and affective contingency-representation which was the subject of Chapter 5 on the kinds of cognitive apparatus and operation that have been reviewed in this chapter seems evident: the development of beliefs-proper relies heavily on the rational execution of the tasks allotted to the analytic mind; the development of fantasies and their related neurotic beliefs depends on the mindware deficits and cognitive miserliness which the tripartite theory accommodates; the failure to distinguish or type these propositional attitudes accurately is similarly more easily understood in the context of an analytic mind that has these characteristics.

It seems unlikely that the comparative evaluative function of the scenarios generated in the process of pragmatic mental imagery could take place without some of the provisions of tripartite theory, namely, the capacity for decoupling of current concerns and realities so that cognitive rehearsal can proceed. A reasonable resting place for the debate over the relative capacities of perceptual and cognitive processes to explain action is that they coexist in symbiotic relationship. For example, the outputs of cognitive processing inform perception, active not least in the production of action-properties, while the outcomes of perceptually-inspired action in turn modify the goals and operations of mental processing. In addition, the various perceptual processes we have discussed are mutually influential: pragmatic mental imagery requires both contingency-representation, i.e., a means of representing the probable outcomes of behavior and their comparative evaluation, and a common currency in which the probable outcomes of future behavior can be portrayed and for the decisive comparison to take place.

Specifically, the beliefs that can control neurotic behavior that we have identified in connexion with slot machine gambling all depend on mindware gaps and contamination, often in a way that leads to exaggerated valuation of the reinforcement thought to be contingent on acting sooner rather than later and thus contingency-representations that predict a highly attractive pattern of emotion. The *gambler's fallacy* – the belief the odds must imminently change – works because the player believes that, since both winning and losing outcomes are possible, a run of losses must portend a win. The odds remain identical from play to play, however. This fallacy is based on a mixture of mindware gaps, the lack of knowledge or understanding of risk and probability, and mindware contamination, the misinformation that the outcomes of an individual's play are bound to "average out" in some way that means their luck is bound to change from time to time. Continued play is therefore made more likely. This belief influences the anticipated pattern of emotion for further gambling, a contingency-representation that presents utilitarian and informational reinforcement as highly probable. This contingency-representation is responsible for response automaticity.

Even if an individual possesses sufficient mindware resources to understand risk and probability, she may still succumb to impulsivity if gambler's fallacy beliefs based on misinformation are held and influence choice at an emotional level. In this case, the operation of Type 2 processes may not be decisive enough to guarantee a cessation in playing. Although decoupling may commence, there may be overwhelming pressure on the process of sustained decoupled cognitive simulation to permit the cool consideration of available behaviors and their probable outcomes because of interjections from Type 1 processes that constantly raise the likelihood of a win on the next play. This makes it easier for the player to succumb to habitual responding without the interference of internalized self-criticism that would urge caution.

A similar broad pattern is apparent in the case of the "near-miss" fallacy where mindware gaps in the form of a lack of requisite knowledge or reasoning skills and mindware contamination in the form of acceptance of false information act as stimuli for response automaticity. The perception of the sights and sounds that accompany two identical symbols gives rise to the interpretation that these are signs of winning. The outcome of this is the belief that one is doing well and likely to gain three identical symbols. The contingency-representations that predict this behavior promise an attractive pattern of emotion contingent on further playing. This is responsible for response automaticity.

The belief that a near-miss is a signal that an outright win is more probable is sustained by the notion that it indicates that one's skill at the game is increasing. Skill at games of ability such as archery can result in the achievement of performances that increasingly approximate an outright win. Scoring several hits that narrowly miss the bull's eye after a period of being unable to hit the target at all can therefore signal that one is getting better. But there is no analogy here for games of chance. Apparently "just failing" in games that depend on probabilities over which one has no control is no evidence whatever for the idea that one is gaining expertise. There is a fixed probability of scoring two identical symbols which is entirely independent of how skillful one may be; there is another fixed probability of scoring three such symbols (and a prize) which is independent of both skill and the number of times one has scored a so-called near-miss.

Belief that the near-miss reveals skill acquisition therefore reflects at least one mindware gap, to the extent that the player who entertains it fails to appreciate risk and probability, and at least one kind of mindware contamination to the effect that games of chance are like games of personal ability in that one can improve one's performance in both through skill acquisition. Given these, the visual and auditory signaling that accompanies scoring two identical symbols can be interpreted as getting better at the game and thus justifying continued play. The contingency-representation of the anticipated pattern of reinforcement that will accompany future play is also likely to enhance response automaticity.

The entrapment fallacy is akin to what economists call the sunk cost fallacy: having invested so much in a project that looks increasingly unlikely to pay off, it is worth investing more rather than losing one's outlay to date. Similarly, having played a game of chance for so long that one has spent a large amount, it is apparently foolish to stop playing because one thereby imagines that that would be to lose the "investment" already made. The mindware gap here takes the form of failure to appreciate that, if the investment already incurred is incapable of proving profitable, nothing is to be gained by adding to it. In the case of gambling, the odds against winning are not changed by one's having incurred a large outlay already. The false belief that one stands a greater chance of capitalizing on foregone

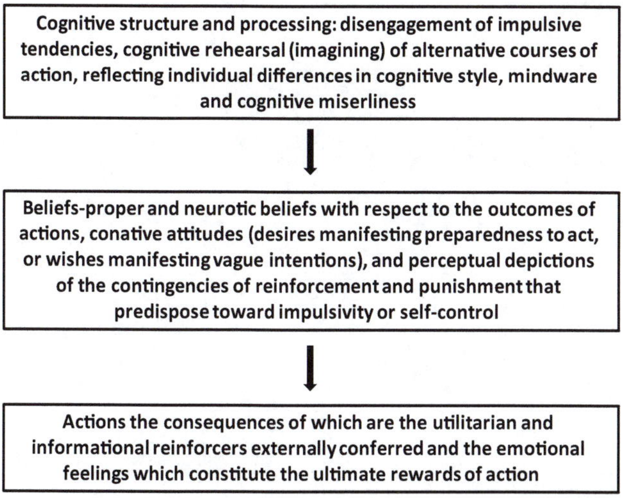

Cognitive structure and processing: disengagement of impulsive tendencies, cognitive rehearsal (imagining) of alternative courses of action, reflecting individual differences in cognitive style, mindware and cognitive miserliness

↓

Beliefs-proper and neurotic beliefs with respect to the outcomes of actions, conative attitudes (desires manifesting preparedness to act, or wishes manifesting vague intentions), and perceptual depictions of the contingencies of reinforcement and punishment that predispose toward impulsivity or self-control

↓

Actions the consequences of which are the utilitarian and informational reinforcers externally conferred and the emotional feelings which constitute the ultimate rewards of action

FIGURE 6.2 **Cognitive interpretation, intentional interpretation, and action.**

uneconomical speculation by increasing one's outlay bears no relation to the probability of winning.

In summary, the posited sequence for understanding what makes action action is shown in Figure 6.2.

Notes

1 One possibility is to relate them to cognitive style and cognitive level, respectively.
2 For further detail, see Foxall (2016a).
3 Note, however, that these authors omit resources.
4 This last being the standpoint from which I write.

7

BEHAVIOR, ACTION, AGENCY

Abstract

The preceding argument is based on the view that what transforms consumer activity into consumer choice is the temporal conflict between purchasing or consuming immediately and deferring these pleasures. Consumer choices form a spectrum from everyday purchasing which is minimally consequential to compulsive and addictive consumption that generates far more serious outcomes. Everyday shopping usually entails minor conflict but addiction is an example of a more major struggle. The book has sought to link *context*, conceived in terms of the pattern of rewards and sanctions that consumption occasions, and *cognition*, the consumer's conception of these outcomes, via the *intentional consumer-situation* which is the immediate precursor of consumer choice. The exposition has been directed toward the conceptual elaboration of this concept: by viewing consumer choice as action rather than behavior, by exploring the role of psychological rationality in consumer decision making, by initiating and applying the concept of perceptual contingency-representation as a central component of consumer-situation, and by expanding the personal level of exposition, that concerned with the subjective experience of the consumer. This concluding chapter summarizes the argument and considers a broader perspective.

Introduction

The argument pursued in preceding chapters is based on the view that what transforms consumer activity into consumer choice is the temporal conflict between purchasing or consuming immediately and deferring these pleasures. Consumer choices form a spectrum from everyday purchasing which is minimally consequential to compulsive and addictive consumption that generates far more serious outcomes. Everyday shopping usually entails minor conflict but addiction is an example of a more major struggle. It is time to summarize and point to future avenues of theorization.

General summary

The Behavioral Perspective Model (BPM) is involved in all three stages of the Intentional Behaviorism research strategy, assuming extensional and intentional perspectives as required by, first, theoretical minimalism, a stage which eschews intentional language such as "desiring" and "believing," and, second, psychological explanation which entails the formulation and critical evaluation of an intentional consumer-situation in order to explain consumer action by reference to desires, beliefs, emotions, and perceptions. In both cases, the heart of the model is the consumer-situation, which, as the immediate precursor of consumer behavior and consumer action, links the stimuli that comprise the current consumer behavior setting with the elements of consumer experience of which current behavior is a function.

In the extensional model of consumer behavior, the consumer-situation is conceptualized as the interaction between (a) the discriminative stimuli and motivating operations that make up the physical and social setting and (b) the consumer's learning history, the sum total of previous relevant behaviors and their reinforcing and punishing outcomes. The consumer-situation is, more specifically, that which links the present stimulus field and the consumer's learning history. In the pursuit of theoretical minimalism, the consumer-situation is an entirely extensional device concerned only to predict consumer choice on the basis of an approach that is as close as possible to a natural behavioral science of consumption. The extensional BPM is concerned with how this extensional consumer-situation links the consumer's stimulus field and her learning history. In such a model, the consumer-situation can be understood simply as the interaction of its two elements as each primes the other for behavior: *consumer behavior setting x learning history*. This means that, in practice, learning history often is ignored because there is no way to access it and present it in operational terms. It consists largely of the discriminative stimuli that are relevant to the attainment of utilitarian and informational reinforcement contingent on the performance of particular consumer behaviors. Learning history can be ascribed in general terms: for example, the experiences likely to have been the lot of a 50-year-old male consumer in an affluent marketing-oriented economy who is seeking a birthday gift for his partner can be imagined in an informed manner to produce a generalized history of consumption with respect to this task. But there is often no way in which the specifics of such a history and the ways in which it precisely invests the stimuli that compose the consumer's physical and social setting with the capacity to endanger discriminative behavior can be ascertained. But the extensional model has, nevertheless, proved invaluable as a means of exploring aspects of consumer choice not accessible to other methodologies. The consumer-situation in this theoretically minimal model is sufficiently specifiable in measurable extensional terms, and, even though there may be difficulties in realizing this fully, it has proven a valuable means of conceptualizing, measuring, and predicting consumer choice (Foxall, 2017).

The extensional consumer-situation is something that exists only for the investigator who is attempting to predict the behavior of an organism, comprising as it does a log of the organism's prior behavior and its outcomes and an understanding of the stimulus field that constitutes the current behavior setting. No attention is accorded, within the confines of radical behaviorism, the question of *where* the learning history inheres or how the organism *perceives* the stimulus field. This is illustrated in the upper part of Figure 2.5. It is not that the investigator is unaware of the possibility that the organism has some kind of experience of the contingencies of reinforcement and punishment: only that this understanding does not enter into the investigator's paradigm.

In the intentional perspective, the consumer-situation comprises the intentionality of the consumer, her desires, beliefs, emotions, and perceptions with respect to previous consumption and potential consumption. In the process of intentional interpretation in which the intentional consumer-situation is reconstructed, the consumer-situation is composed of (a) the contingency-representations that are the immediate perceptual antecedents of action, and (b) the sustaining beliefs that lead to the interpretations that guide the formation and conative tendencies of these perceptions (i.e., the conative tendencies to which they can lead). The task of constructing an intentional interpretation of consumer choice is to explore how the intentional consumer-situation links the consumer's stimulus field and her learning history, which now is conceived in terms of her intentionality. The elements of the three-term contingency now become the intentional objects of the consumer's mentation. The intentional consumer-situation is therefore concerned with how the consumer represents the world of contingencies.

This raises questions such as how contingencies of reinforcement and punishment can be mentally represented, the nature of perception, and its intentionality. Earlier chapters answered these questions through the formulation of the concept of *contingency-representation*, and doing so in two ways. The first is through consideration of what intentional representation itself is, as this has been discussed by philosophers of mind such as Dretske (1988). The second is through the work of another philosopher, Bence Nanay (2013a), who has considered in some depth the role of perception in the determination of action. Although I disagree with his analysis on several points, it is an exemplar of how to approach the search for the unique contribution of perception to the explanation of action because it is skeptical of the widespread explanations in terms of desires and beliefs which dominate philosophical discussion in this area and which have been at the heart of the Intentional Behaviorism research program. There are in fact three reasons for considering Nanay's approach: first, as a critical standpoint from which to appraise earlier work on the intentional-contextual explanation of consumer choice in which cognitive decision making has assumed a central explicatory role; second, as a guide to the way in which the perceptual approach to explaining consumer choice that

I take in this volume can be comparatively evaluated; and, third, because Nanay proposes a means by which the predictive capacity of the second stage of Intentional Behaviorism, namely, the account of consumer choice as a function of the intentional consumer-situation, can be assessed.

Although contingency-representation has cognitive and conative dimensions, it is the affective which provides the most immediate, perceptual precursor of action. In order for emotions to be considered contingency-representations, it is necessary that there are sound reasons for their being perceptual and for believing them to be systematically related to the contingencies of reinforcement. Chapter 5 examined the evidence for these claims, concluding that contingency-representation inheres in emotional responses to the environments of purchase and consumption. But contingency-representations, in the form of emotional responses, are not the sole components of the intentional consumer-situation which also includes the beliefs that would be necessary to sustain both the emotional responses themselves and the overt behaviors that follow from them. In the case of the more extreme consumer action under consideration, many of these beliefs are a-rational rather than rational and may even border on the fantastical.

A further important dimension to the intentional consumer-situation that derives from its place in the explanatory scheme proposed by Intentional Behaviorism is the intentional consumer-situation, which describes the intentionality of the consumer who is viewed as an idealized intentional system, a rational maximizer of utilitarian and informational reinforcement subject to her budgetary constraint. This idealized view has to be (i) tested in terms of its predictive capacity and, if it is successful, (ii) cashed out in terms of a framework of cognitive functioning that is shown empirically to generate the kinds of intentionality on which the intentional consumer-situation trades. The predictive capacity of the model is examined via straightforward predictions of consumer action, though these are likely to be highly generalized (Foxall, 2016b). The intentional consumer-situation is primarily concerned with the perceptual and emotional experience of the consumer. But since Intentional Behaviorism accepts that perception is cognitively penetrated, the specific beliefs that influence perception itself also form a part of the intentional consumer-situation.

Emotions are candidates for contingency-representations because they are (a) perceptions of past and present contingencies of reinforcement and punishment that can influence action by activating desires and other conative processes, (b) systematically related to the contingencies of reinforcement in terms of which consumer-situations are conceptualized, and (c) immediate precursors of actions that are appropriate to the contingencies of reinforcement that they represent. Moreover, (c) is empirically demonstrable in terms of success semantics. This understanding is integrative of the whole thesis put forward here insofar as it suggests that we can use the extensional model to work out the pattern of reinforcement the consumer receives, and on this basis determine the pattern of emotion that is the ultimate reward of her consumer-action. The perception we can ascribe in this way can be critically examined according to whether the consumer's action based thereupon is successful. If this is accomplished, the final stage, which critically examines the intentional interpretation by reference to extant empirically justified models of cognitive structure and functioning, can be undertaken.

The cognitive interpretation links context and cognition by detailing the ways in which the beliefs that comprise part of the intentional consumer-situation are generated. It therefore deals with the cognitive structures that influence the formation and retention of the beliefs that influence perception in the operation of the intentional consumer-situation. The analysis is concerned with the ways in which the cognitive consumer-situation links the consumer's situation with the cognitive processes that generate the beliefs that influence her perceptual experience. The consumer may act rationally but the beliefs that are the output of cognitive processing may not only fail to meet the criteria of economic rationality but also be a-rational, even fantastical, in psychological terms.

The appeal to perception and emotion in the critical examination of Intentional Behaviorism allows the immediate precursor of consumer choice, which in the BPM is assumed to be the *consumer-situation*, to be evaluated in mental terms that are not confined to the ubiquitous desire x belief formulation that provides the central model of decision making in numerous disciplines (Bermúdez, 2009). It is not my intention to replace the desire x belief model – indeed, it is important to the framework of conceptualization and analysis on which this monograph is based. But it is necessary for that very reason to subject it to critical analysis. Hence, I take with the utmost seriousness Nanay's proposal that perception in the form of pragmatic representation is a central component of the immediate mental precursor of action which can displace the desire x belief model deserves serious attention. Nanay's suggestion of the concept of *pragmatic representation* as the immediate mental antecedent of action is a critical standpoint for the development of the concept of contingency-representation that I introduce in this book as an essential component of the intentional consumer-situation.

All of the contents of the intentional consumer-situation, cognitive, affective, and conative, can be considered contingency-representations of one sort or another. However, while the perceptual nature of contingency-representation is emphasized initially, I go on to present the hypothesis that the perceptual component of contingency-representation is predominantly emotional in character, an affective evaluation of the contingencies of reinforcement and punishment that comprise the context of consumer choice. The contingencies are represented also by desires and beliefs, which in contrast to perceptions are conceptual or propositional. In developing the account of the intentional consumer-situation, I examine its conceptual components in relation to this perceptual/emotional evaluation and as psychological influences on action that are rooted in deeper cognitive functioning. Contingency-representation emerges, therefore, as composed of cognitive, conative, and affective elements that are conceptually separate but which combine in representing the contingencies and their influence on action.

The discussion of the propositional attitudes that shape human action from the perspective of psychoanalytically-based theory of mind permits this intellectual quest to move beyond the assumption often made in the philosophy of mind that adult humans' thought can be taken as rational. This is clearly not the case for much consumer choice, notably that which is based on the steep discounting of the future that is part of the essential definition of compulsiveness and addiction, but also for the much more prevalent kinds of consumer behavior that show a degree of impulsivity. An account of consumer choice that is dependent on cognitive theory must show that it is capable of dealing with both rationality/irrationality and a-rationality. For this account, I have turned to psychoanalysis to provide an analysis of psychological as opposed to economic rationality.

An important component of Intentional Behaviorism is the insistence that the intentional interpretations of consumer action that it generates be consistent with cognitive theory. The development of the concept of contingency-representation and the use of psychoanalytic analysis makes it possible to discuss more precisely, within the context of the cognitive theory which has been employed in this research program, the nature of the psychological consumer-situations posited in the course of explaining consumer choice, including the mentation necessary to provide a cognitive account that underpins and justifies the intentional interpretation. The assumption that the tripartite cognitive theory of Stanovich (2009) can perform as one of the mainstays of explaining consumer choice (Foxall, 2016a, 2016b) can now itself be examined in light of its capacity to undergird the intentional account of consumer action that is necessary if a post-extensional explanation is to be offered.

It is unlikely that the comparative evaluative function of pragmatic mental imagery could take place without some of the provisions of tripartite theory, namely, the capacity for decoupling of current concerns and realities so that cognitive rehearsal can proceed. But we will not know this until we have considered contingency-representation in detail. If we take Nanay's point that beliefs and desires may at times form part of the mental antecedents of action – that they may furnish the intentional consumer-situation – but that pragmatic representations are in any case necessary and that they may often be sufficient, we can make a case for a dual-process model of cognition and perception. Moreover, the outputs of desires x beliefs processing may inform perception, being especially active in the production of action-properties. Pragmatic mental imagery requires both contingency-representation, i.e., a means of representing the probable outcomes of behavior and their comparative evaluation, and a common currency in which the probable outcomes of future behavior can be portrayed and for the decisive comparison to take place.

Classes of action

Ascribed intentionality and ascribed intensionality

A large part of this volume has been concerned with the definition of behavior and action, intentionality and intensionality. Behavior has been understood as activity under the control of external stimulation; action, as controlled by, or at least requiring explanation in terms of, intentions such as desires, beliefs, emotions, and perceptions. Intentionality is simply aboutness, while intensionality is a linguistic phenomenon concerned with the meaning of sentences. None of this suggests, of itself, a source of personal control, free will, or agency, and I do not wish to go further than this despite some realist philosophers' assumption that explanation in intentional terms is indicative of personal agency. An interesting question, nevertheless, is whether there is another form of action and intentionality, one over which the individual can exert some degree of personal control by virtue of her comprehension of the intensional character of the reasons employed in the explanation of her action. Would such intentional control over one's actions on the basis of a demonstrable understanding of intensionality constitute "agency"?

Agency is often conceived of as the capacity to inaugurate action on one's own initiative rather than as a result of causal influences acting upon one, be they environmental stimuli, genetic endowments, or real intentional entities such as desires and beliefs. As such, agency is probably never encountered in an absolute sense; rather, it enters explanations by way of providing a relative estimate of the degree to which an action is the result of autonomous reasoning and selection. Agency, then, is the capacity to look at the reasons one has for behaving and being able to criticize them on the basis of their relationship to real-world criteria so that some can be acted upon while others are rejected. This is not absolute agency or autonomy since one is still acting for reasons but one has the intellectual capacity to examine one's reasons and select the most appropriate and adaptive to guide one's action. We might refer to this as *reasoned agency* in contradistinction to the *as if agency* on the basis of which we construct the intentional consumer-situation on the basis of *ascribed action* by using the intentional stance (Dennett, 1987). To the extent that an individual overcomes her neurotic beliefs in favor of beliefs-proper, and the extent to which she can employ pretending, imagining, supposing, hypothesizing, and even fantasizing as aids to planning future actions without being seduced by them into committing to maladaptive actions, she is exhibiting reasoned action. It seems reasonable to assume that an organism that can demonstrably accomplish these intellectual feats and base her actions on the conclusions reached differs significantly from one whose actions can be understood only through the ascription to them of intentionality. In the first case, there is evidence of first-personal rationality and reasoning-for-action; in the second, there is only the ascription of intentionality to explain the behavior of an organism for which no stimulus field can be identified. Of course, at base, the reasoned intentionality apparent in the first case is knowledge by description rather than knowledge by acquaintance, third-personal data for heterophenomenology rather than directly-accessed first-personal experience. Ultimately, therefore, even this intentionality is being ascribed by the investigator. But the individual who can demonstrate her capacity to distinguish among these propositional attitudes is distinct from one who cannot or, being able to does not, and this demonstration of reasoning is an intensional skill that sets this kind of agent apart.

If we pursue this possibility, we might propose two classes of action: that which is ascribed on the basis of the intentional stance in an act of explanation that purports to do no more than overcome the unavailability of the stimulus field required for an extensional analysis. This is action described intentionally on the basis of the consumer's history and circumstances in the act of ascription by which we have assumed the intentional consumer-situation to be constructed. In Table 7.1, this intentionally-ascribed action is designated A_1. In Dennett's terms, all there is to being an intentional system of this kind, having desires and beliefs, is to be

TABLE 7.1 Behavior, action, and agency

	Behavior	Action: ascribed intentionality (A1)	Action: ascribed intensionality (A2)
Stimulus field	Empirically available stimulus field that is amenable to being related to observed activity in an experimental or quasi-experimental situation.	No stimulus field is available. Intentional interpretation, based with modification on Dennett's intentional stance, predicts action.	No stimulus field available. Intensional stance explains.
Role of agency	No agency. Direct environmental causation.	"As if" agency.	"Reasoning-based" agency.
Role of propositional attitudes	No resort to propositional attitudes in explanation of behavior.	Propositional attitudes attributed by investigator to account for observed action.	Demonstrated typing of propositional attitudes by actor as guide for action.
Analogies with representational systems	No representation.	RS Type I. Symbols. Verbal symbol (i.e., vocal sound or writing that has become paired with S^D for reinforcers and now functions as an S^D in its own right). Can be interpreted by others (or the individual) as symbolizing the reinforcer. *Content and function are decided by others (i.e., the social community).*	RS Type III. Both content and function are intrinsically determined. These are wholly internal indicators.

predictable by these means; we are making no ontological claims beyond materialism. The second kind of action is similarly explained but in a more detailed manner: its description rests on the consumer's demonstrated ability to reason intensionally for herself. This action is designated A_2 in the table. In this case, we still employ the intentional stance to predict the system and we still make no ontological claims of extra-physicality.

In both cases, intentional capacities or properties are ascribed on the basis of knowledge by description, though in the second there is greater evidence of the nature of knowledge by acquaintance, the subjective intellectual experience of the consumer.

Agency would be attributed in the case of A_1 by explaining the system through the ascription to it of intentionality. We would then be treating the predicted system *as if* it were an agent that acts independently of a stimulus field. However, we have no scientific evidence to this effect (whatever form that would need to take). However, a system which demonstrates A_2 on the basis that it can type, for itself, the propositional attitudes that guide its actions, distinguishing for instance between beliefs-proper and neurotic beliefs or fantasies, has demonstrated its capacity to use intensional language and to be guided by its conclusions in the determination of its actions. This demonstrated intensionality and the action that ensues are both independent of ourselves as extraneous systems: both the content and the function of the intensionality are intrinsic to the system that we observe.

Action and representational systems

The ascription of intentionality to predict and explicate the action of a system involves allocating content as well as function; the system is, therefore, an example of what Dretske calls a representational system Type I (RSI). Some animal activity would, therefore, count as action because our only means of explaining it is the use of intentional language, there being no environmental stimuli on the basis of which an account of the activity can be provided (see, for instance, Brakel, 2016). However, this is intentionality *we* ascribe as investigators. Again, we are users of Dennett's intentional stance, ascribing desires and beliefs to a system in order to predict, and partially explain, its behavior. We might well agree with Dennett in this case that this is all there is to having intentionality: i.e., being a system that is predictable by means of ascribing appropriate intentionality to it. We are ascribing "as if" agency to the system but this is a statement about us, not it. However, the system that can type the propositional attitudes that guide its actions is more than this. It has intrinsic intentionality (evidenced by demonstrated intensionality). This to me is the essence of agency.

In the case of A_2, based on personally-demonstrated reasoning, the individual employs the use of intensional language in accounting for why she acted in a particular way, and is able to parse propositional sentences relating to her actions in ways that demonstrate the difference between types of propositional attitude; for example, to distinguish fantasies from beliefs-proper. In this case, the intentionality is ascribed on the basis of the individual's propositional verbal behavior, and the content is given (by the individual and/or the verbal community). Only the function is supplied by the investigator who uses the content to account for the consumer's action. If, for example, a consumer says, "I believe that avoiding excess sugar in one's diet is essential to health," we can take the content as intrinsic and merely add the function of this belief: it is likely to result in her avoiding sugar. In this case, in which the evidence on which the ascription is made takes the form of a propositional attitude, the representation is an example of a representational system Type II (RSII).

But A_2 action can be subdivided into that which is explained in terms of propositional knowledge, knowledge by description, and that which is explained in terms of perceptual experience, knowledge by acquaintance, even though this is known to the researcher only propositionally and only expressible by the experiencer in propositional terms too. Hence, in summary, we distinguish:

> *Action defined on the basis of the ascription of intentionality.* In this, A_1, we ascribe the propositional attitudes that are appropriate to the consumer's observed action. Appropriate to might mean (a) consistent with, (b) explanatory of, or (c) causative of. The only evidence we have is for (a). And, as investigators, we supply both content and function to the explanation: therefore, the system is classified in Dretskean terms as a representational system Type I (RSI).

> *Action defined on the basis of the ascription of intensionality.* In this, A_{2a}, where the action on which we base the ascription of intentionality is the consumer's verbal behavior embodying propositional attitudes which her ambient verbal behavior indicates she is capable of parsing intensionally and on the basis of which she apparently acts, we ascribe intensionality. The content is given by the propositional attitudes in question; we are here ascribing propositional knowledge, knowledge by description. In the process, the consumer supplies the content of her propositions and we, as investigators, add the function in terms of the observed action which they explain: the representational system is, therefore, of Type II (RSII).

> *Action defined on the basis of the ascription of perceptual experience.* In this, A_{2b}, where we ascribe knowledge by acquaintance in the form of perceptual contingency-representations to the consumer, albeit on the basis of her propositionally-expressed knowledge by description, we are allocating perceptual experience of which she supplies both the content and the function: we are dealing here with a representational system Type II (RSII).

Misrepresentation

Humans who mistake their neurotic beliefs for beliefs-proper on the basis of the secondary mentation that surrounds them are clearly misrepresenting the context of their actions, the contingencies of reinforcement and punishment that regulate their choices. Recall that, as Dretske (1988) points out, misrepresentation is a necessary characteristic of Type III representational systems: only a system that possesses original or intrinsic intentionality *can* misrepresent in this way. The capacity to misrepresent is a prerequisite of having this intrinsic intentionality. Hence, those who mistake their neurotic beliefs for beliefs-proper and act on them with the assurance that they reflect the contingencies accurately are still Type III representational systems: their beliefs are in error but are corrigible. This consideration may well be the basis for the ability of humans to undertake bundling. The intensionality of the human consumer viewed as a Type III representational system is the only place in which we have encountered the possibility of intrinsic misrepresentation. It does not arise in the case of consumer behavior of which explanation does not entail representation at all; it is not a feature of our treatment of A_1 whether this is simply a matter of the attribution of both content and function.

Conclusion

Let there be no mistake. None of the foregoing indicates progression beyond the bounds of the intentional stance. We are rendering the actions of consumers more intelligible by ascribing intentionality of one sort or another to them on the basis of those and other of their actions. At no point have we devised a means of permitting first-personal perceptual experience to enter directly into scientific analysis. Our explanations are based firmly and exclusively on third-personal propositional knowledge by description. But the suggestion has been made that, in the case of A_{2b}, which depends on the consumer's perceptual experience in order to explain her action, we have come closer to exploring her autophenomenal reality in taking account of her intensional capabilities than is the case for the intentionality ascribed on the basis only of her observed non-verbal actions.

So (deep breath), while this still does not amount, of course, to a means of making the first-personal phenomenology of the actor publicly available without conceptual adornment and capable of entering into a scientific analysis, while we are still making attributions from a third-personal perspective, and while we are dealing with knowledge by description of the actor's intentionality rather than knowledge by acquaintance of her intensionality, there may be an important qualitative difference between the kind of ascription of intentionality involved in taking the intentional stance, with its revelation of "as if" agency, and the ascription of intensionality to the actor who can type propositional attitudes and act accordingly. Of course, such an actor may merely dissemble: her reasoning may be mere rationalization rather than a revelation of her true motivation. But this is not always the case. We are dealing here with a different level of action and agency from that of the creatures to which we ascribe third-personal intentionality simply because we lack a stimulus field by which to predict their activities.

GLOSSARY OF KEY TERMS

Action Action is activity for which no account can be provided in terms of empirically available stimuli. Taking the operant paradigm as the basis of extensional explanation, for instance, we are unable to fulfill the requirements of explanation by means of the three-term contingency which is necessary to explain the activity as behavior. Several perspectives are here: notably, the realist approach which assumes beliefs and desires actually exist and directly cause actions to occur, and the conceptual approach which recognizes that there are activities that require the use of intentional language in order to render them comprehensible but which makes no ontological assumption about the reality of these intentional entities. And, of course, there are intermediate positions; personally, I do not deny that beliefs and desires may be said to exist as summations of strongly held thoughts and feelings, but I make no assumptions about their actually entering into a causal chain with action as its outcome. The important thing about action is that, in the absence of a stimulus field that predicts and partially explains behavior, the only alternative is to employ intentional language and thereby explain the activity as action. We may refer to this as *ascribed action* because the intentionality which explains it is ascribed *by us* as investigators, predictors, or explicators of the activity we observe. It is not something that we would care to say is intrinsic to the system the activity of which we are predicting or explaining. To ascribe intentionality in this way in order to predict and partially explain activity is precisely what Dennett means by adopting the intentional stance.

Action and behavior: A conceptual distinction Note that behavior and action may be topographically identical, indeed may consist of the self-same activity. What distinguishes them is the way in which they are explained: by appeal to the stimulus field which can be experimentally (or – permissible but less rigorous – correlationally) in the case of behavior, by the deployment of intentional language (the intentional idioms that inhere in talk of desiring, believing, emoting, and perceiving) in the case of action. These intentional qualities are ascribed in the case of ascribed intentionality, but demonstrated by the subject (usually verbally) in the case of demonstrated intentionality. There is a sense in which both ascribed and demonstrated intensionality are third-personal attributions of course. But the heterophenomenological evidence is much closer to the individual's phenomenology in the case of demonstrated intensionality.

Behavior Behavior is bodily movement that is expressed by an intransitive verb – my arm's moving – while action is bodily movement expressed intransitively – my moving my arm: hence, we distinguish, following Hornsby (1981), activity$_I$ from activity$_T$. Whereas behavior is explained (or at least predicted) on the basis of an ambient stimulus field, action is activity for which no such stimulus field is empirically available: it is explained, therefore, in terms of the intentionality (principally desires, beliefs, emotions, and perceptions) of the individual.

Behavior is, therefore, activity in the explanation of which a stimulus field can be identified and employed. The criteria of explanatory efficacy are the predictability of the behavior. Alternatively, we might express this as: when a stimulus field adequately predicts an activity, the activity is behavior. The explanation is couched entirely in extensional language and the causation of the activity is attributed to the controlling environment. Hence, there is no role of propositional attitudes in the explanation of behavior. Alternatively, this might be expressed as: behavior provides a dependent variable which is a function of independent variables that are environmental events. As Skinner puts it, "the variables of which behavior is a function will be found in the environment" (1977, p. 1). There is no ascription of agency in the case of behavior, if by this is meant the personal agency that is usually thought of as an intrapersonal, especially psychological, instigator of behavior.

Beyond cognition? The three-stage path to psychological explanation proposed by Intentional Behaviorism provides a means of approaching the ascription of intentionality and cognition in the explanation of human economic activity. However, the possibility is raised by Nanay (2013a) that models which emphasize desires and beliefs as precursors of action might be superseded by a simpler mechanism based on perceptual processes. It is worthwhile, therefore, to pose the question of whether the intentional theory that Intentional Behaviorism employs in its second stage of intentional interpretation or the cognitive theory that it employs in its final stage of cognitive interpretation might indeed be complemented or even superseded by perceptual conceptions. The aim is to suggest a more immediate mechanism for the production of activity than is allowed for in the standard models, a mechanism which humans might share with non-human animals.

Cognitive interpretation The major source of critical examination of the intentional interpretation is employed, however, in the final stage, *cognitive* *interpretation*, in which the extent to which the intentional interpretation can be borne out by well-tested theories of cognitive structure and functioning is assessed. Together, the intentional interpretation and the cognitive interpretation provide psychological explanation. There are elaborate and well-tested cognitive theories of information processing that deal with this question, notably the dual-process theories (and, especially, tri-process theory), which argue that the tensions between a tendency toward impulsivity and a reflective tendency that takes account of the longer-term implications of sudden action eventuate in a response to environmental opportunities and threats.

Hence, the link between context and cognition is the consumer-situation which takes the form of, first, a behavior-level description of the immediate precursor of choice and, subsequently, intentional- and cognitive-level depictions of the context of consumer choice which provides its explanatory texture.

Constructing the intentional consumer-situation The process of intentional interpretation contains four steps. The intentional interpretation, first, has to specify the observed action that is not under the control of a stimulus field, the *target activity*. In the present case, the activity we have to explain is the *persistent* slot machine gambling of players whose performances lead to two identical symbols rather than the three required for a win which would yield a financial reward. We have to answer the questions: What is the consumer maximizing? What intentionality can be ascribed to her in order to render this behavior intelligible, given that there is no stimulus field to provide an operant interpretation? The lack of an operant interpretation is due to the consequences of the gambling having precisely the opposite effect to that predicted by operant psychology, namely, that the punishment provided by losing (gaining two identical symbols when three are required) actually leads to increased play (*pleasure* depends on failing; punishment is reinforcing!).

Second, the intentional interpretation of this behavior begins with the specification of the goal or desire toward the fulfillment of which the target activity is directed. We assume the consumer maximizes a combination of utilitarian and informational reinforcement. But there is no or very little utilitarian reinforcement in the form of actually winning money. If we assume the consumer's behavior is reinforced by means of informational consequences in the form of performance feedback, we must recognize that this is erroneous since it applies to situations in which the consumer's behavior results in failure. The informational reinforcement provided by the sounds and sights given off by the machine are not actually rewards but are *interpreted* as such. Since informational reinforcement is dependent on social and individual judgment about what is a reward, we can ascribe a degree of agency to the consumer who decides personally what is rewarding (in much the same way that individuals may collectively determine what will count as a reinforcer). There may be social support for this as others who are playing or observing comment enthusiastically, "That was a near-win!"

Third, is the construction of an account of the consumer's perceptual experience that is consistent with this pattern of action. This is accomplished by reconstructing the content of the contingency-representations that the consumer would require in order to perform the target action. This is conducted, initially, in *cognitive terms*, and takes the form of a statement of the contingencies of reinforcement and punishment that are consistent with the maintenance of this action. (This cognitive component of the contingency-representation is necessary just as there is a cognitive component of the pragmatic representation. However, for reasons already presented, the concept of pragmatic representation will not do for this purpose.) In the present case, this requires the specification of the cognitively-based, if eccentric, *perception* that the SSR exceeds the LLR at t_1, which flies in the face of the objective perception that the reverse is the case but that the attainment of the LLR requires patience. Next, the contingency-representation is reconstructed *in emotional terms*: a statement of the emotions that maintenance of the target action would rely upon.

Finally, there comes the construction of the beliefs necessary to sustain the observed pattern of action. These consist in beliefs-proper which are reality-tested propositional attitudes, and neurotic beliefs which are fantasies plus the "evidence" provided by subjective psychically-testing that is divorced from evaluation by comparison with the real world. These differing kinds of belief have implications for the ascription of psychological rationality.

Consumer choice It is the presence of hyperbolic temporal discounting that leads to the selection of a smaller, sooner reward (SSR) over a larger, later reward (LLR) that distinguishes the concept of consumer *choice* from that of consumer activity or consumer behavior. Although the characteristic context in which this kind of dilemma is considered is that of extreme consumer choice as in compulsion and addiction, it is frequently encountered, albeit in smaller degree, in many other modes of consumption. The inability of the extensional model to deal with consumer activities that cannot be traced to a stimulus field necessitates a psychological explanation. While the empirical availability of such a stimulus field would make possible an experimental or correlational analysis to establish the environmental variables of which the behavior is a function, its absence removes the possibility of an extensional explanation and makes the use of intentional language and therefore intentional explanation inevitable. In this intentional account, the consumer-situation is defined in terms of the consumer's desires, beliefs, emotions, and perceptions as they relate, specifically, to her consumption history and the contingencies of reinforcement and punishment that have regulated her past consumer actions and that promise to influence them in the future. Previous exposition of consumer choice in the context of Intentional Behaviorism has concentrated on beliefs and desires: the present concern is with the role of perception and emotion in the delineation of the consumer-situation and their relationship to consumer decision making and the formation of beliefs.

Contingency-representation In the intentional consumer-situation, the immediate precursor of consumer action is the perceptual representation of the contingencies of reinforcement and punishment. The cognitive penetration of modules is presented as a necessary element in a perceptual system that aims at prediction in relation to the provision of guidelines to behavior. Perceptual contingency-representations are, therefore, of paramount importance in linking context and cognition, and these perceptual representations of the contingencies of reinforcement and punishment are vital to the selection of an appropriate action from among those available. Insofar as they accomplish this, contingency-representations make action action.

See Contingency-representation and Type III representational systems; Perception; Pragmatic representation; Representation

Contingency-representation and Type III representational systems Perception which represents has both content and functions that the perceiving system ascribes independently of external systems. Contingency-representations have content (what they say about the environment) that can only be supplied by the perceiver's learning history and her interpretation of the nature of the stimuli that compose the behavior setting. They have functions that she alone can supply in deciding what to do next. It is contingency-representation of this kind that makes action action. Cognitive and conative contingency-representations also show this intrinsic content and function but do so through linguistic usages. The determination of whether a propositional attitude is a belief-proper or a neurotic belief or some other kind of intentionality is that of the individual. By typing the propositional attitudes by which we live, we are treating them intensionally.

Emotional feelings as perceptual contingency-representations The essence of perceptual contingency-representation inheres in certain emotional feelings, namely, pleasure, arousal, and dominance, and their composites, which arise in response to currently experienced and imagined contingencies of reinforcement and punishment. Empirical investigations of emotional feelings in relation to the patterns of reinforcement contingency defined by the BPM indicate that pleasure is reported disproportionately for situations of higher utilitarian reinforcement, arousal for situations of higher informational reinforcement, and dominance for more open situations (Foxall, 1997a, 1997b; 2011; Foxall & Greenley, 1998, 1999, 2000; Foxall & Yani-de-Soriano, 2005, 2006; Foxall et al., 2012; Yani-de-Soriano & Foxall, 2006; Yani-de-Soriano, Foxall & Newman, 2013). However, the possibility that emotions provide the affective component of contingency-representations depends on their being shown to be perceptual.

Perceptual contingency-representations consist, therefore, in the emotional responses of the consumer as they reflect the pattern of reinforcement and punishment that has resulted from her prior engagement with the contingencies. These have two dimensions: the actual emotional experience of the consumer in previous consumer-situations and the emotional responses she feels when contemplating the contingencies of reinforcement and punishment that enmesh actions that might be performed now or in the near future: this is the essence of the intentional consumer-situation that is ascribed in the course of constructing an intentional interpretation.

Only the relevant emotional feelings, considered as perceptions, constitute contingency-representations but they do not stand in isolation from cognition and conation. Perception is inevitably cognitively penetrated while emotional feelings are linked to motivational concerns. Especially as the consumer acquires a learning history, what she comes to know about the likelihood of future reinforcement and punishment, based on her rumination on and appraisal of her previous behavior and its outcomes, influences what and how the contingencies of reinforcement and punishment are perceived emotionally. This guides perceptions of current contingencies of reinforcement and punishment and is the source of the relevant cognitive penetration of perception. It can be codified as a series of rules. The neonate's cognitive contingency-representation is limited to whatever rules have been acquired in the course of phylogenetic history. As the individual develops, her cognitive component is supplemented by rules laid down in the course of her ontogenetic development, her learning history. But in what does this learning history consist? We can, therefore, speak about this learning history in terms of cognitively penetrated contingency-representations that inhere in consumers' emotional feelings gained through the experience of contingencies of reinforcement and punishment. It follows that consumer choice cannot be understood in terms of perceptual processes divorced from cognitive and conative considerations. The belief x desire model is highly relevant to this understanding. Emotional feelings are closely linked to motivational pressures.

Intentional Behaviorism The Intentional Behaviorism research program is concerned with the nature, place, and role of intentionality, including cognition, in the psychological explanation of consumer choice. Intentional explanation proposes how action relates to and is explained by the intellectual processes and events by means of which the actor comes to behave sensibly given the demands of the context at hand.

Intentional Behaviorism seeks to establish the point at which intentional explanation becomes necessary and the form it should take. It does so through the exhaustion of the capacity of an extensional model to explain observed behavior, and turns to psychological explanation only when the stimulus field necessary for this behaviorist explanation is no longer empirically available. In the course of this initial investigation, the peculiar benefits of a minimalist explanation of choice are revealed, a positive outcome in its own right and also invaluable in the pursuit of both a comprehensive understanding of consumer choice and its psychological explanation. An exemplar of the failure of the lack of a stimulus field for the explanation of consumer choice is provided by the commonplace necessity of choosing between a smaller reward, immediately available, and a larger reward that will take time. For the original sources of Intentional Behaviorism, see Foxall (2004, 2007, 2008, 2009), and for recent applications to consumer choice, Foxall (2016a, 2016b). A review of the theoretically minimalist extensional research program of consumer behavior analysis is also available: Foxall (2017).

See Cognitive interpretation; Intentional interpretation; Theoretical minimalism; Constructing the intentional consumer-situation

Intentional interpretation The inability of extensional language to explain behavior is thus revealed in this process by the absence of the empirically available stimulus field on which radical behaviorism essentially relies. The only alternative is to employ intentional language. In the second stage, *intentional interpretation*, the consumer's observed action is accounted for by the ascription of the intentionality that renders it intelligible on the assumption that the consumer is a rational, utility-maximizing system. In this way, first, the desires, beliefs, emotions, and perceptions necessary for an intentional account are established so that, second, the interpretation can be empirically tested in terms of its predictive capacity. Although the predictions required for this evaluation of the intentional interpretation are likely to be rather general, they may be augmented in the case of perceptual contingency-representations through the application of Ramsey's success semantics as refined by Nanay to apply to perceptions rather than beliefs.

The resulting intentional idioms constitute the intentional consumer-situation, the immediate antecedent of consumer action, and perform this role by virtue of their capacity to represent the contingencies of reinforcement and punishment, past and present, that influence consumer choice. An important facet of perceptual contingency-representation is provided by the emotional experiences generated by the contingencies of reinforcement and punishment that govern consumer environments.

Intentional interpretation does not obviate the need for the stage of theoretical minimalism; rather, the stage of consumer behavior analysis is essential to the ascription to the consumer of the desires (goals in the form of utilitarian and informational reinforcement maximization rather than the more nebulous notion of utility maximization found in microeconomics) and the nature of the consumer behavior setting and its representations of the potential outcomes of consumer action.

See Intentional Behaviorism

Intentionality and intensionality Our understanding of the nature of behavior, action, and agency is closely tied to the question of whether and how intentionality and intensionality are involved in their explanation. While *intentionality* is aboutness, the possession of content, *intensionality* is a linguistic phenomenon. Intensionality is found in sentences that employ psychological verbs ("attitudes") that relate to propositions, *that* clauses (hence, "propositional attitudes"). Such propositions are referentially opaque, manifesting the non-substitutability of coextensive terms if they are not to sacrifice the truth value of the sentence in which they are found. Moreover, the intentional objects they contain display intentional inexistence and need not actually be a feature of the real world. In all these respects, sentences expressed in intentional language differ from those expressed in extensional language which avoids intentional idioms. The roles of intentionality and intensionality in explanation are clarified by the consideration of the varieties of activity we designate behavior and action.

Perception Expositions of the intentional consumer-situation have to date concentrated on the beliefs and desires required to account for consumer action, and the present approach redresses this by drawing attention to the perceptual and emotional components of intentional interpretation. Perception is understood as conscious awareness of one's environment, an intentional modular process that differs conceptually from cognition and conation and which represents the environment in terms of the agent's capacity to function adaptively within it. This book has not attempted to present a comprehensive account of the philosophy of perception (for which, see, inter alia: Fish, 2010; Prinz, 2002b; Searle, 2015; Siegal, 2011) but is, rather, confined to what is necessary to pursue the argument with respect to contingency-representation.

Pragmatic representation En route to the development of the conception of contingency-representation, Nanay's proposal that pragmatic representation comprises the immediate (perceptual) precursor of action is examined. Its value in raising the nature of the immediate precursor of action and the ways in which it must be conceptualized is brought out. However, there are two problems with the idea of pragmatic representation if it is considered a contender for the kind of contingency-representation that has been identified as desirable. First, it is oblivious to the cognitive penetration of perception; second, it does not in fact take the contingencies of reinforcement and punishment into consideration. The concept of perceptual contingency-representation is presented as experience that is sensitive to the import of prior action and the need to link the explanation of action to its context. It embodies both the consumer's learning history and the probable consequences of current and future action. It comprises cognitive, conative, and affective dimensions, and is amenable to appraisal in terms of success semantics.

Representation The nature of representation in the context of Dretske's typology includes, first, arbitrary symbols like road signs and maps used to delineate the environment so that appropriate behavior may ensue: these are Type I representational systems (RSI); second, the signs such as animal tracks of which we establish the significance: these are Type II representational systems (RSII); and, third, those natural indicators like perceptions that have the function of intrinsically representing and so guiding action: these are Type III representational systems (RSIII). These intrinsic indicators are independent of the cognitive operation of any other system; they mediate environmental events and the internal mechanisms that "read" them in order to generate responses that ensure the survival and reproduction of the individual. As intrinsically intentional representations, they point the way to the perceptual means by which consumers respond to prospective contingencies of reinforcement and punishment, and suggest how the intentional consumer-situation may be constructed. This is how perceptual contingency-representations are understood.

Success semantics, contingency-representation, and action The import of Ramsey's success semantics is that the content of a belief inheres in the success conditions of the actions to which it leads. Some difficulties with success semantics can be overcome, according to Nanay, if its claims are applied to simpler antecedents of action than beliefs, namely, perceptions, specifically pragmatic representations. However, this militates against the contribution that success semantics can make to the scientific evaluation of mental events since perceptions are not empirically available for third-personal investigation. A solution lies in stating an individual's beliefs on the basis of her verbalizations and determining the perception that would have the same content. This stated content can then be evaluated by comparison with the manifest content of a belief or perception that reflected the success conditions of the action to which it led. This procedure not only renders a scientific analysis based on the predictive capacity of cognitive and perceptual contingency-representations to be undertaken as a check on the veracity of an intentional interpretation but also supports the conclusion that the explanation of action in terms of perceptions such as pragmatic representations and contingency-representations cannot be divorced from an analysis in terms of the desires x beliefs model.

Theoretical minimalism The research strategy employed in order to elaborate the psychological consumer-situation, Intentional Behaviorism, has three stages. The first, theoretical minimalism, builds and tests to destruction an extensional model of consumer choice, a process in which the need for intentional and cognitive explanation is revealed as well as the form it needs to take. The extensional consumer-situation, which is the immediate precursor of consumer behavior, comprises the consumer's learning history and the current consumer behavior setting which are both (in principle, at least) specifiable in terms of empirically available, manipulable stimuli by which her behavior can be predicted. Extensional explanation consists in the capacity to undertake such prediction with accuracy. In this process, the aspects of consumer choice that can be explained only in terms of environmental stimulation are revealed and this is in itself an invaluable component of the Intentional Behaviorism research strategy.

See Intentional Behaviorism

BIBLIOGRAPHY

Ainslie, G. (1986). Beyond microeconomics: Conflict among interests in a multiple self as a determinant of value. In J. Elster (Ed.), *The Multiple Self*. Cambridge: Cambridge University Press, pp. 133–175.

Ainslie, G. (1989). Freud and picoeconomics. *Behaviorism*, 17, 11–19.

Ainslie, G. (1992). *Picoeconomics: The Strategic Interaction of Successive Motivational States within the Person*. Cambridge: Cambridge University Press.

Ainslie, G. (2001). *Breakdown of Will*. Cambridge: Cambridge University Press.

Ainslie, G. (2007). Emotion: The gaping hole in economic theory. In B. Montero & M. D. White (Eds), *Economics and the Mind*. London and New York: Routledge, pp. 11–28.

Ainslie, G. (2010). Procrastination: The basic impulsive. In C. Andreou & M. D. White (Eds), *The Thief of Time*. Oxford University Press, pp. 11–27.

Ainslie, G. (2011). Free will as recursive self-prediction: Does a deterministic mechanism reduce responsibility? In J. Poland & G. Graham (Eds), *Addiction and Responsibility*. Cambridge, MA: MIT Press, pp. 55–87.

Ainslie, G. (2013). Money as MacGuffin: A factor in gambling and other process addictions. In N. Levy (Ed.), *Addiction and Self-control: Perspectives from Philosophy, Psychology, and Neuroscience*. Oxford: Oxford University Press, pp. 16–37.

Ainslie, G. (2016). The cardinal anomalies that led to behavioral economics: Cognitive or motivational? *Managerial and Decision Economics*, 37, 261–273.

Ainslie, G. & Monterosso, J. (2003). Hyperbolic discounting as a factor in addiction: A critical analysis. In R. E. Vuchinich & N. Heather (Eds), *Choice, Behavioural Economics and Addiction*. Oxford: Pergamon, pp. 35–70.

Alcaro, A., Huber, R. & Panksepp, J. (2007). Behavioral functions of the mesolimbic dopaminergic system: An affective neuroethological perspective. *Brain Research Review*, 56, 283–321.

Alhadeff, D. A. (1985). *Microeconomics and Human Behavior*. Berkeley, CA: University of California Press.

Altman, J., Everitt, B. J., Glautier, S., Markou, A., Butt, D. et al. (1996). The biological, social and clinical bases of drug addiction: Commentary and debate. *Psychopharmacology*, 125, 285–345.

American Psychiatric Association (2013). *Diagnostic and statistical manual of mental disorders*, fifth edition. Washington, DC: APA.

Anscombe, G. E. M. (1957). *Intention*. Oxford: Blackwell.

Bach, K. (1978). A representational theory of action. *Philosophical Studies*, 34, 361–379.

Baker, L. R. (1991). Dretske on the explanatory role of belief. *Philosophical Studies*, 63, 99–111.

Baker, L. R. (1995). *Explaining Attitudes: A Practical Approach to the Mind*. Cambridge: Cambridge University Press.

Banich, M. T. (2009). Executive function: The search for an integrated account. *Current Directions in Psychological Science*, 10, 89–94.

Barkley, R. A. (1997a). Behavioral inhibition, sustained attention, and executive functions: Constructing a unified theory of ADHD. *Psychological Bulletin*, 121, 65–94.

Barkley, R. A. (1997b). *ADHD and the Nature of Self-control*. New York: Guilford Press.

Barkley, R. A. (2001). The executive functions and self-regulation: An evolutionary neuro-psychological perspective. *Neuropsychology Review*, 11, 1–29.

Barkley, R. A. (2012). *Executive Functions: What They Are, How They Work, and Why They Evolved*. New York: Guilford Press.

Barkley, R. A. (2013). Attention-deficit-hyperactivity disorder, self-regulation, and executive functioning. In K. D. Vohs & R. F. Baumeister (Eds), *Handbook of Self-regulation: Research, Theory, and Applications*, second edition. New York: Guilford Press, pp. 551–563.

Barrett, L. F. (2005). Feeling is perceiving: Core affect and conceptualization in the experience of emotion. In L. F. Barrett, P. M. Niedenthal & P. Winkielman (Eds), *Emotion and Consciousness*. New York: Guilford Press, pp. 255–285.

Barrett, L. F., Lewis, M. & Haviland-Jones, J. M. (Eds) (2016). *Handbook of Emotions*, fourth edition. New York: Guilford Press.

Barrett, L. F., Mesquita, B., Ochsner, K. N. & Gross, J. J. (2007). The experience of emotion. *Annual Review of Psychology*, 38, 173–401.

Barrett, L. F., Niedenthal, P. M. & Winkielman, P. (Eds) (2005). *Emotion and Consciousness*. New York: Guilford Press.

Bauer, I. M. & Baumeister, R. F. (2013). Self-regulatory strength. In K. D. Vohs & R. F. Baumeister (Eds), *Handbook of Self-regulation: Research, Theory, and Applications*, second edition. New York: Guilford Press, pp. 64–82.

Baumeister, R. F. & Tierney, J. (2012). *Willpower: Rediscovering the Greatest Human Strength*. New York: Penguin.

Bechara, A. (2005). Decision-making, impulse control and loss of willpower to resist drugs: A neurocognitive perspective. *Nature Neuroscience*, 8, 1458–1463.

Bechara, A. (2011). Human emotions in decision making: Are they useful or disruptive? In O. Vartanian & D. R. Mandel (Eds), *Neuroscience of Decision Making*. Hove and New York: Psychology Press, pp. 73–95.

Bechara, A. & Damasio, D. R. (2005). The somatic marker hypothesis: A neural theory of economic decision. *Games and Economic Behavior*, 52, 336–372.

Bechara, A., Damasio, H. & Damasio A. R. (2000). Emotion, decision making and the orbitofrontal cortex. *Cerebral Cortex*, 10, 295–307.

Bechtel, W. (2008). *Mental Mechanisms: Philosophical Perspectives on Cognitive Neuroscience*. London and New York: Psychology Press.

Bechtel, W. & Abrahamsen, A. (2002). *Connectionism and the Mind: Parallel Processing, Dynamics, and Evolution in Networks*, second edition. Oxford: Blackwell.

Bechtel, W. & Richardson, R. C. (1993). *Discovering Complexity: Decomposition and Localization as Strategies in Scientific Research*. Princeton, NJ: Princeton University Press.

Bennett, M. R. & Hacker, P. M. S. (2003). *Philosophical Foundations of Neuroscience*. Oxford: Blackwell.

Bennett, M. R. & Hacker, P. M. S. (2008). *History of Cognitive Neuroscience*. Chichester: Wiley-Blackwell.

Bermúdez, J. L. (2003). *Thinking without Words*. Oxford: Oxford University Press.

Bermúdez, J. L. (2005). *Philosophy of Psychology: A Contemporary Introduction*. New York and London: Routledge.

Bermúdez, J. L. (2009). *Decision Theory and Rationality*. Oxford: Oxford University Press.

Bernat, E., Patrick, C. J., Benning, S. D. & Tellegen, A. (2006). Effects of picture content and intensity on affective physiological response. *Psychophysiology*, 43, 93–103.

Berridge, K. C. (2007). The debate over dopamine's role in reward: The case for incentive salience. *Psychopharmacology*, 191, 391–431.

Berridge, K. C. & Kringelbach, M. L. (2015). Pleasure systems in the brain. *Neuron*, 86, 646–664.

Berridge, K. C. & Robinson, T. E. (1993). The neural basis of drug craving: An incentive-sensitization theory of addiction. *Brain Research Reviews*, 18, 247–291.

Berridge, K. C. & Robinson, T. E. (1995). The mind of an addicted brain: Neural sensitization and wanting versus liking. *Current Directions in Psychological Science*, 4, 71–76.

Berridge, K. C. & Robinson, T. E. (1998). What is the role of dopamine in reward: Hedonic impact, reward learning, or incentive salience? *Brain Research Reviews*, 28, 309–369.

Berridge, K. C. & Robinson, T. E. (2003). Parsing reward. *Trends in Neurosciences*, 26, 507–513.

Berridge, K. C. & Robinson, T. E. (2012). Drug addiction as incentive sensitization. In J. Poland & G. Graham (Eds), *Addiction and Responsibility*. Cambridge, MA: MIT Press, pp. 21–53.

Berthoz, A. (2003). *Emotion and Reason: The Cognitive Neuroscience of Decision Making*. Oxford: Oxford University Press.

Bickel, W. R. & Yi, R. (2008). Temporal discounting as a measure of executive function: Insights from the competing neuro-behavioral decision system hypothesis of addiction. *Advances in Health Economics and Health Services Research*, 20, 289–309.

Bickel, W. K., Jarmolowicz, D. P., Mueller, E. T. & Gatchalian, K. M. (2011). The behavioral economics and neuroeconomics of reinforcer pathologies: Implications for etiology and treatment of addiction. *Current Psychiatry Reports*, 13, 406–415.

Bickel, W. K., Jarmolowicz, D. P., Mueller, E. T., Gatchalian, K. M. & McClure, S. M. (2012). Are executive function and impulsivity antipodes? A conceptual reconstruction with special reference to addiction. *Psychopharmacology*, 221, 361–387.

Bickel, W. K., Kowal, B. P. & Gatchalian, K. M. (2006). Understanding addiction as a pathology of temporal horizon. *Behavior Analyst Today*, 7, 32–47.

Biggers, T. (1981). The function of dominance-submissiveness within Mehrabian's theory of emotion. PhD thesis. Florida State University.

Biggers, T. & Pryor, B. (1982). Attitude change: A function of emotion-eliciting qualities of environment. *Personality and Social Psychology Bulletin*, 8, 94–99.

Biggers, T. & Rankins, O. E. (1983). Dominance-submissiveness as an effective response to situations and as a predictor of approach-avoidance. *Social Behavior and Personality*, 11(2), 61–69.

Blackburn, S. (2005). Success semantics. In D. H. Mellor & H. Lillehammer (Eds), *Ramsey's Legacy*. Oxford: Oxford University Press, pp. 22–36.

Blair, C. & Ursache, A. (2013). A bidirectional model of executive functions and self-regulation. In K. D. Vohs & R. F. Baumeister (Eds), *Handbook of Self-regulation: Research, Theory, and Applications*, second edition. New York: Guilford Press, pp. 300–320.

Boag, S., Brakel, L. A. W. & Talvitie, V. (Eds) (2015a). *Philosophy, Science, and Psychoanalysis: A Critical Meeting*. London: Karnac.

Boag, S., Brakel, L. A. W. & Talvitie, V. (Eds) (2015b). *Psychoanalysis and Philosophy of Mind: Unconscious Mentality in the Twenty-first Century*. London: Karnac.

Brady, M. S. (2015). Feeling bad and seeing bad. *Dialectica*, 69, 403–416.

Brakel, L. A. W. (2001). Phantasies, neurotic beliefs, and beliefs-proper. *American Journal of Psychoanalysis*, 61, 363–389.

Brakel, L. A. W. (2002). Phantasy and wish: A proper function account of a-rational primary process mediated mentation. *Australasian Journal of Philosophy*, 80, 1–16.

Brakel, L. A. W. (2009). *Philosophy, Psychoanalysis, and the A-rational Mind*. Oxford: Oxford University Press.

Brakel, L. A. W. (2010). *Unconscious Knowing and Other Essays in Psycho-philosophical Analysis*. Oxford: Oxford University Press.

Brakel, L. A. W. (2013). *The Ontology of Psychology: Questioning Foundations in the Philosophy of Mind*. New York and London: Routledge.

Brakel, L. A. W. (2015a). Two fundamental problems for philosophical psychoanalysis. In S. Boag, L. A. W. Brakel & V. Talvitie (Eds), *Philosophy, Science, and Psychoanalysis: A Critical Meeting*. London: Karnac, pp. 119–143.

Brakel, L. A. W. (2015b). Unconscious knowing: psychoanalytic evidence in support of a radical epistemic view. In S. Boag, L. A. W. Brakel & V. Talvitie (Eds), *Psychoanalysis and Philosophy of Mind: Unconscious Mentality in the Twenty-first Century*. London: Karnac, pp. 193–237.

Brakel, L. A. W. (2016). Animals are agents. *Animal Sentience*, 103, 1–3.

Brakel, L. A. & Shevrin, H. (2003). Freud's dual process theory and the place of the a-rational. *Behavioral and Brain Sciences*, 26, 527–528.

Brand, M. (1948). *Intending and Acting*. Cambridge, MA: MIT Press.

Brentano, F. (1874). *Psychology from an Empirical Standpoint*. Leipzig: Meiner.

Burgess, A. (1990). *You've Had Your Time*. London: William Heineman.

Cabanac, M. & Bonniot-Cabanac, M.-C. (2007). Decision making: Rational or hedonic? *Behavioral and Brain Functions*, 3, 45.

Cardinal, R. N., Parkinson, J. A., Hall, J. & Everitt, B. J. (2002). Emotion and motivation: The role of the amygdala, central striatum, and prefrontal cortex. *Neuroscience and Biobehavioral Reviews*, 26, 321–352.

Carnap, R. (1959). Psychology in physical language. In A. J. Ayer (Ed.), *Logical Positivism*. Glencoe; IL: Free Press, pp. 165–198.

Caruthers, P. (2006a). The case for massively modular models of mind. In R. Stainton (Ed.), *Contemporary Debates in Cognitive Science*. Oxford: Blackwell, pp. 3–21.

Caruthers, P. (2006b). *The Architecture of the Mind*. Oxford: Oxford University Press.

Caruthers, P. & Chamberlain, A. (Eds), *Evolution and the Human Mind: Modularity, Language and Meta-Cognition*. Cambridge: Cambridge University Press.

Carver, C. S. & Scheier, M. F. (2013). Self-regulation of action and affect. In K. D. Vohs & R. F. Baumeister (Eds), *Handbook of Self-regulation: Research, Theory, and Applications*, second edition. New York: Guilford Press, pp. 2–21.

Chisholm, R. M. (1957). *Perceiving: A Philosophical Study*. Ithaca, NY: Cornell University Press.

Chomsky, N. (1980). *Rules and Representations*. Oxford: Blackwell.

Churchland, P. M. (2012). *Plato's Camera: How the Physical Brain Captures a Landscape of Abstract Universals*. Cambridge, MA: MIT Press.

Compiani, M. (1996). Remarks on the paradigms of connectionism. In A. Clark & P. Millican (Eds), *The Legacy of Alan Turing. Volume II: Connectionism, Concepts, and Folk Psychology*. Oxford: Oxford University Press, pp. 45–66.

Corr, P. J. (2008a). *The Reinforcement Sensitivity Theory of Personality*. Cambridge: Cambridge University Press.

Corr, P. J. (2008b). Reinforcement sensitivity theory (RST): Introduction. In P. Corr (Ed.), *The Reinforcement Sensitivity Theory of Personality*. Cambridge: Cambridge University Press, pp. 1–43.

Corr, P. J. & Krupić, D. (2017). Motivating personality: Approach, avoidance, and their conflict, *Advances in Motivation Science*, 4, 1–51.

Crane, T. (2002). *The Mechanical Mind: A Philosophical Introduction to Minds, Machines and Mental Representations*, second edition. London and New York: Routledge.

Crane, T. (2009). Internationalism. In B. P. McLaughlin, A. Beckerman & S. Walter (2009) (Eds), *The Oxford Handbook of Philosophy of Mind*. Oxford: Oxford University Press, pp. 474–493.

Curry, B., Foxall, G. R. & Sigurdsson, V. (2010). On the tautology of the matching law in consumer behavior analysis, *Behavioural Processes*, 84, 390–399.

Damasio, A. (1994). *Descartes' Error: Emotion, Reason, and the Human Brain*. New York: Putnam.

Damasio, A. (1999). *The Feeling of What Happens: Body, Emotion and the Making of Consciousness*. London: Vintage.

Dancy, J. (2000). *Practical Reality*. Oxford: Oxford University Press.

Davidson, D. (2001). How is weakness of will possible? In D. Davidson, *Essays on Action and Events*. Oxford: Oxford University Press, pp. 21–42.

Dawkins, R. P. (1976). *The Selfish Gene*. Oxford: Oxford University Press.

Dawkins, R. P. (1982). *The Extended Phenotype*. Oxford: Oxford University Press.

Delgado, M. R. & Tricomi, E. (2011). Reward processing and decision making in the human striatum. In O. Vartanian & D. R. Mandel (Eds), *Neuroscience of Decision Making*. New York and Hove: Psychology Press, pp. 145–172.

Demaree, H. A., Everhart, D. E., Youngstrom, E. A. & Harrison, D. W. (2005). Brain lateralization of emotional processing: historical roots and a future incorporating "dominance". *Behavioral and Cognitive Neuroscience Reviews*, 4, 3–20.

Deonna, J. A. & Teroni, F. (2012). *The Emotions: A Philosophical Introduction*. London and New York: Routledge.

Deonna, J. A. & Teroni, F. (2015). Emotions as attitudes, *Dialectica*, 69, 293–311.

Dennett, D. C. (1969). *Content and Consciousness*. London: Routledge and Kegan Paul.

Dennett, D. C. (1987). *The Intentional Stance*. Cambridge, MA: MIT Press.

Dennett, D. C. (1991). *Consciousness Explained*. New York: Little, Brown.

Dennett, D. C. (1996). *Kinds of Minds: Towards an Understanding of Consciousness*. London: Weidenfeld & Nicolson.

Dittmar, H. & Bond, R. (2010). I want it and I want it now: Using a temporal discounting paradigm to examine predictors of consumer impulsivity. *British Journal of Psychology*, 101, 751–776.

Dokic, J. & Engel, P. (2001). *Frank Ramsey: Truth and Success*. London: Routledge.

Dokic, J. & Engel, P. (2004). Ramsey's principle reinstated. In D. H. Mellor & H. Lillehammer (Eds), *Ramsey's Legacy*. Oxford: Oxford University Press, pp. 8–21.

Dokic, J. & Lemaire, S. (2015). Are emotions evaluative modules? *Dialectica*, 69, 271–292.

Döring, S. A. (2015). What's wrong with recalcitrant emotions? From irrationality to challenge of agential identity. *Dialectica*, 69, 381–402.

Döring, S. A. & Lutz, A. (2015). Beyond perceptualism: Introduction to the special issue. *Dialectica*, 69, 259–270.

Dretske, F. (1981). *Knowledge and the Flow of Information*. Cambridge, MA: MIT Press.

Dretske, F. (1988). *Explaining Behavior: Reasons in a World of Causes*. Cambridge, MA: MIT Press.

Dretske, F. (1991). How beliefs explain: Reply to Baker. *Philosophical Studies*, 63, 113–117.

Dretske, F. (1995). *Naturalizing the Mind*. Cambridge, MA: MIT Press.

Dretske, F. (2001). Where is the mind? In A. Meijers (Ed.), *Explaining Beliefs: Lynne Rudder Baker and Her Critics*. Stanford, CA: Center for the Study of Language and Information, pp. 39–49.

Evans, D. & Cruse, P. (2004). *Emotion, Evolution, and Rationality*. Oxford: Oxford University Press.

Evans, J. St. B. T. (2007). *Hypothetical Thinking: Dual Processes in Reasoning and Judgement*. Hove: Psychology Press.

Evans, J. St. B. T. (2010). *Thinking Twice: Two Minds in One Brain*. Oxford: Oxford University Press.

Faucher, L. & Tappolet, C. (Eds) (2008a). *The Modularity of Emotions*. Calgary, Alberta: University of Calgary Press.

Faucher, L. & Tappolet, C. (2008b). Introduction: Modularity and the nature of emotions. In L. Foucher & C. Tappolet (Eds), *The Modularity of Emotions*. Calgary, Alberta: University of Calgary Press, pp. xii–xxxi.

Fish, W. (2010). *Philosophy of Perception*. New York and London: Routledge.

Fishbein, M. & Ajzen, I. (2010). *Predicting and Changing Behavior*. New York: Psychology Press.

Fodor, J. (1983). *The Modularity of Mind*. Cambridge, MA: MIT Press.

Fodor, J. (2000). *The Mind Doesn't Work that Way*. Cambridge, MA: MIT Press.

Foxall, G. R. (1983). *Consumer Choice*. London: Macmillan; New York: St. Martin's Press.

Foxall, G. R. (1997a). The emotional texture of consumer environments: A systematic approach to atmospherics. *Journal of Economic Psychology*, 18, 505–523.

Foxall, G. R. (1997b). Affective responses to consumer situations. *International Review of Retail, Distribution and Consumer Research*, 7, 191–225.

Foxall, G. R. (1997c). *Marketing Psychology: The Paradigm in the Wings*. London and New York: Palgrave Macmillan.

Foxall, G. R. (1999). The Behavioural Perspective Model: Consensibility and consensuality. *European Journal of Marketing*, 33, 570–596.

Foxall, G. R. (2004). *Context and Cognition: Interpreting Complex Behavior*. Reno, NV: Context Press.

Foxall, G. R. (2005). *Understanding Consumer Choice*. London and New York: Palgrave Macmillan.

Foxall, G. R. (2007a). *Explaining Consumer Choice*. London and New York: Palgrave Macmillan.

Foxall, G. R. (2007b). Intentional behaviorism. *Behavior and Philosophy*, 35, 1–56.

Foxall, G. R. (2008). Intentional behaviorism revisited. *Behavior and Philosophy*, 37, 113–156.

Foxall, G. R. (2009). Ascribing intentionality. *Behavior and Philosophy*, 37, 217–222.

Foxall, G. R. (2010). Invitation to consumer behavior analysis. *Journal of Organizational Behavior Management*, 30(2), 92–109.

Foxall, G. R. (2011). Brain, emotion, and contingency in the explanation of consumer behaviour. *International Review of Industrial and Organizational Psychology*, 26, 26–52.

Foxall, G. R. (2016a). *Addiction as Consumer Choice: Exploring the Cognitive Dimension*. London and New York: Routledge.

Foxall, G. R. (2016b). *Perspectives on Consumer Choice: From Behavior to Action, From Action to Agency*. London and New York: Palgrave Macmillan.

Foxall, G. R. (2016c). Metacognitive control of categorial neurobehavioral decision systems. *Frontiers in Psychology (Theoretical and Philosophical Psychology)*, 7(170), 1–18.

Foxall, G. R. (Ed.) (2016d). *The Routledge Companion to Consumer Behavior Analysis.* London and New York: Routledge, pp. 417–430.

Foxall, G. R. (2016e). Consumer heterophenomenology. In G. R. Foxall (Ed.), *The Routledge Companion to Consumer Behavior Analysis.* London and New York: Routledge, pp. 417–430.

Foxall, G. R. (2017). *Advanced Introduction to Consumer Behavior Analysis.* Cheltenham, UK and Northampton, MA: Edward Elgar.

Foxall, G. R. (in preparation). *Intentional Behaviorism: The Philosophical Basis of Economic Psychology.* New York: Elsevier.

Foxall, G. R. & Greenley, G. E. (1998). The affective structure of consumer situations. *Environment and Behavior,* 30, 781–798.

Foxall, G. R. & Greenley, G. E. (1999). Consumers' emotional responses to service environments. *Journal of Business Research,* 46, 149–158.

Foxall, G. R. & Greenley, G. E. (2000). Predicting and explaining responses to consumer environments: An empirical test and theoretical extension of the Behavioural Perspective Model. *Service Industries Journal,* 20, 39–63.

Foxall, G. R. & Sigurdsson, V. (2012). When loss rewards: The near-miss effect in slot machine gambling. *Analysis of Gambling Behavior,* 6(5)–22.

Foxall, G. R. & Sigurdsson, S. (2016). When loss rewards: The near-miss effect in slot machine gambling. In Foxall, G. R. (Ed.), *The Routledge Companion to Consumer Behavior Analysis.* London and New York: Routledge, pp. 242–257.

Foxall, G. R. & Yani-de-Soriano, M. M. (2005). Situational influences on consumers' attitudes and behavior. *Journal of Business Research,* 58, 518–525.

Foxall, G. R., Yani-de-Soriano, M., Yousafzai, S. & Javed, U. (2012). The role of neurophysiology, emotion and contingency in the explanation of consumer choice. In V. K. Wells & G. R. Foxall (Eds), *Handbook of Developments in Consumer Behaviour.* Cheltenham, UK and Northampton, MA: Edward Elgar, pp. 461–522.

Frankish, K. & Evans, J. St. B. T. (2009). The duality of mind: An historical perspective. In J. St. B. T. Evans & K. Frankish (Eds), *In Two Minds: Dual Processes and Beyond.* Oxford: Oxford University Press, pp. 1–29.

Freud, A. (1937). *The Ego and the Mechanisms of Defence.* Trans. C. Baines. London: Hogarth. (Originally published, Vienna 1936.)

Freud, S. ([1900] 1953). The interpretation of dreams. In J. Strachey (trans.), *The Standard Edition of the Complete Psychological Works of Sigmund Freud, Volumes 4–5.* London: Hogarth Press.

Freud, S. ([1911] 1958). Formulations on the two principles of mental functioning. In J. Strachey & A. Freud (Eds), *The Standard Edition of the Complete Works of Sigmund Freud, Volume 12.* London: Hogarth Press, pp. 218–226.

Freud, S. ([1895] 1964). Project for a scientific psychology. In J. Strachey (trans.) *The Standard Edition of the Complete Psychological Works of Sigmund Freud, Volume 1.* London: Hogarth Press.

Frijda, N. H. (2008). The psychologist's point of view. In M. Lewis, J. M. Haviland-Jones & L. F. Barrett (Eds), *Handbook of Emotions,* third edition. New York: Guilford Press, pp. 68–87.

Gelder, B. de (1996). Modularity and logical cognitivism. In A. Clark & P. Millican (Eds), *The Legacy of Alan Turing. Volume II: Connectionism, Concepts, and Folk Psychology.* Oxford: Oxford University Press, pp. 147–168.

Gelder, B. de & Vroomen, J. (1994). A new place for modality in a modular mind. *Cahiers de Psychologie Cognitive,* 13, 84–91.

Gilboa, S. & Rafaeli, A. (2003). Store environment, emotions and approach behavior: Applying environmental aesthetics to retailing. *International Review of Retail, Distribution and Consumer Research,* 13, 195–211.

Gollwitzer, P. M. & Oettingen, G. (2013). Planning promotes goal striving. In K. D. Vohs & R. F. Baumeister (Eds), *Handbook of Self-regulation: Research, Theory, and Applications*, second edition. New York: Guilford Press, pp. 162–185.

Gray, J. A. (1982). *The Neuropsychology of Anxiety: An Enquiry into the Functions of the Septo-hippocampal System*. Oxford: Oxford University Press.

Gray, J. A. & McNaughton, N. (2000). *The Neuropsychology of Anxiety*. Oxford: Oxford University Press.

Groeppel-Klein, A. (2005). Arousal and consumer in-store behavior. *Brain Research Bulletin*, 67, 428–437.

Hackett, P. M. W. (2016). *Psychology and Philosophy of Abstract Art: Neuro-aesthetics, Perception and Compensation*. London: Palgrave Macmillan.

Hebb, D. O. (1949). *The Organization of Behavior: A Neuropsychological Theory*. New York: Wiley.

Heil, J. (1998). *Philosophy of Mind*. London: Routledge.

Heil, J. (2013). Mental causation according to Davidson. In G. D'Oro & C. Sandis (Eds), *Reasons and Causes: Causalism and Anti-causalism in the Philosophy of Action*. Basingstoke: Palgrave Macmillan, pp. 75–96.

Helm, B. W. (2015). Emotions and recalcitrance: Reevaluating the perceptual model. *Dialectica*, 69, 417–433.

Herrnstein, R. J. & Vaughan, W., Jr. (1980). Melioration and behavioral allocation. In J. E. R. Staddon (Ed.), *Limits to Action: The Allocation of Individual Behavior*. New York: Academic Press.

Heyes, C. (2000). Evolutionary psychology in the round. In C. Heyes & L. Huber (Eds), *The Evolution of Cognition*. Cambridge, MA: MIT Press, pp. 3–22.

Heyes, C. & Huber, L. (Eds) (2000). *The Evolution of Cognition*. Cambridge, MA: MIT Press.

Hofmann, W., Friese, M., Schmeichel, B. J. & Baddeley, A. D. (2013). Working memory and self-regulation. In K. D. Vohs & R. F. Baumeister (Eds), *Handbook of Self-regulation: Research, Theory, and Applications*, second edition. New York: Guilford Press, pp. 204–225.

Hornsby, J. (1981). *Actions*. London: Routledge and Kegan Paul.

Jacob, P. & Jeannerod, M. (2003). *Ways of Seeing: The Scope and Limits of Visual Cognition*. Oxford: Oxford University Press.

Jarmolowicz, D. P., Reed, D. D., DiGennaro Reed, F. D. & Bickel, W. K. (2016). The behavioral and neuroeconomics of reinforcer pathologies: Implications for managerial and health decision making. *Managerial and Decision Economics*, 37, 274–293.

Jeannerod, M. (1994). The representing brain: Neural correlates of motor intention and imagery. *Behavioral and Brain Sciences*, 17, 187–245.

Jeannerod, M. (1997). *The Cognitive Neuroscience of Action*. Oxford: Blackwell.

Johnston, E. & Olson, L. (2015). *The Feeling Brain: The Biology and Psychology of Emotions*. New York: Norton.

Jones, K. (2008). Quick and smart? Modularity and the pro-emotion consensus. In L. Faucher & C. Tappolet (Eds), *The Modularity of Emotions*. Calgary, Alberta: University of Calgary Press, pp. 3–27.

Kahneman, D. (2011). *Thinking, Fast and Slow*. London: Allen Lane.

Kennett, J. (2001). *Agency and Responsibility: A Common-sense Moral Psychology*. Oxford: Oxford University Press.

Kirton, M. J. (2003). *Adaption—Innovation in the Context of Diversity and Change*. London and New York: Psychology Press.

Koob, G. E. F. (2013). Neuroscience of addiction. In B. S. McCrady & E. E. Epstein (Eds), *Addictions: A Comprehensive Guidebook*, second edition. New York: Oxford University Press, pp. 17–35.

Koob, G. F. & Le Moal, M. (2001). Drug addiction, dysregulation of reward, and allostasis. *Neuropsychopharmacology*, 24, 97–129.

Koob, G. F. & Le Moal, M. (2006). *Neurobiology of Addiction*. London: Academic Press.

Koob, G. F., Arends, M. A. & Le Moal, M. (2014). *Drugs, Addiction, and the Brain*. Oxford: Academic Press.

Koole, S. L., van Dillen, L. F. & Sheppes, G. (2013). The self-regulation of emotion. In K. D. Vohs & R. F. Baumeister (Eds), *Handbook of Self-regulation: Research, Theory, and Applications*, second edition. New York: Guilford Press, pp. 22–40.

Kringelbach, M. L. (2010). The hedonic brain: A functional neuroanatomy of human pleasure. In M. L. Kringelbach & K. C. Berridge (Eds), *Pleasures of the Brain*. Oxford: Oxford University Press, pp. 202–221.

Kringelbach, M. L. & Phillips, H. (2014). *Emotion: Pleasure and Pain in the Brain*. Oxford: Oxford University Press.

Lacewing, D. (2015). Emotion, perception, and the self in moral epistemology. *Dialectica*, 69, 335–355.

LeDoux, J. E. (1998). *The Emotional Brain*. New York: Simon & Schuster.

LeDoux, J. E. (2000). Emotional circuits in the brain. *Annual Review of Neuroscience*, 23, 155–184.

Lupyan, G. (2015). Cognitive penetration of perception in the age of prediction: Predictive systems are penetrable systems. *Review of Philosophy and Psychology*, 5, 547–569.

Lutz, A. (2015). The phenomenal character of emotional experience: A look at perception theory. *Dialectica*, 69, 313–334.

Lyons, W. (1995). *Approaches to Intentionality*. Oxford: Clarendon Press.

Madden, G. J. & Bickel, W. K. (Eds) (2010). *Impulsivity: The Behavioral and Neurological Science of Discounting*. Washington, DC: American Psychological Association.

Malafouris, L. (2013). *How Things Shape the Mind: A Theory of Material Engagement*. Cambridge, MA: MIT Press.

Malcolm, N. (1977). *Thought and Knowledge*. Ithaca, NY: Cornell University Press.

McClure, S. M., Laibson, D. L., Loewenstein, G. & Cohen, J. D. (2004). Separate neural systems value immediate and delayed monetary rewards. *Science*, 306(5695), 503–507.

McGinn, C. (2004). *Consciousness and its Objects*. Oxford: Oxford University Press.

McGinn, C. (2006). *Shakespeare's Philosophy: Discovering the Meaning behind the Plays*. New York: Harper.

McGurk, H. & MacDonald, J. (1976). Hearing lips and seeing voices. *Nature*, 264, 746–748.

McNaughton, N. & Corr, P. J. (2004). A two-dimensional neuropsychology of defense: Fear/anxiety and defense distance. *Neuroscience and Biobehavioral Reviews*, 28, 285–305.

McRae, K., Ochsner, K. N. & Gross, J. J. (2013). The reason in passion: A social cognitive neuroscience approach to emotion regulation. In K. D. Vohs & R. F. Baumeister (Eds), *Handbook of Self-regulation: Research, Theory, and Applications*, second edition. New York: Guilford Press, pp. 186–203.

Mehrabian, A. (1979). Effect of emotional state on alcohol consumption. *Psychological Reports*, 44, 271–282.

Mehrabian, A. (1980). *Basic Dimensions for a General Psychological Theory*. Cambridge, MA: Oelgeschlager, Gunn & Hain.

Mehrabian, A. & Riccioni, M. (1986). Measures of eating-related characteristics for the general population: Relationships with temperament. *Journal of Personality Assessment*, 50, 610–629.

Mehrabian, A. & Russell, J. A. (1974). *An Approach to Environmental Psychology*. Cambridge, MA: MIT Press.

Mehrabian, A. & Russell, J. A. (1975). Environmental effects on affiliation among strangers. *Humanitas*, 11, 219–230.

Mehrabian, A. & de Wetter, R. (1987). Experimental test of an emotion-based approach to fitting brand names to products. *Journal of Applied Psychology*, 72, 125–130.

Miller, E. K. & Wallis, J. D. (2009). Executive function and higher-order cognition: Definition and neural substrates. In L. R. Squire (Ed.), *Encyclopedia of Neuroscience, Volume 4*. Oxford: Academic Press, pp. 99–104.

Millikan, R. G. (2004). *Varieties of Meaning*. Cambridge, MA: MIT Press.

Mischel, W. & Ayduk, O. (2013). Willpower in a cognitive affective processing system: The dynamics of delay of gratification. In K. D. Vohs & R. F. Baumeister (Eds), *Handbook of Self-regulation: Research, Theory, & Applications*, second edition. New York: Guilford Press, pp. 83–105.

Mithen, S. (1996). *The Prehistory of the Mind: A Search for the Origins of Art, Religion and Science*. London: Thames & Hudson.

Moore, S. & Oaksford, M. (Eds) (2002). *Emotional Cognition*. Amsterdam and Philadelphia: John Benjamins.

Morris, J. D., Klahr, N. J., Shen, F., Villegas, J., Wright, P. et al. (2008). Mapping a multidimensional emotion in response to television commercials. *Human Mind Mapping*, 30, 789–796.

Müller, A. & Mitchell, J. E. (Eds) (2011). *Compulsive Buying: Clinical Foundations and Treatment*. London and New York: Routledge.

Nanay, B. (2011). Do we see apples as edible? *Pacific Philosophical Quarterly*, 92, 305–322.

Nanay, B. (2012). Action-oriented perception. *European Journal of Philosophy*, 20, 430–446.

Nanay, B. (2013a). *Between Perception and Action*. Oxford: Oxford University Press.

Nanay, B. (2013b). Success semantics: The sequel. *Philosophical Studies*, 165, 151–165.

Naqvi, N., Shiv, B. & Bechara, A. (2006). The role of emotion in decision making. *Current Directions in Psychological Science*, 15, 260–264.

Nichols, T. T. (2017). *The Death of Expertise: The Campaign against Established Knowledge and Why It Matters*. New York: Oxford University Press.

Nichols, T. T. & Wilson, S. J. (2015). Working memory functioning and addictive behavior: Insights form cognitive neuroscience. In S. J. Wilson (Ed.), *The Wiley Handbook on the Cognitive Neuroscience of Addiction*. Chichester: Wiley-Blackwell, pp. 55–77.

Oliveira-Castro, J. M., Cavalcanti, P. & Foxall, G. R. (2016a). What consumers maximize: Brand choice as a function of utilitarian and informational reinforcement. *Managerial and Decision Economics*, 37, 360–371.

Oliveira-Castro, J. M., Cavalcanti, P. & Foxall, G. R. (2016b). What do consumers maximize? The analysis of utility functions in light of the Behavioral Perspective Model. In G. R. Foxall (Ed.), *The Routledge Companion to Consumer Behavior Analysis*. London and New York: Routledge, pp. 202–212.

Osgood, C. E., May, W. H. & Miron, M. S. (1975). *Cross-cultural Universals of Affective Meaning*. Urbana, IL: University of Illinois Press.

Osgood, C. E., Suci, G. J. & Tannenbaum, P. H. (1957). *The Measurement of Meaning*. Urbana, IL: University of Illinois Press.

O'Shaughnessy, J. & O'Shaughnessy, N. J. (2003). *The Marketing Power of Emotion*. New York: Oxford University Press.

Over, D. E. (2003). *Evolution and the Psychology of Thinking: The Debate*. Hove and New York: Psychology Press.

Panksepp, J. (1998). *Affective Neuroscience*. Oxford: Oxford University Press.

Panksepp, J. (2005). On the embodied neural nature of core emotional affect. *Journal of Consciousness Studies*, 12, 158–184.

Panksepp, J. (2007). The neuroevolutionary and neuroaffective psychobiology of the proso-cial brain. In R. I. M. Dunbar & L. Barrett (Eds), *The Oxford Handbook of Evolutionary Psychology*. Oxford: Oxford University Press, pp. 145–162.

Perkins, D. N. (1995). *Outsmarting IQ: The Emerging Science of Learnable Intelligence*. New York: Free Press.

Peters, J. & Büchel, C. (2011). The neural mechanisms of inter-temporal decision mak-ing: Understanding variability. *Trends in Cognitive Science*, 15, 227–239.

Peterson, R. L. (2007). *Inside the Investor's Brain: The Power of Mind over Money*. Hoboken, NJ: Wiley.

Petry, N. M. (2005). *Pathological Gambling: Etiology, Comorbidity, and Treatment*. Washington, DC: American Psychological Association.

Phelps, E. A. & Sokol-Hessner, P. (2012). Social and emotional factors in decision-making: Appraisal and value. In R. J. Dolan & T. Sharot (Eds), *Neuroscience of Preference and Choice: Cognitive and Neural Mechanisms*. Amsterdam: Academic Press, pp. 207–223.

Pickering, A. D. & Smillie, L. D. (2008). The behavioral activation system: Challenges and opportunities. In P. J. Corr (Ed.), *The Reinforcement Sensitivity Theory of Personality*. Cambridge: Cambridge University Press, pp. 120–154.

Politser, P. (2008). *Neuroeconomics: A Guide to the New Science of Making Choices*. New York: Oxford University Press.

Price, C. (2005). *Emotion*. Milton Keynes: Open University Press.

Prinz, J. J. (2002a). Consciousness, computation, and emotion. In S. Moore & M. Oaksford (Eds), *Emotional Cognition*. Amsterdam and Philadelphia: John Benjamins.

Prinz, J. J. (2002b). *Furnishing the Mind: Concepts and their Perceptual Basis*. Cambridge, MA: MIT Press.

Prinz, J. (2003). Emotions embodied. In R. Solomon (Ed.), *Thinking about Feeling*. New York: Oxford University Press.

Prinz, J. J. (2004). *Gut Reactions: A Perceptual Theory of Emotion*. Oxford: Oxford University Press.

Prinz, J. J. (2006). Is the mind really modular? In R. J. Stainton (Ed.), *Contemporary Debates in Cognitive Science*. Oxford: Blackwell, pp. 22–36.

Prinz, J. J. (2008). Is emotion a form of perception? In L. Faucher & C. Tappolet (Eds), *The Modularity of Emotions*. Calgary, Alberta: University of Calgary Press, pp. 137–160.

Radoilska, L. (2013). *Addiction and Weakness of Will*. Oxford: Oxford University Press.

Ramsey, F. P. ([1927] 1990). Facts and propositions. *Aristotelian Society Supplementary Volume*, 7, 153–170. Reprinted in Mellor, D. H. (Ed.) (1990). *F. P. Ramsey: Philosophical Papers*. Cambridge: Cambridge University Press.

Ridgway, N., Kukar-Kinney, M. & Monroe, K. B. (2008). An expanded conceptualization and a new measure of compulsive buying. *Journal of Consumer Research*, 35, 622–639.

Roberts, R. C. (1988). What an emotion is: A sketch. *Philosophical Review*, 97, 202–203.

Rolls, E. T. (1999). *Emotion and the Brain*. Oxford: Oxford University Press.

Rolls, E. T. (2005). *Emotion Explained*. Oxford: Oxford University Press.

Rolls, E. T. (2008). *Memory, Attention, and Decision-making*. Oxford: Oxford University Press.

Rolls, E. T. (2009). From reward value to decision-making: Neuronal and computational principles. In J.-C. Dreher & L. Tremblay (Eds), *Handbook of Reward and Decision Making*. Amsterdam: Academic Press, pp. 97–133.

Rolls, E. T. (2012). *Neuroculture: On the Implications of Brain Science*. Oxford: Oxford University Press.

Rolls, E. T. (2014). *Emotion and Decision-making Explained*. Oxford: Oxford University Press.

Rolls, E. T., Grabenhorst, F. & Leonardo, F. (2009). Prediction of subjective affective state from brain activations. *Journal of Neurophysiology*, 101, 1294–1308.

Ross, D. (2012). The economic agent: Not human, but important. In U. Mäki (Ed.), *Philosophy of Economics*. Amsterdam: Elsevier, pp. 691–736.

Ross, D., Sharp, C., Vuchinich, R. E. & Spurrett, D. (2008). *Midbrain Mutiny: The Picoeconomics and Neuroeconomics of Disordered Gambling*. Cambridge, MA: MIT Press.

Runyan, J. D. (2014). *Human Agency and Neural Causes: Philosophy of Action and the Neuroscience of Voluntary Agency*. New York: Palgrave Macmillan.

Russell, B. (1912). *The Problems of Philosophy*. London: Home University Library of Modern Knowledge.

Russell, J. A. & Barrett, L. F. (1999). Core affect, prototypical emotional episodes, and other things called *emotion*: Dissecting the elephant. *Journal of Personality and Social Psychology*, 76, 805–819.

Russell, J. A. & Mehrabian, A. (1976). Environmental variables in consumer research. *Journal of Consumer Research*, 3, 62–63.

Russell, J. A. & Mehrabian, A. (1978). Approach-avoidance and affiliation as functions of the emotion-eliciting quality of an environment. *Environment and Behavior*, 10, 355–387.

Ryle, G. (1949). *The Concept of Mind*. London: Hutchinson.

Sadler-Smith, E. (2009). A duplex model of cognitive style. In L. Zhang & R. J. Sternberg (Eds), *Perspectives on the Nature of Intellectual Styles*. New York: Springer, pp. 3–28.

Sahlin, N.-E. (1990). *The Philosophy of F. P. Ramsey*. Cambridge: Cambridge University Press.

Samuels, R. (2000). Massively modular minds: Evolutionary psychology and cognitive architecture. In P. Caruthers & A. Chamberlain (Eds), *Evolution and the Human Mind: Modularity, Language and Meta-cognition*. Cambridge: Cambridge University Press, pp. 13–46.

Samuels, R. (2005). The complexity of cognition: Tractability arguments for massive modularity. In P. Carruthers, S. Laurence & S. Stich (Eds), *The Innate Mind: Structure and Contents*. Oxford: Oxford University Press, pp. 107–121.

Samuels, R. (2006). Is the human mind massively modular? In R. J. Stainton (Ed.), *Contemporary Debates in Cognitive Science*. Oxford: Blackwell, pp. 37–55.

Schultz W. (2000). Multiple reward signals in the brain. *Nature Reviews Neuroscience*, 1, 199–207.

Schultz, W., Preuschoff, K., Camerer, C., Hsu, M., Fiorillo, C. D. et al. (2008). Explicit neural signals reflecting reward uncertainty. *Philosophical Transactions of the Royal Society B*, 363, 3801–3811.

Sandis, C. (Ed.) (2009). *New Essays on the Explanation of Action*. London and New York: Palgrave Macmillan.

Sandis, C. (2012). *The Things We Do and Why We Do Them*. London and New York: Palgrave Macmillan.

Schnaitter, R. (1999). Some criticisms of behaviorism. In B. A. Thyer (Ed.), *The Philosophical Legacy of Behaviorism*. Dordrecht: Kluwer, pp. 209–249.

Searle, J. R. (1983). *Intentionality: An Essay in the Philosophy of Mind*. Cambridge: Cambridge University Press.

Searle, J. R. (1995). *The Construction of Social Reality*. New York: Free Press.

Searle, J. R. (2000). Consciousness. *Annual Review of Neuroscience*, 23, 557–578.

Searle, J. (2001). *Rationality in Action*. Cambridge, MA: MIT Press.

Searle, J. R. (2010). *Making the Social World: The Structure of Human Civilization*. Oxford: Oxford University Press.

Searle, J. R. (2015). *Seeing Things as They Are: A Theory of Perception*. Oxford: Oxford University Press.

Segal, H. (1979). *Klein*. Glasgow: Fontana/Collins.

Shettleworth, S. J. (2000). Modularity and the evolution of cognition. In C. Heyes & L. Huber (Eds), *The Evolution of Cognition*. Cambridge, MA: MIT Press, pp. 43–60.

Shettleworth, S. J. (2010). *Cognition, Evolution, and Behavior*. Oxford: Oxford University Press.

Schroeter, L., Schroeter, F. & Jones, K. (2015). Do emotions represent values? *Dialectica*, 69, 357–380.

Shea, N., Boldt, A., Bang, D., Yeung, N., Heyes, C. & Frith, C. D. (2014). Supra-personal cognitive control and metacognition. *Trends in Cognitive Sciences*, 18, 186–193.

Siegal, S. (2011). *The Contents of Visual Experience*. Oxford: Oxford University Press.

Skinner, B. F. (1950). Are theories of learning necessary? *Psychological Review*, 57, 193–216.

Skinner, B. F. (1953). *Science and Human Behavior*. New York: Macmillan.

Skinner, B. F. (1969). *Contingencies of Reinforcement: A Theoretical Analysis*. Englewood Cliffs, NJ: Prentice Hall.

Skinner, B. F. (1971). *Beyond Freedom and Dignity*. New York: Cape.

Skinner, B. F. (1974). *About Behaviorism*. New York: Knopf.

Skinner, B. F. (1977). Why I am not a cognitive psychologist. *Behaviorism*, 5, 1–10.

Slovic, P., Finucane, M. L., Peters, E. & MacGregor, D. G. (2004). Risk as analysis and risk as feelings: Some thoughts about affect, reason, risk, and rationality. *Risk Analysis*, 24, 311–322.

Smillie, L. D. (2008). What is reinforcement sensitivity? Neuroscience paradigms for approach–avoidance process theories of personality. *European Journal of Personality*, 22, 359–384.

Solomon, R. C. (2008). The philosophy of emotions. In M. Lewis, J. M. Haviland-Jones, & L. F. Barrett (Eds), *Handbook of Emotions*, third edition. New York: Guilford Press, pp. 3–16.

Stainton, R. J. (Ed.) (2006). *Contemporary Debates in Cognitive Science*. Oxford: Blackwell.

Stanovich, K. E. (2004). *The Robot's Rebellion*. Chicago, IL: Chicago University Press.

Stanovich, K. E. (2009a). Distinguishing the reflective, algorithmic, and autonomous minds: Is it time for a tri-process theory? In J. St. B. T. Evans & K. Frankish (Eds), *In Two Minds: Dual Processes and Beyond*. Oxford: Oxford University Press, pp. 55–88.

Stanovich, K. E. (2009b). *What Intelligence Tests Miss: The Psychology of Rational Thought*. New Haven and London: Yale University Press.

Stanovich, K. E. (2011). *Rationality and the Reflective Mind*. Oxford: Oxford University Press.

Stanovich, K. E. & West, R. F. (2000). Individual differences in reasoning: Implications for the rationality debate? *Brain and Behavioral Sciences*, 23, 645–726.

Stanovich, K. E. & West, R. F. (2003a). The rationality debate as a progressive research program. *Behavioral and Brain Sciences*, 26, 531–533.

Stanovich, K. E. & West, R. F. (2003b). Evolutionary versus instrumental goals: How evolutionary psychology misconceives human rationality. In D. E. Over (Ed.), *Evolution and the Psychology of Thinking: The Debate*. Hove and New York: Psychology Press.

Stanovich, K. E. & West, R. F. (2011a). A taxonomy of rational thinking problems. In R. E. Stanovich, *Rationality and the Reflective Mind*. Oxford: Oxford University Press, pp. 95–119.

Stanovich, K. E. & West, R. F. (2011b). Intelligence as a predictor of performance on heuristics and biases tasks. In R. E. Stanovich, *Rationality and the Reflective Mind*. Oxford: Oxford University Press, pp. 121–154.

Stanovich, K. E., West, R. F. & Toplak, M. E. (2012). Intelligence and rationality. In R. Sternberg, & S. B. Kaufman (Eds), *Cambridge Handbook of Intelligence*. Cambridge: Cambridge University Press, pp. 784–826.

Sterelny, K. (2003). *Thought in a Hostile World: The Evolution of Human Cognition*. Oxford: Blackwell.

Sternberg, S. (2011). Modular processes in brain and mind. *Cognitive Neuropsychology*, 28, 156–208.

Steward, H. (2012). *A Metaphysics for Freedom*. Oxford: Oxford University Press.

Tai, S. H. C. & Fung, A. M. C. (1997). Application of an environmental psychology model to in-store buying behavior. *International Review of Retail, Distribution and Consumer Research*, 7, 311–337.

Tappolet, C. (2016). *Emotions, Values, and Agency*. Oxford: Oxford University Press.

Terrace, H. S. (1984). Animal cognition. In H. L. Roitblatt, T. G. Bever & H. S. Terrace (Eds), *Animal Cognition*. Hillsdale, NJ: Lawrence Erlbaum, pp. 7–28.

Tomasello, M. (2014). *A Natural History of Human Thinking*. Cambridge, MA: Harvard University Press.

Tomasello, M. (2016). *A Natural History of Human Morality*. Cambridge, MA: Harvard University Press.

Tooby, J. & Cosmides, L. (1992). The psychological foundations of culture. In J. H. Barkow, L. Cosmides & J. Tooby (Eds), *The Adapted Mind*. Oxford: Oxford University Press, pp. 19–136.

Toronchuk, J. A. & Ellis, G. F. R. (2013). Affective neuronal selection: The nature of the primordial emotion systems. *Frontiers in Psychology*, 3, 589.

Van Kenhove, P. & Desrumaux, P. (1997). The relationship between emotional states and approach or avoidance responses in a retail environment. *International Review of Retail, Distribution and Consumer Research*, 7, 351–368.

Villiers, P. A. de & Herrnstein, R. J. (1976). Toward a law of response strength. *Psychological Bulletin*, 83, 1131–1153.

Vohs, K. D. & Baumeister, R. F. (Eds) (2011). *Handbook of Self-regulation: Research, Theory, and Applications*, second edition. New York: Guilford Press.

Vuchinich, R. E. & Heather, N. (Eds) (2003). *Choice, Behavioral Economics and Addiction*. Amsterdam: Pergamon.

Wager, T. D., Barrett, L. F., Bliss-Moreau, E., Lindquist, K. A., Duncan, S. et al. (2008). The neuroimaging of emotion. In M. Lewis, J. M. Haviland-Jones & L. F. Barrett (Eds), *Handbook of Emotions*, third edition. New York: Guilford Press, pp. 249–271.

Whyte, J. T. (1990). Success semantics. *Analysis*, 50, 149–157.

Wallach, L. & Wallach, M. A. (2013). *Seven Views of Mind*. London and New York: Psychology Press.

Whiting, D. (2012). Are emotions perceptual experiences of value? *Ratio*, 25, 93–107.

Whyte, J. T. (1993). Purpose and content. *British Journal for the Philosophy of Science*, 44, 45–60.

Whyte, J. T. (1997). Success again: Replies to Brandom and Godfrey-Smith. *Analysis*, 57, 84–87.

Yani-de-Soriano, M. & Foxall, G. R. (2006). The emotional power of place: The fall and rise of dominance in retail research. *Journal of Retailing and Consumer Services*, 13, 403–416.

Yani-de-Soriano, M., Foxall, G. R. & Newman, A. (2013). The impact of the interaction of utilitarian and informational reinforcement and behaviour setting scope on consumer response. *Psychology and Marketing*, 30, 148–159.

Zettle, R. D. & Hayes, S. C. (1982). Rule-governed behavior: A potential framework for cognitive-behavioral therapy. In P. C. Kendall (Ed.), *Advances in Cognitive-behavioral Research and Therapy*. Academic Press, New York, pp. 73–117.

INDEX

Abrahamsen, A. 43
Accomplishment 8–10, 72–9, 94
Accumulation 8–10, 72–9, 94
action 36*n*7, 128–32, 147, 155; and
  behavior 1–2, 14–16, 147–8; and
  beliefs-proper 132; bifurcation
  of 14–16; BPM as a model of 4–6;
  classes of 141–4; identification
  of 103–6; and intensionality 141–4;
  and intentionality 141–4; and neurotic
  beliefs 57, 131–2; and representational
  systems 144–6
action-properties 80, 88, 89, 119–20, 133
activity: defined 14–15
addiction 17–21, 36*n*12, 78, 110, 130, 131,
  136–7, 141, 150
agency 15, 36*nn*7–8, 37*n*20, 106, 130–1,
  136–46, 142–4, 146–9; "as-if" 146; and
  intensionality 153–4
Ainslie, G. 14, 27, 35*n*6, 97, 117, 125
Ajzen, I. 63*n*7
akrasia 3, 11, 17–21, 22–31, 36*n*13,
  125, 131; and definition of consumer
  choice 16–17; Platonic view of 36*n*14
algorithmic mind 33–4*n*4, 114*n*5, 120–5
amygdala 67, 73
anxiety 73, 74, 77–8
approach behaviors 5, 13, 24, 67, 71, 72–4,
  75, 76, 77, 93; and basal ganglia 72; and
  mesocorticolimbic dopamine system 72
a-rationality 3, 17, 19, 95–9, 104,
  111–13, 114*n*5, 115*n*7, 122–3, 126–7,
  131, 139–41

Arends, M. A. 78
avoidance behaviors 5, 26, 67, 69, 71, 72, 73,
  74, 75, 77, 87, 93
autonomous mind 33–4*n*4, 120–2; and
  cognitive miserliness 124–5

Baker, L. R. 54
Barrett, J. F. 67, 90*n*5
basal ganglia 72
Bechtel, W. 43, 46
behavior 14–16, 15, 148; *see also* action
Behavioral Approach System (BAS)
  72–3, 74–9
Behavioral Inhibition System (BIS)
  73, 74–9
Behavioral Perspective Model (BPM) 1,
  4, 8–10, 10*n*1, 55, 56, 65, 91*n*9, 137–41;
  extensional model 137–8; intentional
  model 138–41
behaviorist explanation 46–8
beliefs: and action 144–5, 147; cognitive
  foundations 116–22; content of
  36*n*10, 65, 81, 155; as contingency-
  representations 3, 19, 20, 31, 39–40,
  53, 61, 103–13, 137–41, 150, 151;
  in contrast to perceptions 57, 80,
  85–8, 153, 154; desire x belief model
  1, 2, 12, 51, 57–60, 80, 117–19,
  140–1, 148, 152, 155; direction of fit
  41, 106; in heterophenomenology 86;
  indispensability of 87–8; in intentional
  consumer-situation 95–6, 95–115, 150;
  in intentional systems theory 79;

Taylor & Francis eBooks

Helping you to choose the right eBooks for your Library

Add Routledge titles to your library's digital collection today. Taylor and Francis ebooks contains over 50,000 titles in the Humanities, Social Sciences, Behavioural Sciences, Built Environment and Law.

Choose from a range of subject packages or create your own!

Benefits for you

- » Free MARC records
- » COUNTER-compliant usage statistics
- » Flexible purchase and pricing options
- » All titles DRM-free.

REQUEST YOUR **FREE** INSTITUTIONAL TRIAL TODAY

Free Trials Available
We offer free trials to qualifying academic, corporate and government customers.

Benefits for your user

- » Off-site, anytime access via Athens or referring URL
- » Print or copy pages or chapters
- » Full content search
- » Bookmark, highlight and annotate text
- » Access to thousands of pages of quality research at the click of a button.

eCollections – Choose from over 30 subject eCollections, including:

Archaeology	Language Learning
Architecture	Law
Asian Studies	Literature
Business & Management	Media & Communication
Classical Studies	Middle East Studies
Construction	Music
Creative & Media Arts	Philosophy
Criminology & Criminal Justice	Planning
Economics	Politics
Education	Psychology & Mental Health
Energy	Religion
Engineering	Security
English Language & Linguistics	Social Work
Environment & Sustainability	Sociology
Geography	Sport
Health Studies	Theatre & Performance
History	Tourism, Hospitality & Events

For more information, pricing enquiries or to order a free trial, please contact your local sales team:
www.tandfebooks.com/page/sales